Private Practices

Private Practices:
Girls Reading Fiction and Constructing Identity

Meredith Rogers Cherland

Taylor & Francis
Publishers since 1798

| UK | Taylor & Francis Ltd, 4 John St., London WC1N 2ET |
| USA | Taylor & Francis Inc., 1900 Frost Road, Suite 101, Bristol, PA 19007 |

First published 1994

A Catalogue Record for this book is available from the British Library

ISBN 0 7484 0225 X
ISBN 0 7484 0226 8 (pbk)

Library of Congress Cataloging-in-Publication Data are available on request

Typeset in 10/13pt Baskerville
Typeset by RGM, Southport

Printed in Great Britain by Burgess Science Press, Basingstoke on paper which has a specified pH value on final paper manufacture of not less than 7.5 and is therefore 'acid free'.

DEDICATION

For my grandmothers,

Georgianna Marion Louise Neveu and Mary Edwina Fowler.

Contents

Contents

Series Editor's Preface

While Meredith Cherland was completing *Private Practices*, we swapped electronic mail about the weather. At the time, it was − 20 Celsius in Regina, Saskatchewan and + 45c in Townsville, Queensland: the extremes of human endurance tested at opposite outposts of empire. As I read about Karen and Jerrica and the other Oak Town children's responses to *Julie of The Wolves* — and as I watched the ceiling fans beat hot air in circles — I recalled the traditional themes of Canadian literature: struggle against nature, hostile environment and the cold.

These themes unfold on the divide of gender. Canadian literature by Robertson Davies, Farley Mowat and others set 'man' against hostile elements and landcapes. Yet much of the work of Canadian women authors like Alice Munro, Gabrielle Roy and Margaret Atwood focuses on women's struggles against hostile communities, social institutions and cultures. Their work builds complex psychological landscapes of gender relations and identity. In Atwood's *Surfacing* and *Roughing it in the Bush* — staples of Canadian high school literature study — psychological inferiority and conflict are projected onto the landscape.[1]

How cultures define the physical and psychic 'inside' and 'outside' as gendered domains is the focus of Daphne Spain's recent work, *Gendered Spaces* (1993). Spain argues that it is in the social organisation of space that public and private, civic and domestic spheres are physically established and divided. What struck me while I was reading Cherland's ethnography is how much of Canadian life is physically 'inside'. Such matters of location and site — gendered and cultural geographies — mediate and shape how and when one works, the kinds of leisure activities one does, and the conduct of everyday lives (Soja, 1989).

The Canadian girls studied here use reading as a public and private practice to work through the complexities of gender and sexual identity, their life possibilities and pathways. A great deal of their reading occurs in 'private lessons' — practices of autodidactic (self-teaching) literacy undertaken far away from the public eye. Often these events take place in the spaces of their homes, living rooms and bedrooms. Of course, the notion of a 'room of one's own' is resonant in feminist theory and political practice. But it also figures centrally in the mythology of the modern family. That mythology is tied closely to postwar economic prosperity and cultural formation in Canada, the US, Australia and other English-speaking countries (Johnson, 1993). And it is reiterated in the folk culture around suburban, White communities, in songs from the Beach Boys to the Bangles, in 'teenage' movies and programs from *Heathers* to *Doogie Howser*. There is so much about Oak Town that typifies the postwar dream: the Anglo nuclear family in the suburbs, Dad with a steady job, cars and appliances, sports and shopping centres, and, at the heart of this, a suburban home and lifestyle with your own room and your own books.

In Canadian and American, Australian and British Oak Towns, children today live in a world of postmodern spaces, of post-literary literacy, of powerful media texts for the shaping of hybrid gendered and cultural identities. In this setting, Cherland's finely-grained study presents what at first glance is an anachronism: the sheer volume of institutional work and effort that still goes into constructing literature as 'prestigious knowledge'. Particularly in the face of commodified, multi-mediated culture, the persistence of the novel is remarkable. The bourgeois reading public first developed in 18th and 19th century Europe and, with the rise of the novel, mass reading became a gendered, private practice (Huyssen, 1987). Then and now, part of the allure of literature to the middle class has been its power to make the cultural 'Other' available in narrative. The effect for Oak Town is not dissimilar: in Cherland's words, 'knowledge someone else had produced seemed to the Oak Town children more legitimate than what they knew themselves'.

But literary reading remains one of those everyday practices about which we have unlimited folk wisdom but few local, empirical accounts. Despite the recent focus in cultural studies on the social production of meaning by audiences, viewers and fans — few studies actually track and document people's everyday uses of literature and practices of literary reading.

In *Private Practices*, Cherland takes us with Jerrica, Samantha and others into their rooms, where they read *Babysitters' Club* books and *Bridge to Teribithia* late into the night after 'official' bedtime. Their parents pursue their own forms of literary education, building expectations about appropriate reading for men and women: fiction for women, utilitarian non-fiction for men. In the school, packaged literature curriculum prescribes content and 'literary development' in ways that generate regimes of boredom — perhaps not the 'damage of schooling' that Cherland anticipates — but at best a sanitised and commodified literary experience. In the face of this institutional agenda, the girls' readings are deliberate attempts to change the subject, to position themselves in relation to texts and their social worlds. But in spite of the girls' significant emotional and social investment in reading fiction, boys dominate public talk around literary texts, expressing their readings and 'discourses of action' forcefully and exclusively.

Throughout, Cherland invokes cross-cultural comparisons from the Amish, the Vai, inner city African-American youths and others — as if to remind us to view Oak Town as outsiders. For me, this required that I suspend the apparent 'naturalness' of my own schooling in literature, which despite its quite different (urban Asian-American) context was based on a similar mythology of the intrinsic power and value of literature. If we hold this mythology up to a sociological light, other issues and questions appear: Why does this particular Anglo-Canadian community — one of cultural and economic privilege — invest so much institutional time and effort in the building up of literary practice? Does it reflect a core belief in the moral value and cultural benefits of literature, as many of the adults and teachers suggest? Is it due to schools' traditional investment in the production of literary practice and knowledge? Is it for purposes of cultural capital, as Cherland argues? Or is it, as Linda Christian-Smith's (1990) work indicates, a product of the complex political economy of books, publishing and other media for the selling of 'gender'?

Cherland insists that what will count as literature is the construct of particular communities and cultures. In Oak Town, reading literature involves the selection and shaping of gendered identity and textual practices. This sets up a complex, contradictory relationship between schooling and the textual formation of gender. At once, 'Girls may learn to "read" and do school more easily than boys when what counts as reading requires compliance', while the school provides public texts where 'people of colour, working women and single mothers [are] invisible'. At the same time, the girls actively use reading as a mode of 'resistance to teachers' control of their time and to the imposed curriculum'. For many, this was their only visible agency against the authority of teachers and text.

Much of the literary theory that has driven research, teaching and curriculum work has been sociologically naive, and *Private Practices* is a major contribution to our understanding of the social networks and gender relations around reading practices. For the girls of Oak Town 'reading' is one space where the private and public meet — where identity meets ideology, where desire meets discourse. What matters is how communities and institutions, teachers and students construe and build these social practices, how 'private reading practices are publicly constructed'. Accordingly, one of Meredith Cherland's most instructive public lessons is that the power of literature is constructed and not natural, learned and not given.

Allan Luke
Townsville, Queensland, Australia
April 1994.

Notes

1 I am indebted to Wendy Waring, Curtin University of Technology, for this observation.

References

Christian-Smith, L. (1990) *Becoming a Woman Through Romance*, New York: Routledge.

Huyssen, A. (1986) *After the Great Divide: Modernism, Mass Culture, Postmodernism*, Bloomington: Indiana University Press.

Johnson, L. (1993) *Modern Girl: Girlhood and Growing Up*, Sydney: Allen & Unwin.

Soja, E. (1989) *Postmodern Geographies: The Reassertion of Space in Critical Social Theory*, Cambridge: Polity Press.

Spain, D., (1993) *Gendered Spaces*, Chapel Hill, NC: University of North Carolina Press.

Preface

> The best feminist analysis . . . insists that the inquirer herself be placed in the same critical plane as the overt subject matter . . . the class, race, culture and gender assumptions, beliefs and behaviors of the researcher herself must be placed within the frame of the picture that she attempts to paint . . . Thus, the researcher appears to us not as an invisible, anonymous voice of authority, but as a real, historical individual with concrete, specific ideas and interests. (Sandra Harding, 1987)

My two grandmothers led similar lives. Both were born in 1875. Both lived on the east coast of the United States. Between them, over the course of fifty years, my grandmothers had five husbands, all of them laborers (a butcher, a railroad worker, a carpenter, a union steward and a machinist). They were widowed five times — three times by accidents, twice by disease. They both took in laundry and worked as chambermaids and waitresses to feed their several children. By the time I was born in 1947, my grandmothers had lived to see their own children become established in lives of post-war prosperity, and to see their first grandchildren attending suburban public schools. I have an old photograph of one of them at the age of 10, standing pale and exhausted beside the machine she ran in a textile factory in Massachusetts.

I have lived a privileged life: because I am White, many schools have been open to me (except those reserved for men and some that cost too much). I have never been hungry. I have had good health and adequate medical care. I learned to read in the first grade. My parents, who could not get as much education as they wanted, valued education and saw it as a guarantee of comfort and security. They encouraged me and supported me through twenty years of schooling.

I was the fifth person in my extended family to finish high school. The year I graduated, public schools were being integrated in Selma, Alabama. By the time the Women's Movement reached me, I had completed a Master's degree in English literature and started work as a junior high-school English teacher in downtown Boston. By day, I taught immigrant children, some of whom went hungry. By night, I read feminist authors and attended consciousness-raising groups. I gained some awareness of what my grandmothers' and parents' urban childhoods must have been like, and I learned to burn with anger at social injustice and personal oppression.

Twenty-one years have passed since I left Boston. I have been a teacher educator at a Canadian university for the last fifteen of them. My husband of nineteen years teaches high school. We live with a teenage daughter and a son.

My education, both formal and informal, has led me to understand the facts of my life and of my grandmothers' lives against the backdrop of history (and, more recently, feminist revisionist history) and in terms of considerations of class, race and gender. I have used Marxian analyses to arrive at an understanding of the economic system that required a lifetime of unremitting physical labor from my grandmothers, and the class system that contributed to their husbands' deaths. In my own work and teaching, I have used Omni and Winant's (1986) theory of racial formation to understand the American Civil Rights Movement I witnessed, and Ogbu's (1985) analysis of race as enacted in schools to understand my own privileged position and school success. At the same time, feminist theory has encouraged me to do more than just accept my 'natural' place in the world. It has provided enlightening explanations for the suffering of women I loved, compelled me to take an interest in the lives of the women I work with, and led me to make the experiences of female children the focus of my research.

Anthropology has offered me a way to make culture visible through enthography — to show the details of how femininity is socially constructed. Finally, in recent years, Carole Edelsky and Allan Luke have shown me that the enterprise of literacy education — the career choice of my youth — is a site of struggle for social control and for social justice.

Theories of women's experiences, education and literacy come together in my work because I want to know more about the lives my grandmothers led, about my own experiences, and about the world my children will inhabit. This book is an attempt to share my view of the world, to throw some light on the complexities of children's lives, and to move the world one step closer to justice.

Meredith Rogers Cherland
January 1994

Acknowledgments

This book is based upon my doctoral dissertation, and grew out of work that my doctoral advisor, Dr Carole Edelsky of Arizona State University, taught me to do. Her insights were an important part of this analysis and shaped the way I came to see my experiences in Oak Town. She was, and remains, my excellent teacher, and has my profound gratitude.

In a similar way, Allan Luke showed me how to write a book, and guided me through the reading that enriched this writing. He is a fine editor and teacher, and I want to thank him for his generous help.

I also thank the people of Oak Town (especially those who were in Grade Six during the year of this study) who welcomed me into their school and their homes and made it possible for me to learn about their lives. I won't forget them. I thank, in addition, the Saskatchewan Middle Years Association for its financial support of the pilot project which led to the Oak Town work. And I thank Florence Bishop and Barbara Elliott for feminist community, for provocative ideas, and for the affirmation they have provided me with over the past ten years and more.

Carole Edelsky, Salina Shrofel and Joel Taxel read drafts and offered helpful comments on work in progress, while Carolyn Beitel gave me help at the computer — as well as moral support. My children were patient, and my husband Carl cheerfully kept our household running during 'the year of the book'. My thanks to all of them.

Parts of Chapter 4 have appeared previously in *Texts of Desire: Essays on Fiction, Femininity and Schooling*, edited by Linda K. Christian-Smith. Here, they are revised and reprinted with the permission of The Falmer Press.

Chapter 1

A Constructed World

I stood at the book table at morning recess time. Kids were milling around this sixth-grade classroom, eating and visiting, strolling out to their lockers in the hallway and back again. I watched Leah and Sarah talking at their desks. Both had permed, chin-length hair, parted on the side and clipped with a pretty barrette. They wore pastel sweaters with knee-length black pants, spotless white socks and white runners. Leah had an apple, Sarah a muffin.

I straightened out the books on the table and tried to make the covers visible. Matt Peterson, the teacher, had pushed the table right up against the wall under a bulletin board displaying three large laminated illustrations of Lloyd Alexander's *The Book of Three*. Matt had drawn the pictures himself, using pastels. Done in shades of rust and green and gold and brown, these all showed the character of Taran on horseback, fierce and heroic, drawn sword in hand, battling several ugly creatures at a time.

Leah wandered over to the table and picked up a paperback with a photo on the front. The title said *Satin Slippers #1: To Be a Dancer*. She told me, 'I've read this one. You can get all these *Satin Slippers* books at Coles bookstore. I have the first six, and I'm going to be getting #7. My mother thought they looked good, so she started buying them for me.'

Sarah joined us. 'She did? She just bought them for you?'

'Yuh,' said Leah. 'We were in the store, and she just said to me, "Oh, Leah, this looks like a great set!" And when I got to reading them, I liked them too, but first my mother just fell in love with the cover of them. She bought me the first three because she liked the cover so much.'

I looked at the cover. It was made from a photograph of a tall, slim young woman in pink tights and leotard with a gauzy skirt and toe shoes. She stood by a tall window in a graceful pose, long blonde hair flowing, arms extended. It was a hazy photo, in soft focus.

Sarah said, 'I read this one, the first one, and it was okay. But I just love the cover too. I stare and stare.'

The end-of-recess bell rang and the two girls moved to their desks with everyone else. It was silent reading time. Sarah took *Satin Slippers #1* with her and placed it flat on her desk. She sat, hands in her lap, gazing at the cover.

How does a researcher explain the meaning of a scene like this one? She writes a book. This is a book about gender and reading. It is about gender as a cultural construction, and about the reading of fiction as it happens within cultures. It is about the social negotiation of gender, and about the reading of fiction as a social practice. It is intended to engage those concerned with education in a consideration of how children's lives, and their own work, are created and shaped by cultural forces.

This is a book about seven girls, and the year during which they were all 11 and 12 years old. It is about the affluent North American homes they came from, the school they attended, and the world they lived in. It is about the books they read, and about *how* they read them. This is a story of childhood, of aesthetic pleasure and psychic pain, and of growing up in a particular sociocultural context.

This is a story that I have constructed. I am the story's narrator, the person who tells the story from a certain vantage point and with a certain voice. I am the person who has chosen the events that comprise the story. I have arranged them and shadowed them with my meanings to support my own values and serve my own vested interests and intents. In this way, I have done what every researcher and every storyteller does: I have seen people and events in the light of my own belief systems, experiences, and discourses, and I have told what I hope is a compelling and authentic story that is consistent with what I believe about the world.

A researcher cannot be 'objective'. Yet she does have choices about whether, and how, to make her political and other beliefs visible to those who will read her work. What follows is an explanation of my theories — that have shaped this book — and my ways of talking about the world.

A View of Reality

What is real? Where in the world does meaning reside? Where and how do people assert agency in everyday life? I believe that reality is different for different people, and that meaning is created by people in social interaction. This sociological theory of symbolic interactionism suggests that both reality and the social order are created by people as a process of joint action (Blumer, 1969).

According to symbolic interactionism, people live in a world of objects which become meaningful according to how others relate to them — according to how others act in ways that reveal the meanings they attach to those objects. The early-twentieth-century sociologist George Herbert Mead put it this way (1934): living things are involved in relationships of mutual determination with the environment and are not merely responsive to the pre-existing world around them. In other words, living things negotiate the world's meaning *together*. Working from these assumptions, when I enter schools and classrooms as a researcher, I expect to see people *negotiating* meaning, and in that process constructing their shared social and cultural reality.

I expect to see people — in interaction — creating a context for real events, and I expect to see the language events they create in turn creating the context. Thus I see reality as *reflexive*. I believe that while a social order exists, 'its existence always appears within interaction' (Mehan and Wood, 1975, p. 184). That is to say that most of the time, people feel and experience the privileges and the restrictions of their place within the larger social order in their interactions with other people. It is not, therefore, any *abstract* knowledge of how society is structured that makes real the existence of societal structure. What makes these structures real are all the concrete details involved in dealing with other people.

And yet, it is clear that while individuals create the social order by enacting it, they do not personally invent it. Not every form of social interaction will do. Particular social interactions are required that display, and are constrained by, a knowledge of 'an other and prior and *independent* world' (*ibid.* p. 186). The world, in other words, is both *of* our making and *beyond* our making (Mehan and Wood, 1975). When I enter elementary-school classrooms, I listen to a conversation, see the larger social order at work in shaping it, *and*, at the same time try to see how that conversation is in fact *creating* the social order before my very eyes.

I do not regard what goes on in classrooms as completely improvisational and emergent in nature. Obviously, patterns of belief and action do persist over time. The concept of 'aligning actions' (Stokes and Hewitt, 1976) explains this persistence. Aligning actions are actions by which participants align their individual patterns of acting to one another so as to create joint or social acts. Such actions are felt to be 'normatively appropriate or required, typical and/or probable with respect to the people and the situations involved'. By this account, cultures consist of such recognized and preferred ways of thinking, feeling, and acting. I enter elementary-school classrooms prepared to see the culture influencing people in interaction, and expecting also that I will eventually be able to discern these patterns both of 'aligning actions' and of shared cultural meanings. In the case of this study, I expected that some of those shared meanings would concern, and *shape*, what counts as 'gender', and that still others would concern, and shape, 'reading'.

When you undertake research from this view of reality, it is questions of meaning that become focal. My work grows out of interpretive research traditions in anthropology and sociology, insofar as it focuses on individuals' meanings. But in addition I scrutinize these meanings, looking for 'aligning actions' and asking questions about group identities, group beliefs and group actions. These are the questions of ethnography, which deals with the description of individual cultures.

Ethnography is consistent with a symbolic interactionist view of reality as something that people create in social interaction. Ethnographers spend a good deal of time with the people they study, working to understand and document the shared meanings of the people they describe, as well as attempting to acquire an *insider's* viewpoint. Ethnographic traditions in anthropology and sociology have thus required the ethnographer to move beyond his or her own cultural viewpoints to see the world as the people they study see it.

But what happens when an ethnographer approaches the research task with a strong political orientation and an education in Neo-Marxist, feminist and other critical theory? What if the ethnographer sees the culture she is studying in the light of her own personal beliefs about power relations and authority? A category of research called 'critical ethnography' has grown out of a dissatisfaction with those social accounts of structures — such as class and patriarchy — in which real human actors never appear, as well as out of a dissatisfaction, on the other hand, with those cultural accounts of human actors in which broad structural constraints, like patriarchy and racism, never appear (Anderson, 1989). Although critical ethnography puts an *interpretive* focus on human agency and local knowledge, so as to keep the researcher's pre-existing theory from entirely determining the findings of a study, it also suggests that the participants' own meanings explain and perpetuate social phenomena.

It is perhaps most illuminating to view the critical ethnographic project as amounting to a 'negative critique' performed by an undeniably interested researcher (Brodkey, 1987). Its purpose is to describe consistencies and contradictions, and to give a critique of different perspectives for change. Here, I want to follow Brodkey's advice in making my own stance clear: I do not pretend to be an unbiased, 'objective' and disinterested researcher. I believe that people, both the researched *and* the researcher, create reality in their social interactions, and that various power relationships, as well as my own vested interests, serve to shape the way I interpret the interactions between the people I study. And I am certain that the story presented here is one story of the interaction of my own views of the world with those of the girls, the families, and the teachers of one individual community.

A View of Reading

This book is not a report located in the mainstream of reading research. Reading research in the past decade has diverged along two distinct paths, each one throwing a different light on reading. The established tradition of reading research, rooted in cognitive psychology, assumes that reading is a universally similar psychological process that exists within the minds of individual people. A newer line of reading research, rooted in anthropology and sociolinguistics, looks at reading as an external, social act, performed by people in interaction and in a particular context. Whereas the disciplines of education and psychology have most often focused on discrete elements of reading and writing skills, and have conceptualized literacy as an individual and autonomous form of technology, anthropology and sociolinguistics, on the other hand, have focused on shared social practices and shared conceptions of reading and writing (Street, 1993). This book forms part of the second line of research.

I do not mean to imply that the two streams of research are neatly divided. Within each line of research there is a range of perspectives. Those who highlight the psychological aspects of reading take a variety of positions on the extent to which the psychology of reading is socially shaped, while those who highlight the social practices that constitute reading take a variety of positions on the extent to which a psychology of reading exists. Each line of research contributes to the creation of a discourse which emphasizes certain characteristics of reading over others.

It is misleading to think of reading as a purely psychological process, but quite profitable, on the other hand, to think of it as a social practice. So much is missed when researchers ignore the proposition that no one reads in a social or cultural vacuum. So much is learned when researchers embrace the idea that every person is part of a culture, part of a society, and that each person participates in cultural norms that determine how they act as readers. Research in anthropology has helped to make the point by making visible the cultural norms that shape reading (Heath, 1983; Fishman, 1991; Bloome and Solsken, 1988), while research in socio-linguistics, for its part, has shown us how people create meaning, create reality if you will, through the conversational structures of their talk, giving evidence both of what reading means to them and of their cultural norms for reading (Cook-Gumperz, 1986; Michaels, 1986; Au, 1980). In work informed by these ideas, Bloome and Bailey (1989) have suggested that literacy ought to be studied as an *event* — that is to say, as inherently social and 'other oriented'. In this interpretation, the meaning of literacy is located in the event rather than in people's heads. By examining the relevant events, we can come to view reading not as a cognitive process but instead as 'varied forms of visible social, cultural, and political practices' (Luke and Baker, 1991). This book examines the literacy events and visible practices associated with one particular group of people in order to understand what reading is for them.

Studying literacy events and practices in one particular local setting is a worthwhile enterprise because it deepens and broadens one's knowledge of what reading can signify. Membership in a community is partly defined by the process of knowing and participating in the shared literacy practices that are characteristic of that community (Barton and Ivanic, 1991). The reason for this is that such local literacy practices are inextricably bound up with the social history and social organization of a community, and reveal much about the relationships that exist among different subgroups. In one early study of literacy in a specific community, Scribner and Cole (1981) constructed an ethnography of literacy among the Vai people of Liberia. They found that many Vai men possessed three forms of literacy: they could read and write in Vai — the language they used at home, in trade, and in other everyday settings; they could read and write in Arabic — which they used in religious contexts; and they had acquired English literacy in order to participate in school. However, few Vai *women* learned Arabic or English literacy, because they were not allowed to participate in reading the Qur'an, and they did not (with a few exceptions) attend the secondary English schools. Literacy thus both grew out of and contributed to creating the gendered social structure of the community.

In another such study, Heath (1983) constructed the story of how three culturally different communities in the Piedmont Carolinas of the United States came to use language, and of how teachers in those communities learned both to understand the locals' ways with language and literacy and to legitimate those ways in their classrooms. Two of the communities,

'Trackton' and 'Roadville', were literate communities, but each had its own history, and its own traditions of structuring, using, and assessing reading and writing. In Trackton — a Black working-class community descended from sharecroppers — children learned an oral tradition of creative storytelling, not tied to any literal facts, that provided an arena for oral competition involving both exaggeration and the stressing of the strength of the individual against an adversary. In Roadville — a White working-class community involved, for four generations, in the work of the local textile mills — children learned an oral tradition of storytelling that involved an assertion of community membership and agreement on acceptable behaviors. Roadville stories were 'true' — that is to say, accurate in their retelling of events — and they culminated in a particular point to be made, or lesson to be learned. Trackton and Roadville children came to school with different conceptions of what a 'story' is, conceptions that were in conflict with those promoted by the school. It was also the case that, in both Roadville and Trackton, people shared a variety of literary traditions. In Trackton, people did not accumulate printed material but instead read primarily for instrumental and social-interactional purposes. In Roadville, on the other hand, children were given books, and were read to, at home, before they attended school, and yet, despite this, reading and writing in school were seen primarily as appropriate acts of compliance. Neither community's literacy practices were consistent with the school's.

Analyzing the educational implications of the acquired knowledge of a community's shared literacy practices can have positive consequences for children's lives in schools. In her Piedmont study, Heath found that the school's literacy practices were a better match for those of the townspeople, Black and White, who had been exposed to many of the cultural discourses available to other mainstream middle-class groups across the United States, and who were not as tied to the local literacy uses of any specific community. It is not surprising that the children of the townspeople found it easier to succeed in school than the children of Trackton and Roadville who had to learn to negotiate the differences between the school's ways with words and their own. The teachers of Heath's study were able to use her descriptions of local language and literacy practices to redesign the school's literacy experiences, at least temporarily, in ways that were less alienating and more meaningful for the children.

Other ethnographies have also centered on a community's meanings for literacy, and on mismatches between the literacy practices of a community and the literary practices of its schools. For example, in a study of the literacy practices of the Amish people, Andrea Fishman (1991) found that Amish girls would not participate in those school literacy activities, such as dialogue journals, that challenged Amish conceptions of identity and knowledge. Self-assertiveness was regarded as improper for girls, and writing was regarded only as a means of recording information. As a consequence, the girls saw dialogue journals as too self-assertive by their community's standards, and the kind of writing required by such journals as an improper use of literacy.

More often, it is the school that rejects the literacy practices of the community, rather than the community which rejects the literacy practices of the school. In a study of the vernacular writing of Philadelphia high school students (Camitta, 1993), it was found that teachers thought of students' writing to each other as deviant or non-standard, and did not see at all the social purposes served by such writing. Because teachers would not recognize its value, vernacular writing went 'underground' and became artificially disconnected from the process of literacy education as it was officially conducted. It is this kind of contrast between the literacy practices of certain communities (such as the Roadville and Trackton communities, the Amish colony, and the Philadelphia teens), on the one hand, and the literacy practice of their schools, on the other hand, that demonstrates the need to frame local uses of literacy within a cultural context.

While understanding literacy certainly requires in-depth accounts of actual literacy practices as found in many different local settings (Street, 1993), it also seems to me to require a broad awareness of the historical and cultural forces that have shaped, and are still shaping, both the community's and the school's respective literacy practices. People transform literacy to their own cultural concerns and immediate interests, and it is in this way that literacy practices change. Whether one examines the literacy practices of the Somalis, as such practices come to be used to heighten nationalistic fervor (Lewis, 1993), or the literacy practices of Latin American immigrants, as these are used to enable participation in a new society (Klassen, 1991), or the literacy practices of the Hmong of Philadelphia, as these are used to preserve kinship ties and to negotiate a new social status in an unfamiliar world (Weinstein-Shr, 1993), it is always clear that such practices change in response to social forces. This is consistent with the reflexive view of reality that I have already discussed: literacy changes in response to social forces, because it plays a part in *constructing* the various interlocking dimensions of a society (ethnicity, class, race, and gender) which then come together to *create* these social forces. *Growing Up Literate: Learning from Inner-City Families* (Taylor and Dorsey-Gaines, 1988), a work which makes an ethnographic study of parenthood and childhood in the context of extreme urban poverty, illustrates this process. The bright and articulate mothers of this story used literacy in sophisticated, time-consuming and intricate ways in order to claim welfare benefits and to negotiate with the demeaning bureaucracies that took the control of their lives out of their own hands. The children of this story, all of whom learned to read easily despite their schools' preoccupation with the discrete skills of literacy, met the demands of the educational institution as they became increasingly alientated from it. Race and class, in this study as in Heath's study, not only worked to shape literacy practices, but, in turn, were also *shaped by* these same practices.

This is also true of gender. Consider, for example, Bloome and Solsken's (1988) study of kindergarten children acquiring literacy. They found that Jack, a child with older siblings, had watched his brothers reading and writing in certain ways and had watched his mother (and not his father) reading and writing in the company of his siblings. Jack learned to treat reading and writing the way his brothers treated reading and writing — namely, as *work*. He used literacy both to earn external rewards, and to display competence to adults. He learned the practices of his culture by watching others, and in this way came to use literacy in culturally appropriate gendered ways. By way of a reflexive process, his literacy practices were shaped by gender, while, in turn, he enacted his gender through literacy. And although, in the first and second grade, Jack, and other young children who went to the same school as him, grew and changed in their literacy practices, those practices continued to be broadly marked for gender in subtle and complicated ways (Solsken, 1993). Solsken concluded that while standard literacy across cultures is often the province of men, it may also be, in some subcultures and social classes, primarily a *female* activity. This is not necessarily contradictory, 'since dominant groups may control activities which are executed by subordinate groups' (*ibid.* p. 215). This hint that literacy practices are aspects not only of culture, but also of their inherent power structures (Street, 1993) speaks of new directions for ethnographic studies of literacy as social practice.

It is in the past ten years that researchers have begun to explore the idea that the acquisition, uses and meanings of different literacies have an ideological character. If ideology is reviewed as the site of tension between authority and power on the one hand and resistance and creativity on the other (Street, 1993), then it can be more easily understood how several ethnographers of literacy have considered the ideological character of gendered literacies. The reading of romances, for example, can partly serve to compensate women for their lack of power and their lack of control over their own lives, as Radway's (1984) study of adult women romance readers in the eastern United States has shown. And the reading of teen romances, moreover, can influence the decisions girls make about their own futures, but can also provide a site for the girls' engagements with the tensions that surround the construction of gender identity (Christian-Smith, 1987).

In the later chapters of this book, I will examine other ethnographies of literacy which explore the tension between the various 'textual effects' that not only contribute to the construction of gender subjectivity but also create the possibilities for self-determination that exist in daily literacy practices (Luke, 1993). Elsewhere, I will have more to say about the complex connections between gender and reading. Here, I am simply making the point that reading is a social practice, shaped by gender, race, and class, that is lived in complicated ways in people's lives.

It seems important to reiterate that in my view, race, class, ethnicity and gender are not so much separate variables as interconnected dimensions in life, dimensions that are created through ways of living that involve both literacy practices and relations of power. The ways in which women live sexual oppression are integrally connected to the ways in which they live race, class and ethnicity — as can be seen in Rockhill's (1993) study of the struggle of Hispanic women in Los Angeles to become literate. These women were unable to do what they wished to do — namely, go to school to learn the English language and thus acquire English literacy — because of the constraints of an ethnic orientation which kept them 'protected' within the home, and because of male control of their lives. Due to their ethnicity, class and gender, they were perceived as having no right to literacy. Many met with physical violence when they attempted to acquire English literacy and to profit from the economic choices it could give them.

There are many forms of violence, and it is not surprising that some of these manifest themselves in connection with reading when one considers the ideological character of literacy, and its uses in connection with the maintenance of power. Violence will appear later in this study of girls' reading in Oak Town, when this book focuses on reading in events, and interactions. But first, the meaning of reading as a *social practice* will be explained, in terms of how the children of the Oak Town community use reading as a means both of participating in their own culture and of constructing their own agency — in ways that sometimes conflict with the literacy practices of their school.

A View of Gender

This book takes an *anthropological* view of gender. In other words, it does *not* treat gender as a matter of biological circumstance. Its assumption is that gender is not inherent in the individual but 'constructed' in a culture when a collection of symbols are invested with meanings that define what it is to be male and female (Ortner and Whitehead, 1981). There are still some who cling to biological determinist and essentialist arguments, but much contemporary anthropology views gender not as something people *are* but rather as something people *do*. People 'do' gender in different ways in different cultures. They are taught and they learn from birth to behave in gender-appropriate ways in all the activities and practices of their daily lives. Indeed, they learn gender so well that they can 'do' it without even thinking consciously about doing it.

This view of gender is consistent with the view of reality I have been discussing above. Close and detailed analysis of the actions that constitute social life shows that being male or female is 'a reflexive accomplishment' (Mehan and Wood, 1975, p. 143). This idea is beautifully illustrated in the work of Garfinkel (1967), who studied a 19-year-old male who chose to dress and live and pass as female. This person, calling herself Agnes, found that being a woman and being accepted as a woman required a ceaseless social performance. Agnes was continually engaged in the work of passing as female. This work involved socially structuring situations in which she could engage in the *practices* of being female. Because she had lived as a male until the age of 16, Agnes had to learn the routine feminine practices her women friends had engaged in unconsciously for many years. She changed her appearance drastically, and she had also to learn the practices necessary for cooking in a kitchen with older women; she learned correct dating practices; and with great difficulty, she learned (eventually) to speak as a woman speaks. In her relationship with the researcher Garfinkel, Agnes felt free enough to ask him occasionally if he thought her actions or her speech were 'normal' (meaning plausibly female). Most often they were. Although Agnes remained anatomically male, she lived in the world and was accepted as a woman. Her life makes it clear that one is made a man or woman within the social order by virtue of the *practices* one employs.

What is also true is that these practices, in turn, serve to produce the gendered social structures of everyday life. Cooking meals and scouring sinks, walking tentatively in high-heeled shoes, pursuing other people's topics in conversation — all these practices do more than make one a woman; they also place one in a certain relation to others, positioning others so as to require them to engage in the practices that in turn make *them* women and men.

Like ethnomethodology, sociology has a long history of describing and accounting for gender differences by examining closely the actions and practices of everyday life.[1] In examining 'gender displays', Goffman (1976 and 1977) described rituals or highly conventionalized portrayals that express masculinity or femininity in North American mainstream culture via such activities as lighting a cigarette, or taking a seat in a crowded room, or via the posture one adopts, for example, when standing still. These 'gender displays' are socially scripted dramatizations of the particular culture's *idealized versions* of masculine and feminine natures. Although most people believe that gender displays grow out of a person's essentially male or female nature, clearly Mehan and Wood and I do not. Such behaviors, we believe, are learned, and are required for the creation of gender. In a more recent approach to the problem, one that makes use of ethnomethodology and feminist work, West and Zimmerman (1987) contend that 'the "doing" of gender is undertaken by women and men whose competence as members of society is hostage to its production. Doing gender involves a complex of socially guided perceptual, interactional, and micropolitical activities that cast particular pursuits as expressions of masculine and feminine "natures"' (West and Zimmerman, 1987, p. 126). This view of gender, much closer to my own, differs from Goffman's in two respects. Where Goffman saw gender as happening most often at key junctures of social activities, so as not to interfere with the activities themselves, West and Zimmerman believe that gender is portrayed within *every* social activity. Where Goffman believed that gender display is optional, West and Zimmerman argue that it is compulsory, that all members of society are required to portray their gender within every social activity: wearing clothes, talking, eating, reading, walking — everything they do with other people. They are 'required' to do this because they are punished, with ridicule or social disruption, if they practice gender-*inappropriate* behavior. In this way, they are held responsible for performing every social act as a man or as a woman.

Gender and Talk

Reading is one such social act. Conversation is another. It is possible to learn a good deal about people's tacit cultural beliefs through the observation and analysis of conversations. There are many sociolinguistic studies which show how it is that people 'do gender' in conversation. Tannen, in a (1990) controversial best seller shows how many men, acting on their tacit assumption that the world's social structure must be organized hierarchically, try to maintain the upper hand in a conversation. In contrast, many women tend to see themselves as embedded in a network of connections, and to view conversations as negotiations for closeness, negotiations in which a consensus is sought. Through two such different approaches to conversations, gender is constructed.

Tannen (1990) has been roundly criticized for ignoring the structured economic, political and micropolitical power differential between women and men, that such conversational strategies grow out of — and at the same time help to create and maintain (Troemel-Ploetz, 1991). She stops short of acknowledging or describing the political context behind gender differences in conversational styles. And like many others carrying out sociolinguistic analyses, she avoids considerations of history and ideology and supposes that the ways in which people talk can be explained in terms of personal motivation and choice. There are, however, a number of people working in this field (Edelsky, 1981; Fairclough, 1989; Fishman, 1978; Goodwin, 1980; Lakoff, 1990; Maltz and Borker, 1982) who *do* analyze the conversational structures that both create and reflect gender inequality and do more to account for the power diffentials displayed in talk. Fishman, for example, shows (1978) how the work of maintaining social interaction through talk falls primarily to women, and declares that it is not a coincidence that in a world where men have more economic and political power than women do it is men's choices of topic that are developed and maintained in a conversation, and it is men who interrupt more. In an analysis of dominance through conversational strategies, McConnell-Ginet (1984) points to a finding of many studies: gender affects how people think they ought to contribute to a conversation, how they actually do contribute, and how their contributions are then perceived. She, like West and Zimmerman and me, sees 'doing gender' in speech as unavoidable.

Gender and Reading

Because gender is a cultural construction and reading is a social practice, gender is also unavoidably present in reading. Several reader-response literary critics have offered one possible explanation for why this is so. They argue that if the reader is female, her experience as a woman will inevitably determine her response to, and her interpretation of, the text in question (Culler, 1982; Bleich, 1978; Holland, 1975; Iser, 1974). Women, because they acquire different backgrounds and have different experiences from those of men, will develop *different* identities, and because of this they will read the same texts in a different way from the way they are read by men. Although these reader-response theorists are widely cited and used by educators, few of them, unfortunately, have made any explicit consideration of gender inequality and its influence on the mind of the reader. Exceptions are Bleich (1989) and Fox (1990).[2]

In contrast, Neo-Marxist and poststructuralist literary studies have been much more inclined to make matters of power and politics visible in their considerations of gender and reading. Shifting the theoretical focus from readers over to texts and contexts, they have stressed the idea that certain works of literature and certain *meanings* for literature have been elevated to privileged positions by social ideologies and by particular hegemonic interests (Williams, 1977; Eagleton, 1983). In a patriarchal society, man is the 'founding principle' and woman the excluded other, so that what has come to be considered literature is male-authored and, in outlook, male-identified; and the representative reader is always assumed to be male. In this historical context, it should not be surprising that the female reader of this male-authored and male-identified literary canon is required, when she reads, to identify herself as male, and thus to identify against herself, in order to share in the meaning of the work (Fetterley, 1978). Not only does she fail to find her own experiences of the world represented in literature, she is also asked to accept male experiences, as presented in what counts as literature, as if they were representative of human experience in general. This is as true for the 11-year-old schoolgirl reading approved works of children's literature in school as it is for adult women readers of the literary canon. Fetterley asks women to adopt the stance of a 'resistant reader' who does not identify as male but instead situates what she reads within a political context involving gender inequality and the neglect of women's experiences in literature.

The idea of a resistant female reader has been an important one in the attempt to understand both the phenomenon of women and girls reading outside the literary canon, and the phenomenon of women and girls reading for their own purposes. Radway's (1984) ethnographic study (mentioned above) of a group of women who were avid readers of Harlequin and other romances explores both phenomena in depth, while at the same time keeping the workings of patriarchy and oppression clearly visible. The housewives and working-class women she studied saw the act of reading romances as both combative and compensatory. Their reading was combative in so far as it allowed these women to refuse the demanding other-oriented role that the prevalent culture was prescribing for them. It was compensatory in the way it provided women vicariously with the emotional gratification, attention, and nurturance that they did not receive enough of in daily life. I have taken seriously Radway's insistence that scholars must attempt not only to document how the act of reading is viewed by the reader herself but also to analyze it within the cultural context in which it occurs.

Someone else who, in her studies of the reading of teenage women within cultural contexts, has taken Radway's point seriously is Linda Christian-Smith — she is mentioned above in connection with ethnographic studies of literacy (1993, 1987, 1989). Working from a poststructuralist perspective which sees language and literacy as the place where a sense of the self, a subjectivity, is constructed, Christian-Smith has studied the reading of romance fiction on the part of middle-class and working-class girls from diverse racial and ethnic backgrounds. Her work analyzes both the ways in which romance novels influence young women and how they come to see both themselves and the possibilities inherent in their lives. It also examines the ways in which young women read 'against the grain', analyzing romance reading as the site of negotiation in political and economic ideological struggles, in the United States, for young women's hearts and minds.

It seems to me that in the work of Radway, Christian-Smith and (lately) others (see Christian-Smith, 1993), the perspectives of anthropology and poststructuralist literary criticism come together so as to allow an examination of how identity is constructed in the reading of fiction. I will be drawing from both these perspectives on gender and reading in attempting to explain what goes on when 11-year-old girls are reading. In examining the events and interactions of their everyday lives, I will be assuming that people are 'doing gender' continuously; that their conversation will reveal their tacit beliefs, beliefs that both reflect and create gender[3]; and that considerations of power and of politics must frame these gendered stories of identity construction.

A View of Schooling

Schooling is never neutral. It is an important means of reproducing cultures, of educating children in the shared meanings of the cultural group that controls the school, and so of perpetuating existing social formations and economic relationships. School, I believe, is a place where 'mechanisms of domination' (Apple, 1979) preserve the stratified structure of a society. This book will be concerned with the critical analysis of society and of schooling. It makes use of critical educational theory, theory influenced by Neo-Marxist thought and shaped by the moral imperative of social justice. Critical educational theory begins with a dissatisfaction with the present nature both of society and of schooling, and seeks to achieve both the empowerment of individual people and the transformation of different social structures (Weiler, 1988).

Some critical educational theories emphasize 'reproduction', meaning the ways in which existing social, gender and class relationships are passed on from one generation to the next (Althusser, 1971; Bowles and Gintis, 1976; Bourdieu, 1977). Other critical theories, on the other hand, emphasize 'agency', signifying the production of meaning through the individual's 'resistance' to imposed knowledge and practices (Giroux, 1983; Willis, 1977; Simon, 1983; Everhart, 1980; McRobbie, 1978).

These terms ('reproduction', 'agency', and 'resistance') have been associated with a broad range of Neo-Marxist theories in which the construction of social reality is seen as a dialectic between individual consciousness and various structural determinants (Weiler, 1988). 'Reproduction' refers to the process by which dominant ideologies of power distribution are demonstrated in the structure, curriculum and pedagogy of the school in such a way that children learn to see them as natural and inevitable, and come to accept and live by them. These ideologies are manifest in the belief systems, discourses, and practices of everyday school life — including rule systems, conventions and rituals, peer relations, structures involved in classroom conversations, and forms of testing — as well as, of course, in the texts that children read and discuss. The process is dialectical in that it is constructed and contested by individuals who engage in 'resistance' by thinking and acting in ways that counter these dominant ideologies, and that seek to disrupt their enactment. When people engage in resistance, or even simple 'play' with rules and practices, they are exercising 'agency', namely the individual's ability to exercise power, and to act so as to produce an effect upon the world. It is my own view, however, that while cultural ideologies are contested via the individual's resistance, the cultural 'hegemony', i.e. the world views promoted by the school and by other societal agencies of ideological and social control, are almost always *preserved*.

Several critical ethnographic studies of schooling have provided powerful portraits of cultural reproduction, agency and resistance at work in specific schools and among particular people. In his (1977) ethnographic study of English working-class boys, Willis found that these boys rejected the school's ideology of society as a competitive arena where anyone who worked hard might succeed intellectually. The boys instead recognized and valued only the *manual* work done by others of *their own social class*, and, significantly, they came to see the kind of intellectual work promoted by the school as destructive in nature. In rejecting intellectual work and abstract knowledge, and in refusing thus to earn the approval of the school, the boys were implicitly accepting the class structure as something inevitable. Their resistance, which amounted to a rejection of dominant work values, did not, unfortunately, lead them to any kind of critical understanding of their place in an advanced capitalist society.

But what of girls' responses to schooling and the way it articulates dominant cultural values? In a (1978) study, McRobbie detailed how 14-to-16-year-old English working-class girls also rejected the values of the school — especially the school's values of propriety and good behavior for female students. The girls refused to be neat, diligent and compliant, as the school insisted they must be, and instead chose to flaunt their sexuality as an act of resistance. McRobbie points out that both the girls' oppression and their subsequent resistance were gender-specific. They were working-class children and they were girls, and this meant that both capitalism and patriarchy had interacting negative consequences for their lives.

Where Willis was concerned (1977) with the reproduction of class under capitalism, McRobbie was primarily concerned (1978) with the reproduction of gender under patriarchy. McLaren's (1986) ethnography of life in an urban Portuguese Catholic middle school in Canada explored another dimension of the dynamics of cultural reproduction by describing the role of religious ideology in schooling. This study of the various subcultures inherent in subordinated groups also involved an analysis of the taught body of knowledge of the school as a social construction that embodied specific ideological interests; and, like the studies carried out by Willis and McRobbie, it showed the dynamics of cultural reproduction as they took place within a terrain marked by 'contestation and struggle' (Giroux, 1986).

In literacy education, where these issues of class, culture, patriarchy and contestation become focal ones, the applications of critical theory are especially interesting. More than twenty years ago, Paolo Freire began to teach people to read and write in order to 'empower' them to engage in social analysis and political activism. He explained that *illiteracy* is a social practice that is political in nature, and is linked both to a cultural hegemony (which it strengthens) and to a form of resistance (which it sometimes embodies) (see Freire and Macedo, 1987). Freire has based his life's work on the premise that literacy can equip people to analyze and challenge the oppressive character-istics of society at large, and through his work he has inspired others to join him in developing critical, justice-seeking pedagogies.

In a contrasting application of critical theory to literacy education, an application which grew out of a study of the Nicaraguan literacy campaign, Lankshear and Lawler examined (1987) both the political nature of literacy instruction and the *lack* of power that can result from the acquisition of certain inadequate forms of literacy. The idea is that acquiring these different forms of literacy can lead students to believe that they are being properly enabled to cope with life, when in reality the forms of literacy they are learning serve only to keep them in their places and to preserve the status quo. These are examples of 'improper literacy', as found in cases where poverty-stricken Black children in the United States are taught to write letters to their Congressmen in the expectation that this will help them to improve their schooling, and in cases where adolescent girls copy down and memorize what the teacher has to say when what the curriculum actually requires is the exercise of creative problem-solving abilities. The point maded by Lankshear and Lawler is that certain forms of literacy can actually work *against* both the individual's empowerment and social change.

How does it happen that the shared meanings which serve the interests of groups in power come to be acted upon even by those whose interests they do *not* serve? Freire writes (1973) of peasants' receiving a view of reality, both from the church and from their landlords, that teaches them a passive and fatalistic attitude. In this view of the construction of the individual psyche, culture is the mediating link between ruling-class interests and everyday life (Giroux, 1992). Critical Neo-Marxist concepts and a dialectical view of cultural reproduction as achieved via schooling suggest both that people continue to accept the oppressive structures of the status quo, when the demonstrations of dominant ideologies serve to position them in certain ways, and that they share with others the meanings given to those ideologies. The desire for agency and for acts of individual resistance can be seen as signs that change and social transformation are possible, but such change is by no means inevitable. Critical theories suggest that in order to facilitate social change through schooling, teachers need to develop radical pedagogies which enable students to think critically about the culture and its institutions and so begin the process of social transformation (Giroux, 1988; Giroux and McLaren, 1989).

This vision of teachers' developing critical pedagogies for empowering students is, for many, a compelling one, one in which teachers engage students in serious dialogue in the classroom (McLaren, 1989; Shor, 1990; Shor and Freire, 1987). Because the purpose of the dialogue is to allow students to contest the ideologies that oppress them, and to appropriate reality for themselves, the teacher works at validating both the students' individual views and the students' individual experiences of the world. Themes from everyday life become the basis for critical inquiry. For example, Freire (1973) asked Chilean farmers to list the names of the things that were most immediate and important in their daily lives (tools, weather forms, foods) and then gave them written versions of these words to learn as their first lessons in literacy. Shor, by contrast, talked with Black teenagers in New York City about the violent and the pleasurable aspects of their daily lives — as appropriate subjects to be written about. In both these cases the pedagogical process enabled students to use their words and their writing ability for a political purpose, namely to communicate both with the landlord, and with school officials.

Critical pedagogies also propose that the teacher provide (and encourage other students to provide) a demonstration that student 'voice' is important and valued, where 'voice' refers to the individual perspectives of the student speakers. Students are to be encouraged to say and write and do what feels 'authentic' and important, and the teacher, for his or her part, is to create classroom situations where students are free to express themselves (Giroux, 1988; McLaren, 1989; Shor, 1990). The idea is to move away from lesson formats and classroom structures wherein only the teacher and the authors of the texts being studied are allowed to determine the content to be considered and the ideologies to be expressed. Students, too, have the right, perhaps even *more* of a right than the teachers do, to name the topics for study, to introduce the reality of their lives into classroom interactions, and to be heard and acknowledged.

The concepts of 'authenticity', and a student 'voice', that have arisen in these discussions of critical pedagogy have, however, been criticized by feminist theorists (Luke and Gore, 1992). Orner, for example, argues (1992) that these concepts implicitly involve realist and essentialist epistemological positions which are unacceptable because they are in conflict with a belief in the social construction of the individual's subjectivity (e.g. the idea that a person is born with an essential self, an individual and unchanging essence, that can be 'expressed'). Because there are 'multiple voices and contradictions present in specific historical sites at specific historical moments' (Orner, 1992, p. 80), there are times when it is not safe for students to speak, even when in the presence of teachers enlightened by critical educational theories.

An illustration of this point occurred at the University of Wisconsin at Madison in 1988, when Elizabeth Ellsworth explored the uses of critical pedagogies while teaching a course called 'Media and Anti-Racist Pedagogies', and found that she could not make her classroom a safe space for students to speak out and talk back to her about their experiences of oppression. Strategies like the 'dialogical method' of Shor and Friere (1987) seemed to give the illusion of equality while leaving the authoritarian nature of the teacher–student relationship intact. Notions of dialogue and democracy that assumed the existence of rational human subjects capable of agreeing on universal moral principles served only to obscure the pressures of the historical moment, as well as the unjust power relations defined by differences in race, class, and gender existing between the students and the teacher (Ellsworth, 1992). I agree that any calls for a critical pedagogy which will foster and support student resistance to the hegemonic structures of the school are problematic, because they do not recognize adequately the contradictory and changeable nature of the individual's subjectivity, and because they do not seem to respect the complexity of the operations by which a cultural hegemony is maintained.

I do, however, want to continue to make use of the concepts of cultural reproduction, agency, and resistance in my discussions of how individual psyches and subjectivities are shaped and produced at school. I have found these concepts extremely useful in explaining and understanding the ways in which the larger social order, on the one hand, and individual subjectivity, on the other hand, come together. These concepts acknowledge fully the view of reality as a social construction; they can accommodate the ethnomethodological emphasis on the reflexivity of reality without contradicting the idea that gender is created in social practices; and yet at the same time they have a political dimension that enriches discussions of both gender and schooling because they acknowledge complex relations of power and inequality.

Perhaps even notions of critical pedagogy can be redeemed — if these can be reworked so as to account for the ways in which individual subjectivities or identities are constructed — and be informed by a sense of the complexities involved when people attempt to overcome differences and work together in classrooms. Because I believe that it cannot be right to abandon entirely the attempt to change schooling practices in the interests of justice, I will return to considerations of critical pedagogy in the final chapter of this book.

A View of Research

Research is never neutral. Every instance of research is informed both by a certain view of what knowledge is, and by the views of the world in general that belong to the researcher. 'Before being a researcher, a person is first a member of a particular culture. It is within that culture that the person's view of the world is constructed' (Sears, 1992, p. 149). A person's view of the world — her lived cultural experiences or values — mediates what she chooses to study, how she studies it and what she finds.

The research that forms the basis for this book is not neutral. It is informed by my beliefs that knowledge is socially constructed, that reading is a social practice, that 'doing gender' is compulsory, and that schooling works to reproduce social inequality. But research is still not neutral even when the researcher *fails* to make her epistemological assumptions explicit. Experimental research that grows out of the dominant culture's obsession with numbers, strong desire for generalizations, and yearning for control is just as likely to serve certain vested interests as is research that grows out of critical theory.

The past twenty years have been a time of turmoil and rapid change in educational research. Research — like this study — that is framed by critical social and educational theories was once viewed as radical and non-mainstream. But it has now become accessible and common — as the shelves full of available case studies, action research reports and critical ethnographic studies show. Critical research, often linked to oppositional social movements like feminism, is both associated with and challenged by the postmodern crisis of confidence in Western conceptual systems, and by a sense of the limits of Enlightenment rationality (Lather, 1992). It is *associated* with postmodern thought because it is part of what can be called a 'postpositivist' (Fiske and Schweder, 1986) movement in educational research which rejects the claim both that objectivity is possible and that only measurable entities are of interest in the field of education. It is *challenged* by postmodern thought because it seeks to empower people to change the world — itself an enterprise extending from the Enlightenment, and a project that many postmodern thinkers view with considerable cynicism.

Poststructuralist theories, however, have proved very useful both in explaining the use of power on behalf of specific interests and in analyzing opportunities for *resisting* it. These theories identify language as the place where our sense of self, our sense of subjectivity, is constructed. 'Subjectivity' can be defined as 'the conscious and unconscious thoughts and emotions of the individual, her sense of herself and her ways of understanding her relation to the world . . . Poststructuralism presupposes a subjectivity which is precarious, contradictory and in process, constantly being reconstituted in discourse each time we think or speak' (Weedon, 1987, pp. 32–33).

A key concept here is that of 'discourse', a term that refers to the use of language (and other means of signifying) to represent certain interests and to convey certain meanings. To illustrate, it may be useful to think of the discourses that surround the identity of 'woman' in the world today. One such discourse is that in which 'woman' is a sexual object — as presented in films and on television, and in shopping-mall advertisements. Another competing discourse represents 'woman' as a political force — as is the case in the press releases of certain feminist political organizations. Still another discourse, embodied in part in *Good Housekeeping* magazine articles, and in cultural artifacts like greeting cards, represents 'woman' as the loving center of the family. Different classes and colors of women, depending on their access to cultural texts, engage with these and other competing discourses. Some women are better positioned and equipped than others, but all struggle to create their sense of self, their own subjectivities in response to these discourses. These struggles are, a question of, *inter alia*, reading positions and practices — in particular, of how women read these texts of desire and identity. Hence, the focus of this book.

These poststructuralist views have implications for research. Although many poststructuralist theorists are not particularly interested in the political applications of their work, feminists and others interested in social justice have been able to make good political use of their ideas because they address forms of social organization — as well as the social meanings and values that create and reflect them — and also address matters of individual consciousness (Weedon, 1987). As a feminist, my research undertaking has been to both describe the changing subjectivities of the girls I studied, and to consider the forces at work in the construction of those subjectivities. This kind of work, I would hope, may lead us, as educators and researchers, to generate alternative practices and interventions in literacy education.

Mine is feminist research, and 'feminisms' are always forms of politics. Taken together, these many feminisms constitute a social movement aimed at changing the power relations that exist between women and men in society. In this way, feminist theories, feminist scholarship and feminist research are all political, belonging to what Lather calls 'an advocacy paradigm' (1992) — because they are openly value-based. They seek to correct the invisibility, and the distortion, of women's experiences in the social sciences, as well as to serve the interests of the people being studied. Having said this, it seems important to reiterate that feminist research is no more ideological than mainstream research — which, by contrast, not only privileges male experience but also, as Harding points out (1987), poses only those questions, and cites only those histories and methdologies, which are of interest to White, Western, bourgeois men.

An appendix to this volume details more of the methods I used to collect data for the study upon which this book is based. I will take up these issues of methodology (the interpretative framework that guided the research project) when I begin describing the Oak Town project later in this chapter. Here, in the interests of clarifying my view of what research is, I want to touch upon concerns that arise in connection with my beliefs about knowledge.

I don't view research as a quest to discover the Truth, because I don't believe that one Truth exists. My job in doing research is, in one sense, to attempt to convey the various Truths held by others (Sears, 1992). While I began from a feminist perspective, so as to open up a space for women's and girls' standpoints and voices, I did not undertake this research to validate any particular theoretical stance. In this sense, I have not used ethnographic methods merely to confirm what I already presume to exist. As much as it is possible, I have read the data with a mind open to and sensitive to the views of the people I have studied, and I have tried not to see them as a problem to which I am the solution.

And yet at the same time it would be misleading of me to claim that my research is simply 'interpretive'. I acknowledge that I am putting the views and experiences of the people I am studying within the framework of my own views and experiences of the world. I believe that it is impossible for me to take a position outside discourse, and I believe that my different interpretations of the data I collect (and even of what appears to me to count as data in the first place) grow out of what I am, and out of the ways in which I see the world. My struggle is to be empathic, rather than objective, and to provide the interpretive framework which, at this historical moment, makes the most sense to me (Sears, 1992).

Let me say this in a slightly different way. As a feminist and as an ethnographer, I set out to present and to privilege the experiences of the girls I studied, as well as *their* own view of reality. I want to represent, as best I can, their own voices — that is to say, the subjectivities they were experiencing and expressing at the time this research was done. I also know that I must keep myself present in the story; and in order to display my own view about what is happening, it is imperative that I undermine my 'researcher stance' and continue to 'interpret' myself as the interpreter of the story (Lather, 1992).

I will close this section on research by making a point in connection with the purposes and uses of feminist research. It has been suggested that feminist research ought to be explicitly committed to changing the social order, both by producing emancipatory knowledge and by empowering 'the researched' (Weiler, 1988; Lather, 1986; Stanley and Wise, 1993). I hope that my own research has produced knowledge that will be useful to emancipatory projects involving feminist consciousness raising, curriculum construction and liberation pedagogies. My research did not attempt to change the lives of the people involved in the study — my access to the children involved could not have been negotiated on those terms. My presence in their classrooms and their homes was tolerated, not invited. I had no right to make direct attempts to change them. It is my hope that this research, and other feminist research, will make a contribution, through the creation of new knowledge, to social and educational movements that will indeed benefit people like those I studied.

The Study

This book is based upon an ethnographic study of the home and school lives of seven sixth-grade girls, and of their reading of fiction. The girls lived in an affluent middle-class Canadian community of 1200 people, located in Ontario, not far from a city with a population of of 150,000. I will call their community 'Oak Town'. The girls involved in the study attended Oak Town School — a 10-year old, well-equipped red-brick school with 350 students — where they were members of two sixth-grade classes.

Most of the people who lived in Oak Town were of Ukrainian, German, and Scots-Irish descent, and were now second- and third-generation Canadians. They described themselves as 'middle class'. Many worked, for their wages, in jobs that required some specialized skill: bookkeeping, firefighting, mechanics, carpentry, computer programming, nursing, and clerical and sales work. Some had their own small businesses. Most families were affluent because they had two sources of income. There were no doctors or lawyers living in Oak Town. There were two new housing developments, and taxes were lower than in the city. Amenities included a nearby shopping mall, clean air and cable television. The people living here saw Oak Town as a comfortable place for families with children, and they felt that their elementary school had an excellent reputation. Oak Town, then, was what many would view as an idyllic suburban community, i.e. one without the overt problems of racial strife, drugs, and postmodern culture that affected life in the nearby city.

My central concern in the study was to answer this question: what did the reading of fiction mean to these girls? I began by thinking that the question was an interpretive one — one that would require the use of qualitative research methods — and that I would, first and foremost, be studying *individuals*. However, it soon became clear to me that describing and interpreting the various meanings that the girls gave to their reading would in fact require a description of the whole culture in which they lived their lives. I had, it seems, committed myself to a full ethnographic project, a form of qualitative research that attempts to identify the tenets of a given *culture*, the unconscious beliefs, customs, mores, and values of a group of people that are built up over time and transmitted from one generation to the next.

Over the course of an entire school year, I collected data in four ways: I made field notes based on observations of the sixth-grade classes at Oak Town School; I interviewed the sixth-grade children, their parents, and their teachers, and transcribed those interviews; I discussed novels with groups of children, recorded our conversations, and transcribed those conversations; and finally, I shared dialogue journals with seven of the girls who were avid readers of fiction, engaging in written conversations with them about the fiction they and I were reading. At the end of the school year I had accumulated more than 2000 pages of data. I read that data over and over again, looking for categories and themes, and writing memos to myself about connections between what was emerging in this data and what I was reading about in literary critiques, in feminist theories, and in critical educational theories. The assertions of this book are based upon this data, although clearly the ways in which I read and rewrote the data were shaped by the various theoretical positions described in this chapter[4].

I hope the reader will also examine Appendix A — which offers a more detailed explanation of the methodology used in this Oak Town study — in order to understand more fully the kind of evidence which supports each of the assertions I make. On the one hand, I want to argue that this work does meet the traditional criteria for excellence in ethnographic research: it is the sheer weight of the ethnographic detail, combined with the close relationships I enjoyed with the people of Oak Town, which together establish the validity of the study upon which this book is based.

At the same time, I also want to step outside the framework of the traditional criteria for judging an ethnographic project and place the study within the context of critical feminist educational discourses. The study has 'validity', not because it correctly represents external Truth, but because its conclusions are consistent with and justified by the data as I have interpreted it.

Feminist research can and does use every existing type of research methodology (Harding, 1987). What makes a piece of research feminist in nature is not just the fact that it uses new methods or approaches but rather the fact that it uses them in *new* ways and for *new* purposes — opening out new vantage points, ways of seeing, and ways of doing. Feminist ethnography attempts to represent *women's* experiences (unlike traditional ethnographic approaches, which only represent *men's* experiences). It attempts to answer questions that women need to have answered; and, as mentioned above, it places the researcher herself within the interpretive framework: a feminist ethnographer should not be invisible in her ethnographic tale.

The dilemma is this: I want to tell this story in a way that is convincing and familiar and immediate for the reader. But there are clear dangers involved in the traditional conventions of ethnographic writing. If I use the techniques of novelistic realism — if I write in the ethnographic present tense and make the people I write about seem fixed and unitary and unchanging, if I make myself invisible in the interests of telling a good story — then I risk obscuring the profound effect that my own ideology has had upon the narrative (Brodkey, 1987). I myself, therefore, need to be present in the text. And yet at the same time I still need to make the presence of the people I studied felt in the text: I need to try to represent their voices, as well as my own.

In trying to accomplish both aims at once, I have avoided the ethnographic present in order to help the reader to remember that this is a study of a certain historical moment, and that 'cultures do not stand still for their portraits' (Clifford, 1986a). And I have written, moreover, in two different 'voices', each of which makes use of a different point of view, different word choices, and a different tone or attitude. When representing the voices of the Oak Town people, I have used colloquialisms and a conversational tone. When offering my own analysis, on the other hand, I have been more formal and academic in tone. Occasionally, I will deliberately interrupt myself to comment upon the story (Brodkey, 1987). I realize that writing in two voices does not guarantee that the representation will be fair or 'accurate'. Nevertheless, Chapters 1, 2, and 3 *do* begin with the 'voices' of the people of Oak Town; for how could I presume to explain their identities without first attempting to present them?

As part of this attempt at such a presentation, I have made use of *narrative vignettes*. Narrative vignettes, although a central and powerful means of presenting data and analyses in qualitative research (Erickson, 1986;

Eisner, 1981; Barone, 1990), also tend, like the use of the ethnographic present tense, to make the narrator invisible. However because ethnography itself is 'a performance emplotted by powerful stories' (Clifford, 1986b, p. 98), I *was* able to create suitable vignettes for this book — by taking excerpts from the field notes made for the study and 'polishing' these to convey my interpretive perspective. These narrative vignettes are intended both as an alternative presentation of my analysis, and as a representation of the voices of the people they portray.

Chapter 2 describes life in Oak Town. Its theme is 'Gender Practices: The Cultural Reproduction of Gender.' It introduces the children and their families — the people whose words, and whose daily lives, have the power to make their culture visible to us. And it presents some of the 'visible practices' by which gender was constructed in Oak Town. Chapter 3, 'Literacy Practices: The Reproduction of Gender in Reading', goes on to consider Oak Town parents and their views on the practice of reading, both in their own lives and in the lives of their children. It details the ways in which reading and gender have intersected across generations, as well as some of the ways in which gender has been *enacted* in reading.

Chapter 4, 'Instructional Practices: Gender and Reading at School,' provides descriptions and an analysis of what happened in school when gendered forms of literacy learnt at home were brought to bear on the school curriculum. Children certainly used school literacy to construct gender. But reading at school was *itself* constructed by cultural views of knowledge and authority, and by cultural views of what it meant to read either as a girl or as a boy.

Chapter 5, 'Identity Practices: Constructing a Gendered Subjectivity', looks more closely at the girls and their reading practices. It describes the relationship between what the girls wanted for themselves in their struggle towards adulthood, on the one hand, and the messages the culture gave them about the gender-appropriate version of adulthood that they could achieve on the other. The reading of fiction became the arena in which girls attempted to see themselves as strong and active agents in the world. But it was also an arena in which they received cultural messages about violence against women.

Chapter 6 considers the implications of this book's analysis for parents and teachers — and anyone else who is concerned about child-rearing and educational problems and practices. The book takes up issues of the cultural reproduction of gender inequality, resistance to that reproduction, and pedagogical practices that support that reproduction. It highlights once again the importance of creating a cultural 'lens' that will create useful perspectives on the problems surrounding literacy and social injustice in the 1990s, in the hope that deeper knowledge of literacy as situated social practice, will encourage social transformation and support social justice.

The challenges that this kind of study poses are significant: to work simultaneously within symbolic-interactionist and feminist frameworks; to account for who I am but, at the same time, tell other people's stories; to show reading and gender accomplished and created by individual people, but keep visible, also, the workings of power and authority; to show cultural forces at work in people's lives, but respect also the power of the individual's will; and to acknowledge, and mourn for, all the damage schooling does, while holding out hope for a better world. The last challenge, that of seeing the damage while remaining hopeful, is the most difficult of all to meet.

But feminism is, and must always be, an enterprise of hope. And there are many in the world of feminist scholarship and research who will keep me company as I make the effort to be hopeful.

I accept the challenge in the words of Adrienne Rich (1978):

My heart is moved by all I cannot save:
so much has been destroyed.

I have to cast my lot with those
who age after age, perversely,

with no extraordinary power,
reconstitute the world.

Notes

1 I am highlighting *disciplines* in this introduction — as well as their various contributions to the world view I have constructed for myself — for several reasons. First, I hope to bring to the foreground the valuable contributions that different disciplines can make to an understanding of the nature of childhood, gender, reading and schooling — for too long, the discipline of education has depended almost exclusively on that of psychology for insight into all of these. Secondly, I want to clearly distinguish these different ways of understanding the world, in order to demonstrate the *distinctive* value of each. Finally, I want to emphasize the fact that in aligning myself with anthropology, I am choosing to work within a discipline that has great potential for illuminating the complexities of schooling, and one that I believe is still undervalued and under used.

Although I do not mean to set myself apart from all those ethnomethodologists or sociologists (like Irving Goffman) who have contributed so much to the way I see the world. I do, on the other hand, want to emphasize how it is that the ideas I am describing contribute more to an *anthropological* approach to the study of culture.

2 Interestingly enough, Rosenblatt's (1938, 1978) work, which has inspired so many of the response theorists who concern themselves with the psychology of children's literary responses, also attempts to account for the sociocultural context in which the response to literature occurs. Rosenblatt has shown herself to be aware of the important role that history and culture play in shaping the background and

experience of the reader, as well as his or her response to certain texts. I take issue, however, with Rosenblatt's emphasis on the individual nature of the response, because I feel she does not give enough attention to the external forces which work to put readers in certain positions, and to construct their views of literature. This excessive emphasis on the individual, and on a stance that seems to credit the individual with the creation of his or her own psyche, has unfortunately made it possible for her followers to ignore what she has to say about the influence of culture.

3 It is not my intention to isolate gender as a single causal factor of oppression, while excluding the related factors of race and class. The people I studied were members of a homogeneous group, privileged by their race, and privileged by their affluence. I will present ethnographic data which concentrates on *gender* in children's social lives (not on race and not on class), in part because gender as a category was the main influence on the way that the people of this study organized their lives. Race and class did not figure in the way they saw themselves. Gender did. I believe that race and class were important in their lives, but that these factors were invisible to them. This matter is part of my ongoing struggle to strike a balance between representing the views of the people I studied, and bringing my own views to bear on their lives.

In addition, as a feminist researcher, I claim my right to privilege female experience and to make it the subject of my book. At the same time, because I believe that the considerations of gender and race and class are fundamentally interrelated, I *will* occasionally take up class and race issues in this study of Oak Town — and in the final chapter.

4 The data for the study actually yielded three themes. My interpretation is that the people of Oak Town were enacting at least three sets of cultural beliefs, both in their reading practices and in the other activities of their daily lives: beliefs about *time*, beliefs about *individualism*, and beliefs about *gender*. This book focuses on their beliefs about gender only and does not attempt to do justice to the other two themes, although these other themes *are* considered in relation to gender in Chapter 1, and elsewhere, to a certain extent.

Chapter 2

Gender Practices: The Cultural Reproduction of Gender in Oak Town

The Families

Let me introduce some of the people who live in Oak Town, namely the families of the seven girls who were at the center of my work there. What follows is meant to present a picture of their lives, and to provide a background of details against which the reader can understand the analysis offered later. This section is based upon data gained from interviews both with the parents and with the girls themselves. Here, I want to capture for the reader the tone that these people adopted when talking about themselves[1].

The Oak Town families were pleased to have their children at Oak Town School, a proud and sprawling red brick structure with green lawns, expensive playground equipment, a skating rink and large playing fields. To the east of the school, within walking distance, lay Oak Town proper, the older part of town where the shade trees were tallest. Karen, Jerrica, Julie and Alisa lived here. Further to the east lay Farmland Meadows, a development of newer houses with stylish brass mailboxes. Marcia, Cara and Samantha lived there, and they had to use the school bus.

Karen Andruchuk, who was 12 years old, lived one block away from the school in a long white bi-level house with two big cars and two vans in the driveway. Part of the lower level of the house was an office: Karen's dad owned and operated apartment blocks in a nearby city, and her mother kept the books for the business. Karen's brother Kevin was in his third year of high school, while her brother Rick was in eighth grade.

Karen's parents, Ed and Helen Andruchuk, were busy people, but although the business demanded their time and attention, they made it clear to me that they tried hard to give their kids their fair share of attention. They told me that they took two family vacations every year, and that they supported the kids' sports and musical activities by driving them places and buying them the equipment they needed. They said they were pleased, all in all, with what they were able to give their children. Both Ed and Helen had grown up in large families in small towns, and neither had the clothes or toys or books in childhood that their children have enjoyed.

As we chatted, Ed and Helen explained that their children were busy people too. Both the boys took karate, guitar and saxophone lessons, and both played basketball. They were conscientious about their homework, and they liked to read the sports page for relaxation. Karen took gymnastics, and spent every possible minute with her girlfriends. She read at bedtime — often trying out *Babysitters Club* books[2] her friends had recommended to her, or animal stories.

Jerrica Scott and her family lived just up the street from the Andruchuks. Jim, Jerrica's dad, worked in computers, while Michelle, her mother, was a homemaker. Jerrica, age 11, had two younger brothers: Lee, who was 9, and Ross, who was 5. Jim was quite active in the community: he told me he coached hockey, played baseball, and was a volunteer firefighter. He said that when he had some extra time he liked computer games and computer hacking. Michelle told me that she was a reader — in fact, someone who read every available minute of the day.

With a small smile, Michelle told me that Jerrica was a reader too, and the best student in her sixth-grade class. Lee, on the other hand, although *he* also read well, preferred to play hockey all weekend, every weekend, all winter long. What with hockey practices Wednesday nights and Sunday afternoon, he didn't find the time to read. 'He's more the active type,' Michelle confided.

Three blocks over from the Scotts, Julie Dallas, aged 11, lived with her parents Alice and Terry. Julie was their oldest child: they also had 7-year-old Nancy and 4-year-old Tim. Terry fixed machinery, while Alice worked part-time in a department store and part-time as an electrical contractor. On Wednesdays, she also babysat for the kids across the street.

Terry and Alice offered me coffee, and seemed pleased at the chance to talk to me about their own kids and their own childhoods. Neither of them, they said, had had much money when they were growing up, and they thus took pride, even now, in being thrifty (they had decided not to spend much money on entertainment, for example). Terry had his hobbies, and Alice was an avid reader. They both enjoyed television, and so did the kids. Both seemed to me to be quietly proud of Julie — her good looks, her good grades in school, and her athletic ability. They thought Julie did a fine job of amusing herself: if she wasn't skating or braiding friendship bracelets, they said, she'd be reading or baking or doing a craft. And Julie had been playing with Alisa Weiss across the street for as long as they could remember.

Alisa, who was also 11 years old, lived with her parents, Don and Charlene Weiss, and her sister Anna, 16 months younger than she. Don Weiss told me he liked his job as a firefighter in a nearby city, although he hoped to earn a promotion to the rank of Captain. That, however, required a written test which he was hesitant about taking. He spoke quietly when he said he'd never been a good student, and that he hardly read anything other than the newspaper. He said that it was Charlene who had been the good student in high school, and had always liked to read. Even now, when she worked two days a week as a caterer, she read as much as she possibly could.

When I asked Charlene about Alisa's reading, she said that she would have liked Alisa to read more than her favorite *Sweet Valley Twins* books and *Archie* comics. Charlene had bought her the Laura Ingalls Wilder books, and the *Anne of Green Gables* books, but Alisa wasn't interested. That was disappointing for Charlene. Still, she felt lucky that Alisa was such a good kid: she got all As in school, she had nice friends, and she was a dependable and reliable person.

Marcia Thomas's family spoke with me in their pretty new house in Farmland Meadows, where they had moved two years before. Marcia's parents expressed their concern that Marcia, age 13, and her brother Jason, age 11, had had a hard time adjusting to life at Oak Town School. Both kids had been way behind in Math, and Marcia had been kept back a year. Their little sister Megan, age 6, liked school more than they did. All three were rock-music fans, and Marcia was, also, an avid reader. All three entertained themselves at home, spending a considerable amount of time in their rooms.

Michael, Marcia's father, worked as a crane operator. He told me that he loved war documentaries on television and that he had read and collected many books on war and history. Sherry, Marcia's mother, worked in an office and liked to relax in the evenings in front of the television, or with a good book. Stephen King was her favorite author. She said she often recommended one of her horror novels to Michael, and that he enjoyed them too. But she felt some concern about her daughter Marcia's interest in Stephen King and other horror stories, and hoped they wouldn't bother someone so young.

Although the Alexanders lived right next door to the Thomases, I could see, having spent time with both girls at school, that Cara Alexander and Marcia Thomas were not close friends. Although both were in sixth grade, Cara was 11 and Marcia was 13, and they had different interests.

Cara's younger brother Jeremy was 8. Her parents, Bill and Patty, told me they had built their house themselves, and had collected and refinished lots of good-quality wooden furniture — Bill had a workshop in the basement where he did that sort of thing. An electrical technician, Bill was also interested in radio control, and in building model planes. Patty worked as a secretary for the nearby city's Catholic School Board. I thought they were both quiet, soft-spoken people. They said they didn't read much fiction. Patty said it was difficult to find time even to read the newspaper.

The Alexanders both agreed that Cara was the reader in the family. In addition she took piano lessons, practicing every day, and in winter she did figure skating twice a week. She always did her homework, but she still found plenty of time to read. Jeremy, on the other hand, according to his parents, didn't read much. He preferred playing hockey, or building something.

Samantha Ulrich, aged 11, lived two blocks away from Cara. She was the oldest child of Norma and Joe Ulrich. Her younger siblings were Daniel (10), Tina (7), and Ben (5). Joe was a carpenter, unemployed at the time of the study, who carried out furniture repairs in his shop out in the garage. Norma was a homemaker, looking for a part-time job. Norma told me shyly that they were Jehovah's Witnesses, and enjoyed that community of friends at their church in the city. Norma said she thought it was harder for her kids at school, their being of a different religion, but it couldn't be helped. She said that she tried to help her children to feel closer to each other, to make up for the lack of friends at school. Once a week, she and Joe took them all into the city for swimming lessons at the YMCA, followed by some time at the library. Norma would find a novel while Ben and Tina played with the toys in the children's library. Joe and Dan would find some 'how-to' books, and Samantha would take out a stack of Young Adult novels. After that, they would all have supper at Burger King.

Norma told me with pride that Samantha had learned to read in kindergarten. Samantha was devoted to her favorite author, Judy Blume, and would read her books all day when she was sick and home from school. That happened often. Samantha was the least healthy of the four children. Norma felt blessed that Samantha liked to spend time with the family, and that she felt close enough to her mother to talk with her about what she read.

Gender Positions and Gender Enactments

Every culture is characterized by a set of discourses which concern *gender*, and which position people to behave and interact in certain gender-appropriate ways. People can accept some aspects of these discourses as containing 'truths', or common-sense statements, about gender, and can act consciously in accordance with them. Other aspects of these gender discourses people may only accept *tacitly*, without consciously articulating their implications for gender, while still, however, acting on the basis of those implications. Other aspects of these discourses people may not accept.

Like children everywhere, the children of Oak Town had been exposed to the gender discourses of the culture in which they lived. These discourses suggested forms or 'rules' for 'doing' gender, and children could see the adults in their lives acting on these rules in more or less consistent ways. Because the children were concerned with learning to do gender appropriately, thus avoiding the social disruption that is a consequence of doing gender incorrectly, they were sensitive to gender positions suggested in the discourses of the culture and they acted upon their increasing knowledge of these gender forms. Thus they dressed and acted and came to think in accordance with the composite of cultural discourses to which they had been exposed since birth. Gender became for them an important social accomplishment.

Dress and Demeanor

In their study of the role of fifth- and sixth-grade peer groups (in a southern US elementary school) in the cultural 'transmission' of gender, Eisenhart and Holland (1983) found that teachers and other adults within the school were very uncomfortable with any display of sexuality on the part of children, and that children learned to avoid any sexual behavior when adults were present. Any hint of a cross-gender sexual relationship drew the teachers' discouragement swiftly and privately. In gender-segregated sex-education classes teachers encouraged students to avoid acting in accordance with a sexual identity for as long as possible (they warned girls about becoming pregnant, and cautioned boys about trying, too soon, to use romantic relationships in order to gain adult status). Children's sexual behavior thus went underground in the school that Eisenhart and Holland studied, precisely because the children knew that adults would not tolerate such behavior. And yet the adults continued to use gender in organizing many aspects of life at the school (such as taking attendance, physical-education classes, lining up for walking to assembly); and, of course, the cultural discourses conveyed in advertising and on television continued to make it clear to the children involved that gender was a major organizational feature of their society. Eisenhart and Holland want to make the point that the peer group, of necessity, became the place where children developed and practiced their sexual identities. The point that I am making here is that in the presence of adults, the children of the Eisenhart and Holland study were *not* free to use sexual behavior as a way to mark the differences between 'boy' and 'girl'.

Neither were the sixth graders of Oak Town. On one occasion, I visited the high school that the Oak Town children would eventually attend, and it seemed to me that much more openly sexual behavior *was* being tolerated here: boys felt free to drape an arm over a girl's shoulder and guide her somewhere; a girl could insert her hand into the back jeans pocket of the boy she walked beside; and teenage couples were exchanging kisses in the hallways. But at Oak Town School, adults did not tolerate sexual behavior among the children. A little *was* there to be seen among eighth and ninth graders, when I had observed children closely over long periods of time and in peer groups, but it was never public. I am making this point at length because I intend to show that *dress* and *demeanor* and not behavior associated with sexual activity were the means by which the children routinely marked their genders.

In *Gender Play: Girls and Boys in School* (1993), Barrie Thorne also analyzes the ways in which school children mark gender. She points out that younger children in North American society are often seen by adults as *asexual* beings. In the two American elementary schools she studied, teachers often acted as if the children did not have sexual identities. In spite of the fact that they had to deal with the reality of 30 children's bodies in the classroom every day, teachers seemed to deal in sanitized and idealized images of children, and to try to get children to conform to those images. As early as fourth grade, children in the schools Thorne studied were using aspects of dress and body adornment to mark gender meanings — to demonstrate a shift from 'the relatively asexual gender system of childhood to the overtly sexual gender system of adolescence and adulthood' (p. 135). By the time the children had reached sixth grade, a well-developed system of dress and public behavior was in use both for distinguishing girls from boys and for expressing sexual meanings in culturally sanctioned ways.

This was also true of the sixth-grade children at Oak Town School: these sixth graders were also using dress, demeanor and leisure-time activities to 'do gender' (West and Zimmerman, 1987). For example, while the sixth grade girls invested a good deal of time and money in displaying their gender through dress, the sixth-grade boys were achieving an entirely different look at less expense. Most boys dressed in jeans or sweatpants, pullover jersey shirts, cotton socks, and Nikes or Reeboks (running shoes), and they had shaggy haircuts, unevenly cut and falling over their ears. A few of the boys, however, used their clothes and hairstyles so as to display their gender in a different way. Aaron and Jim proudly wore their heavy hockey jackets indoors. Carl and Michael bought the bright cotton print pants and tie-dyed tee-shirts that the mall advertised for boys that spring. And Shay always dressed carefully, and with style: he wore outfits that were color coordinated and carefully put together. One day, for example, he dressed entirely in red and black and white: a white cotton turtleneck with black knit pants, white socks, spotless white runners, a white sweater with tall red letters that said UNLV (University of Nevada at Las Vegas), and a red nylon jacket over that with the collar turned up. I thought he looked comfortable and athletic and masculine. No pastels, no jewelry, no curls — just straight lines and solid colors.

Only three or four of the 21 sixth-grade boys dressed carefully. In doing so, they established their gender by appropriating a 'look' for boys that they had seen advertised on television and on sale at the mall. But the boys who did not put any effort into their dress were also proclaiming a gendered message. Their dress said, 'I don't care what I look like because appearance isn't important for me. I am free to be comfortable and attend to other things.' While this was an acceptable fashion statement for a boy to make, it was not acceptable for a girl, and only one of the sixth grade girls occasionally neglected her appearance.

The activities that the boys undertook to fill their extra time at school and at home were, for the most part, physical activities. Thorne (1986), in one study of gender arrangements in an elementary school, found that the boys engaged in more rough and tumble play and more physical fighting than did the girls, and that organized sports were a central activity for boys. This was certainly true at Oak Town School. Whereas the girls preferred to talk and read and mingle at recess, the boys preferred to be physically active. About one third of the boys played organized hockey, and others said they had played hockey in the earlier elementary grades. The boys also cited their outdoor activities (hunting and fishing and working with Dad), and associated quiet games and indoor activities with illness and bad weather.

The girls engaged in quite different activities, and they dressed more elaborately than did the boys.

> It was 8:50 on the morning after a three-day weekend. Lacey stood in the hallway talking to Karen and Alisa. She was wearing pink and gray 'washed look' jeans with zippers up the back of each leg. She had on a pink and navy sweatshirt, pink star-shaped dangling earrings, pink socks and flat gray shoes. She had a white barrette in her curly hair and a pink glass heart on a chain around her neck.
>
> I complimented her on the pretty outfit. Karen said, 'Yeah, isn't it nice?'
>
> Lacey said,'My Dad took us up to the Mall for the weekend, and I got it all there. I got to bring a friend along, so Jennifer came too. My mom even bought her a shirt just like this one!'

Like Lacey, nearly all the sixth-grade girls put both money and careful thought into coordinating their outfits. Nearly all of them had mirrors on the inside of their locker doors. Hairbrushes and combs hung on little hooks beside the mirrors. Several of the girls had long hair. They braided sections of it, curled their bangs, and arranged it with barrettes, a headband, glittery ponytail holders, a clip, or a small colored comb. When Mrs Gagnon, one of the sixth-grade teachers, French-braided her hair in October, every girl whose hair was long enough did the same every day for a week. On school-picture-taking day four of the girls with long hair 'crimped' it with Tanya's crimping iron. Other girls had perms. They often arrived at school with hair still slightly damp from a morning shower. Cara sometimes tied her curls with a strip of pink lace. Alisa used combs to push the sides of her short, curly perm straight up so that her curls clustered on the top of her head, and every girl arranged her hair so that her earrings would show.

Every girl in sixth grade had pierced ears. None of the boys, however, had a peirced ear — not even Shay. The girls wore all kinds of earrings, but dangling earrings seemed to be the most popular. Jackie, I noticed, even had a black-and-white-striped pair to match her black-and-white-striped sweater. Most of the girls told me they had gotten their ears pierced before they started kindergarten. Jerrica and Nicole and Karen each had a second hole, and all the girls talked about infected ears as if they were routine.

The girls were careful about what they wore to school, and they often wore the same seasonal styles. In the fall, black jersey pants and pastel cotton-knit sweaters were favorites, while in the spring, knee-length jeans with pastel-appliqued sweatshirts were favorites. Very often, the socks the girls wore looked brand new, and if they were wearing not flat shoes but running shoes, these were perfectly white and clean.

The girls polished their fingernails, compared their pendants, and tried on a little makeup at lunch. Sometimes, they found that their clothes constricted their physical activity; for example, the skin-tight black-and-flourescent-green bicycle shorts they bought in the spring weren't easy to run in. Most of the girls therefore changed their clothes for their Physical Education classes. The boys, however, did not.

Not one of the girls chose to play outdoors during recess or at noon. Several played instruments in the band, which practiced at noon time, and a few participated in the Drama Club productions, which were rehearsed at noon. When intramural sports and games were scheduled for noon, most of the girls participated, but only two girls signed up for after school soccer when Mrs Gagnon put up a list. It seemed to me that what the girls preferred to do during their free time was to talk to each other. They talked about events at home, about things they'd bought, about movies and television shows they'd seen, and about books they'd read. They talked about boys, their braces, their families, and about each other.

There were times when groups of girls talking together appeared to become uncomfortable and self-conscious. If Shay or a few of the seventh grade boys appeared to be watching a group of girls during recess, the girls became very much aware of their audience: some tossed their hair and giggled loudly, and all carefully refrained from looking in that direction. I did not, however, see any similar kind of behavior among the boys, even when they became aware that I was watching them intently. Instead, they became curious about me and stared back. It seemed as if the girls, several of whom watched MTV (Music Television) regularly, and all of whom had been exposed to fashion magazines and other cultural discourses of femininity, were already thinking of their appearance as if it were a performance, and recognizing that they themselves were the objects of a 'male gaze' (Kaplan, 1987).

Kaplan (1987) uses the concept of 'gender address' to discuss the ways in which films and videos present gender, as well as the attitudes these media express toward each gender. She explains that feminist film theories, emerging from the study of the classical Hollywood film, have identified a 'male gaze' made toward female figures in which the camera assumes a male point of view and positions female figures in ways meaningful to men — as idealized mothers, for example, or as objects of male sexual desire. Although MTV assumes more than one form of gender address, some very popular videos still make use of the traditional 'male gaze' (Rod Stewart's 'Infatuation', for example). The Oak Town children all saw Hollywood films, television movies, and rock videos, but while the girls now acted, in everyday situations, as if someone were watching them, the boys did not.

Violence

Of course, dress and body adornment were not the only means for 'doing' gender. Behavior provided another. After months of watching Oak Town sixth graders, I came to the conclusion that the people of Oak Town accepted and acted on the idea that boys had a right to impose their wills on other people. Boys demonstrated their awareness of this right or privilege in two ways: they bugged people, and they used physical force and violence to achieve their desires. In these ways, also, they 'did' gender.

'Bugging' is a word that both children and adults at Oak Town School used to mean intentionally bothering people and trying to upset them. Christopher admitted with a grin to bugging Alisa. Karen was apprehensive about inviting boys to her birthday party because they bugged people. Marcia said that Jack bugged her. Teachers also got bugged. All of those who bugged were boys. Julie said that although girls did bug back, they almost never *started* the bugging. I think she was right.

I saw bugging at every possible time of day at Oak Town School. It was a feature of daily life there. At recess, Shay could be seen spraying the seventh-grade girls with hairspray. During Physical Education lessons, the boys bounced soccer balls on the floor while Mrs Gagnon tried to give instructions, so that she couldn't be heard. Nick wouldn't let Anthony walk by his desk on the way back from the bathroom. When Anthony went around Jake's desk on his way to his seat, he poked Jake and brushed his neck to bother him on the way by. And in another instance, while James and Jeff and Rob waited in line for Mrs Gagnon to check their Language Arts notebooks, they pushed and shoved each other.

Bugging was not teasing. Teasing was a verbal practice, an interaction that girls were as likely to participate in as boys. When Christopher told Alisa, 'Oh, you're so cute! You look like the puppy in *Bridge to Terabithia*,' he was teasing. When Karen offered Jake a girl's friendship bracelet, she was teasing. Teasing could be ignored. Bugging, however, could not be, because bugging had a physical dimension (whether symbolic or concrete), and was intentionally more upsetting. Bugging intruded on the body, and demanded that the person being bugged pay attention to and acknowledge the presence of the person doing the bugging. The most common response to bugging was to say 'Quit it!' or 'Cut it out!' But the person doing the bugging had the power *not* to stop — *not* to leave the other person alone. He chose — and it was almost always a male — whether or not the bugging, and the interaction, would continue. Bugging was an assertion of the will, an exercise in power and control.

Several of the boys used bugging with sexual overtones as a way of asserting their power over the girls in the school. Among adults this use of bugging would constitute sexual harassment. James, for example, patted or caressed Jerrica and Nicole anywhere below the waist that he could reach when he was near them. He whispered obscenities to them as he walked by their desks to sharpen his pencil. Tom would stare at a girl's chest (after catching her eye) for several minutes at a time. The girls involved were sorely provoked. They were angry, and they dreaded further such encounters, but they did not report the incidents to the teacher or to their parents.[3]

As mentioned above, both the boys who used this type of bugging and the girls who endured it took their cues from their experiences *outside* the classroom. Their experiences of the cultural discourses which reached them through television and through fiction, as well as through their families, supported this kind of behavior, and suggested that boys and men *were* allowed to do these things to girls and women. Images of male power and female passivity surrounded them. During the year of the study, for example, window displays at the nearby shopping mall included photographs of fashionably dressed women lying prone and draped in chains. Television movies during prime viewing time told stories of wife-assault and serial rape. The school library contained fiction for children that featured violence against women (see Chapter 4 for a description of *The Trouble with Wednesdays* by L. Nathanson, for example). I saw 5 of the 21 sixth-grade boys in Oak Town use bugging with sexual dimensions against girls, perhaps because they regarded it as a viable, safe, and effective way of exerting a kind of power over the girls. None of the girls who were bugged in this way complained about it to an adult, perhaps because there were no suggestions available about taking that course of action, while, on the other hand, there *were* suggestions that they would suffer if they did. Let me explain what I mean.

Some of the messages implicit in the cultural discourses operating here were identified and described 20 years ago by feminist theorists. At least a part of the Oak Town girls' silence had to do with the idea that anything associated with sexuality is shameful (Henley, 1977), and that speaking openly of sexual things is somehow contaminating (Brownmiller, 1975). Another contributing cultural message was the idea that physical force is a *male* prerogative (Millet, 1970). All three of these messages are still present in the culture, still analyzed, and still lamented.

The idea that sex is contaminating is a very old one, one suggested in the earliest patriarchal literature. It has been argued that because, from early on in the reign of patriarchies, the ruling deity has always been male, men have had the authority to create our cultural heritage regarding sex — and, come to that, nearly everything else. Women, on the other hand, have been seen as the objects, the receptacles, and the antagonists of male desire. More to the point, sex itself has been seen as something *inhering in women*. It has been thought of specifically as a female quality, not as a human one, as a temptation offered to men by women, and as something therefore unclean and requiring purification (French, 1985). The idea that sex is tainted and unclean is familiar to children in school, as can be seen in the ritualized cross-gender pollution games like 'Cooties' (played by younger children), which Thorne has described (1993) at length.

At Oak Town School there were many indications that the children had picked up on the suggestion that sex was an exclusively female quality, on the one hand, and had a contaminating effect, on the other. During recess, for example, Lacey, and other girls, drew curvaceous female figures in slit skirts and sexy poses on the chalkboard, and then tried to disclaim all knowledge of who might have drawn them. Furthermore, girls' faces burned red when they were forced to speak to their male teacher about matters of menstruation. And in another instance, Sarah wore to school one of the short and revealing shirts being marketed for girls at the Eastside Mall, but then refused to participate in the high jump while wearing it for fear of exposing her chest to public view. Given these other incidents, the fact that girls did *not* speak out against incidents of sexual harassment implies that they felt *shamed* by them.

They probably also felt helpless. Images of the female 'victim' were readily available to the Oak Town children via the discourses conveyed in the electronic and print media that surrounded them. For example, they were thoroughly familiar with the victim's plight in Michael Jackson's video 'Thriller' (described in greater detail below); everyone discussed the Freddy Krueger videos in which female victims were burned and mutilated (although few sixth graders had actually seen these videos); and girls passed novels featuring female victims from hand to hand. On those few occasions where the 'victim' *was* indeed saved, only very rarely was it because of some definite action on her part.

There were also cultural discourses which suggested to children that the use of force was characteristic of masculinity (Morgan, 1990). Football games, Clint Eastwood and Sylvester Stallone movies, reports of modern warfare on the television news — all were rife with the violence that men exercised upon each other. Other discourses, already mentioned, kept the violence and the threat of violence, that men inflicted on women before the children's eyes. It is only recently that other discourses which suggest that women can *resist* sexual harassment have become more visible: 'Take Back the Night' marches came to the nearby city, and Anita Hill (the American law professor who accused US Supreme Court nominee Clarence Thomas of sexual harrass-ment) made the nightly news, *after* the year of this study. Positioned as victims, shamed by behavior associated with sex, and bombarded with the idea that the use of force is characteristically male and a man's right, the Oak Town girls found themselves unable to report incidents of sexual bugging either to their teachers or their parents.

The boys saw bugging as a way of getting and then keeping the attention of another person — as a powerful tool for securing and controlling a particular model of interaction with another person. It was an act of symbolic power — and, as I have been implying, one of symbolic violence (Bourdieu, 1991). It is not a coincidence that the gender endowed by the culture at large with greater material and political power was the gender that used bugging to resist adult authority and to keep the upper hand when dealing with peers. It is also not surprising that boys acted out their gender through more violent forms of behavior.

It was recess time on a cold and snowy morning. Nearly all the sixth graders had chosen to remain inside. Groups of boys occupied the classroom. One group surrounded Shay and Jim who were arm wrestling. The two boys sat across a desk from each other, right elbows on the table, hands locked together. Their faces were set and intent, their eyes focused on distant objects. The strain showed around their mouths. Four other boys watched in silence.

Across the room Christopher and Aaron stood facing each other, arms up over their heads, hands and forearms locked together. They were each pressing with all their available body weight against the other. I turned to Karen, who was searching her desk for something. 'What are they doing?' She looked briefly at Christopher and Aaron. 'Oh, they're playing "Mercy". That's a game the boys play. You just wrestle with somebody like that and try to get the other guy to say "mercy".'

'Mercy' appeared to be a game in which boys used physical force and the threat of physical injury intentionally, in order to demonstrate personal dominance and impose their wills on other people. Like sexual harassment, it is a game of intimidation, an instance of symbolic violence, a manifestation of what Bourdieu (1991) calls 'symbolic power'.

Symbolic power is an instrument of domination, one brought into existence by discourse, and by certain symbols, rather than by actual weapons. The state is the holder of the monopoly of legitimate symbolic power, according to Bourdieu, because the people of the state agree to allow it to keep that monopoly. The state is allowed any number of symbolic acts of imposition — for example, it is allowed to confer the official names of these acts on social programmes, on wars and on institutions. The exercise of symbolic power always rests on a foundation of shared belief and presupposes the active complicity of those subjected to it.

Symbolic power is accomplished through symbolic violence, and both these phenomena rely upon the power of *suggestion*. Intimidation can only be imposed upon a people *predisposed* to feel it in the first place. Those not so predisposed would ignore it. Exposed to cultural discourses promoting the female as 'victim', the Oak Town girls are predisposed to feel the threat inherent in sexual bugging. Symbolic violence is accomplished through a kind of secret code, with various suggestions inscribed in what might be considered insignificant aspects of things, situations, and practices of everyday life. Positioned as victims without the power to resist, girls are inclined to read the suggestion in boys' uninvited touches as assertions of physical power. Symbolic injunctions, intimidations, warnings and threats such as these work to secure the compliance of an individual.

Symbolic violence is an effective weapon because it does succeed in securing compliance, but it is also *insidious* because it influences the 'construction' of subjectivity. Instead of telling the child what she must do, the culture tells her what she *is* (Bourdieu, 1991). MTV, the television news, novels, fashion advertisements, older relatives and the boys at school all told the Oak Town girls what they were: powerless people whose bodies were 'naturally' the objects of others' desires. It is not surprising, therefore, that most accepted the practice of sexual harassment. Bourdieu suggests that people come to accept these violent suggestions inscribed in the practices of everyday life, no matter what their status or class, and no matter what the effect on them, because cultural discourses position them as people who must accept the warning, while they in turn come to interpret themselves as those who must submit. In this way, domination is sustained through interpersonal relations, and symbolic violence is accepted as legitimate.

There were certainly indications that in Oak Town, acting in physically violent ways was accepted as legitimate and seen as gender-appropriate for the boys in the school. For example, the sixth grade boys at Oak Town School had a favorite game that they loved to play during their Physical Education classes, and they never failed to ask for it. Called 'Buns to the Wall,' it was a form of dodge ball. It required that one team form an outer circle, and that the other team stand within the circle thus formed. The people forming the outer circle then threw balls across the circle to each other, trying to hit the people in the center and get them 'out.' The boys on one team gleefully cheered each other on in trying to hit the girls and boys on the other team with the balls, thrown hard and fast. The team that had the greatest number of boys on it always won.

Although the sixth-grade boys enjoyed the game, the sixth-grade girls, with one exception, despised it because the boys were so rough. Karen said the boys thought being rough was 'macho'. She was always afraid that she'd finish the game needing a cast on an arm or a leg. Marcia said she hated getting 'pounded.' Alisa and Julie said they'd really rather not play that game at all: it wasn't safe, and somebody always got hurt.

Mrs Gagnon told me, 'Well, we play that game a lot because the kids just love it. They beg for it.' I heard the noisy classroom group talk that preceded the Physical Education class on more than one occasion, and I would say that the boys did beg for it, but that the girls argued strongly against it. It seems that Mrs Gagnon did not hear the girls. She did share some of their worries about physical injuries, however: 'Sometimes, I know, Jake throws the ball too high and too hard, and that's dangerous. I've asked him to keep it closer to the ground time and time again, but he just won't do that.' Mrs Gagnon may have been worried about Jake's actions but she still allowed Jake to ignore her — perhaps because Jake's behavior seemed inevitable to her, or perhaps because it was apparently acceptable to the other teachers.

In the soccer, basketball and playground games I witnessed, violence, again, was a feature of the boys' play. The violence, which did sometimes result in injuries, took place on the playground under a teacher's supervision and as part of an approved activity. Certain boys, like Jake, ignored teacher directives to be less violent, and certain teachers, like Joleen Gagnon, accepted their behavior with a 'boys will be boys' attitude. Twice, when older boys' playground basketball skirmishes resulted in bloody noses, I saw teachers, before a crowd of witnesses, quietly direct the injured child indoors to wash up and pursue the matter no further.

Most boys behaved violently only in large group situations where many other boys were present. A few of the boys did, however, display violent behavior during personal interactions in the classroom. Tom, in arguing with Tracey one morning before school, intentionally slammed her into her locker door. Her leg grew numb, and remained that way for half an hour. She cried in alarm, rather than in pain. Mrs Gagnon comforted her, and cautioned Tom to be more careful. At noon time one day, Jake shoved Anthony into the brick wall of the hallway, and Anthony wore a purple bruise on his forehead for the rest of the day.

Not all the boys indulged in violent behaviour, however. There were two or three sixth-grade boys who, I noticed, existed socially on the fringes of the group. They rarely bugged people, and I never saw them use violence in personal interactions. Anthony, often lost in a book, was one of those boys. Cody, who was overweight and ostracized for it, was another.

As already mentioned, it was in games and in other large group situations that almost all the boys behaved violently. For example, one afternoon when *all* the sixth graders went outside to fly kites they had made, 10 of the boys, led by Nick, ganged up on Jack, pushing him to the ground and beating him with their fists, and destroyed his kite. The two sixth-grade teachers, who would not answer my questions about why they thought this had happened, ended the incident quickly and did not appear to be angry or excited about it. I concluded that they saw this as fairly routine. The sixth grade girls, however, told me the story later in tones of shock and indignation. When Jack had been attacked and his kite smashed by 10 of the boys on the playground, one boy, Jim, had helped Jack to his feet, taken him into the building, and helped him to recover. Later, he walked Jack home and helped him to mend his kite. In retelling the story, the girls applauded Jim's efforts to be kind, and cited this as his resistance to an ideology of male violence. Karen said it showed that, 'Not all boys are as mean and macho as they're supposed to be.'

The girls knew that boys were 'supposed to be' violent. When Stephanie told a group of girls that Shay had written something obscene on a dry lawn with bug spray and then set it afire, the girls accepted this as normal, boy-like behavior. However, when Stephanie said that Shay had gone on to burn down a garage, Alisa spoke for the majority of the girls when she said: 'Oh, no, I'm sure Shay wouldn't do that. He's not that kind of person. He wants us to think he is, but he really isn't.'

Alisa knew that the boys' acts of symbolic violence had gone too far as soon as they became costly or dangerous for adults. Burning down a garage, for example, would be going too far: steps would have to be taken to deal with something like that. Shay himself told the related story of his friend Ricky: 'Ricky used to go to this school, but he doesn't go here any more. One day he got mad at a teacher and punched her. Now they've got him taking pills.[4] He's much better now, but he still doesn't go to school. He's crazy. Last winter, when the snow was so deep, he went crazy-carpeting off his roof. ' Shay laughed at this story.

Whereas violence directed against adults was not acceptable, violence toward the self *was* sometimes acceptable: dangerous stunts on ski slopes were smiled at; Julie's parents radiated amusement as they told me about their 4-year-old son knocking out three of his baby teeth and scraping the skin off his chin; and boys' hockey injuries were routinely glossed over, and often attributed to the actions of the injuried party himself. If you were a boy and you got hurt, that was life. That was natural.

Being a boy at Oak Town School, then, meant dressing for action and participating in physical activities. It meant being willing to use physical force in sports and games, and in other group settings, in order to secure your wishes and demonstrate your dominance over other people.

It was Phys Ed period for the sixth graders. Mrs Gagnon had her class out on the back playing field for a game of soccer. The October morning was sunny, cold, and windy. Jim and Carl were wearing their Bergen Minor Hockey jackets.

Mrs Gagnon said this game was to be girls-against-the-boys. The boys vocalized their satisfaction. The girls groaned. Mrs G. said she'd play with the girls, to even things up. Who wanted to be the boys' goalie? Miles and Rick and Jim and Carl and Shay volunteered. Mrs Gagnon chose Miles. Who wanted to be the girls' goalie? No one volunteered. Mrs. G waited. Finally she said, 'Come on. We need a girl goalie.'

Finally, Sarah reluctantly raised her hand. 'All right,' she said. 'I'll do it.'

The game began. Mrs. G shouted encouragement to the girls when they had the ball. Jade was a good player, tall and lean and enthusiastic. She ran and followed the ball aggressively. When she had the ball, Hunter yelled encouragement to Jake. 'Get that ball! Take it away from her! It's just a stupid girl!'

Several of the girls were good players. Nicole, Tracey, and Jackie ran right up to the action around the ball. Shoved aside by the boys, they pulled back. Shay and Aaron were good players too. They rushed right up to the action and into it. They fell over each other and rolled away on the ground.

Alisa and Stephanie stood near me at the east end of the field, watching the action in the distance, carrying on a quiet conversation. 'She's only jealous,' said Stephanie.

The game continued and got rougher. Nick came over to the sidelines and handed me his glasses. He said, 'I'm not wearing these in there!'

Tracey got banged in the face with the ball. She stood still, her hands over her face. Jade rushed over to her and put an arm around her shoulder. Everyone's eyes were on them. Tracey was crying a little, and then laughing too. She fished a Kleenex out of her jacket pocket and wiped a little blood from her nose. Mrs Gagnon went over. Jade said, 'Poor baby. She's okay, Mrs Gagnon.' Tracey leaned against Jade for a moment, then stood up straight, shook her head, and ran back onto the field.

The game resumed.

This sixth-grade soccer game at Oak Town School was a demonstration of the boys' willingness to use physical aggression and violence to 'win'. The fact that the girls did not use physical force, and were generally reluctant to participate in situations where force was likely to be used, provides a good illustration of the connection between gender and violence.

The connection between gender and violence goes hand in hand with a *hierarchical* social structure. This is because in order to maintain the power of one group over another, the threat of violence is required (Bourdieu, 1991). Canadian women do not voluntarily work longer hours to earn less money, or work long unpaid hours in the home: the threat of violence helps to keep them at it. The disadvantages they experience come to exist in a number of complex ways, and many different factors, and many different cultural discourses, contribute to them. One such factor, seen in the Oak Town soccer game, is the fact that physical aggression is accepted in our culture as an expression of maculinity, and that because of this fact, men hold a psychological edge over women (Brownmiller, 1975; French, 1987; Hanmer and Maynard, 1987). It is considered 'natural' for boys to use physical force to establish dominance in school. When they do so, they are 'doing' gender.

The cultural discourses that surrounded Oak Town promoted acts of both physical and symbolic violence to the boys who lived there, and Oak

Town teachers and parents, for their part, accepted violent behavior when the boys used it. These same discourses, on the other hand, promoted an attitude of passivity and compliance, as well as a victim stance, to the girls who lived at Oak Town. And it was violence, as we have seen, that was one visible characteristic of life at school. There were individual boys, like Jim, who resisted the ideology of male violence, and girls admired and celebrated their resistance. But violent behavior, in the form of wife-assault and rape and pornography, continued to characterize the North American society of which Oak Town was a part. By 'doing boy' and 'doing girl' in their daily lives, as well as in their personal interactions, the Oak Town children both learned and reproduced the gender inequalities of the society at large (West and Zimmerman, 1987).

Relationships

The people of Oak Town lived their lives as if the girls and the women were responsible for maintaining human relationships. This was because working at relationships was one of the ways in which the Oak Town girls 'constructed' themselves to be different from the boys. When the boys were outdoors or playing physical games during recess, the girls were indoors talking to each other, playing games that involved paper and pencil, or describing the plots of television shows and books they had read. When the boys were hanging around in large groups, the girls were moving in pairs or in groups of three. When the boys got angry with someone, they pounded him, but when the girls got angry with someone, they said hurtful things and left her all alone.

The Oak Town children behaved much like the children who have been described in other studies of gender in elementary schools. In describing one such study, Thorne (1986) summarized the sociological and sociolinguistic research carried out on girls' groups and boys' groups in the elementary school as follows: boys tended to interact in larger, more age-heterogeneous groups (Lever, 1976; Waldrop and Halverson, 1975; Eder and Hallinan, 1978); they engaged in more rough-and-tumble play and physical fighting (Maccoby and Jacklin, 1974); organized sports were both a central activity and a major metaphor in boys' subcultures, and they often constructed their interactions in the form of contests and hierarchies (Savin-Williams, 1976); and finally, language in boys' groups often took the form of direct commands, insults, and challenges (Goodwin, 1980). All of these findings were also descriptive of the Oak Town sixth-grade boys.

The Oak Town girls, like the girls described in other research studies, lived in different ways, in a world that focused more on caring relationships. In addition: they interacted in smaller groups or friendship pairs (Eder and Hallinan, 1978; Waldrop and Halverson, 1975); their play was more cooperative and inclined to turn-taking (Lever, 1976); they had more intense and exclusive friendships, and used more *indirect* ways of expressing disagreement (Goodwin, 1980; Lever, 1976; Maltz and Borker, 1983); and finally, the language used in their groups rarely involved direct commands — instead, they tended to use directives, for example 'Let's do this', which merged the speaker and the hearer (Goodwin, 1980).

Thorne (1986) cautions that we will fail to see much of the complexity involved in gender and cross-gender interactions if we conceive of 'boys' and 'girls' as simple oppositional categories. Her warning seems well taken. Of course, the research 'findings' described above are not universals: gender arrangements and patterns of similarity and difference can, and do, vary according to the factors of situation, race, class, region, and subculture. All that I want to point out here is that research on same-gender children's groups that was conducted 15 years before this Oak Town study did point to the importance of maintaining close human relationships when 'doing girl'.

So does the work of Carole Gilligan and her colleagues at Harvard (Gilligan, 1982; Gilligan, Lyons and Hanmer, 1989). In studying the moral development of adolescent girls and boys, Gilligan concluded that while boys developed an 'ethic of justice' that valued law and looked for general moral principles, girls were more inclined to develop toward an 'ethic of caring' that valued human relationship and looked at individual cases. Girls' worlds were 'relational worlds', and girls grew up working at 'making connections' with other people. Gilligan was describing in psychological terms what Thorne (1993) and others were describing in sociological terms, and what *I* am attempting to describe in anthropological terms, namely an important aspect of 'doing girl'.

One way to 'do girl' in Oak Town was to be a good friend. The sixth-grade girls had certain rules about friendships, and they followed them closely. They could, and did, state the first rule explicitly: friends were *girls*. The other two rules were unstated, but still nonetheless acted upon: friends were girls their own age — most often girls in the same class at school, or girls who lived in the same neighborhood; and secondly, friendships with girls took precedence over romantic relationships with boys.

The first of these rules, or guidelines, for choosing friends was very important, but difficult to live with. Boys could not be girls' friends, and Karen, for one, thought this was too bad. She sounded wistful when she explained to me that girls *couldn't* 'just be friends' with boys, because then everyone assumed that the boy was a boyfriend, and both people involved became subject to teasing and ridicule. Cara agreed, explaining that although a girl could say that a boy was a friend only, no one would believe that her relationship with him wasn't a romantic one. Complying with this rule, the children lived as if friendship and 'romance' (a word which had sexual overtones) were mutually exclusive. Samantha read a book in which the girl who was the main character had a boy for a best friend and another boy who was her 'boyfriend'. She and the boy who was her best friend kept their friendship a secret. They were careful not to speak to each other in public, because they didn't want people to tease them about liking each other. When Samantha described the plot of this book to Cara, Cara said, 'That's just like here.'

I will discuss teasing as a way of maintaining distance between girls and boys later in this chapter. Here, in connection with the rules for friendship, I will simply point out that teasing worked to discourage cross-gender friendships and so enforce gender boundaries — as, indeed, it did in the elementary schools that Thorne studied (1993). An Oak Town girl or boy who tried to be a friend of someone of the other gender was teased about having a romantic relationship.

None of the girls in sixth grade actually did have romantic relationships with any of the boys in the class. Several seemed to think Shay was very attractive. They talked about what the boys looked like, and it was generally agreed among the girls that Shay and Jim and Christopher were 'cute' boys. Shay and Tom were clearly interested in girls in general, but in no girl in particular. Tom would walk by a group of several girls, and address them as a whole: 'Oh, all you pretty girls. I do like girls.' In teacher-assigned group work sessions, Tom would smirk and roll his eyes at the girls in the group, encouraging them to giggle. Shay spent every morning recess watching and teasing and talking to the seventh- and-eighth grade girls whose home rooms were just down the hall. But neither Tom nor Shay singled out any one particular girl for positive attention.

For their part, several of the girls spoke of having boyfriends outside of school: a church friend, or a cousin's friend, or someone they met at a wedding. These boyfriends were people they didn't have to see and deal with on a daily basis, and that made them manageable. From my perspective, it seemed to be unclear to the sixth-grade children exactly how one *would* carry on a romantic relationship in school every day. At any rate, whether for this reason or some other reason, no one did it. But the children did seem to think about romantic relationships as interesting possibilities. Indeed, a few of the girls told me they thought they were ready to try having a boyfriend. In one interview, Marcia said that a person could read *Sweet Valley High* books to find out how it was really done.

As I have said before, the adults of Oak Town did not want to see their children as sexual beings, and the children had learned that it was not acceptable for them to behave in sexual ways in public. In the sixth grade, the children were still using their dress and demeanor to organize the gender system by which they lived; however, because they were approaching and entering into puberty, they were finding themselves moving to a gender system organized instead around heterosexual relationships (Thorne, 1986). Feminist theorists have pointed out that heterosexuality is 'compulsory' in most cultures, because patriarchy requires a system in which women's sexuality is controlled so that paternity can be reliably established (Durocher, 1990). Supported by economic structures that often make women financially dependent upon men, and sanctioned by religious and moral condemnations of homosexual behavior, heterosexuality is not just a choice but rather the organizing and defining principle for constructing adult gender identity, as well as the social structures that frame it. In Oak Town, friendship rules and the teasing that enforced them supported the children's transition to using heterosexuality to do 'gender', both by making mere friendships across the genders unlikely to occur, and by punishing children when they did occur.

Taking their cues, then, from the adults around them, and from the media, the children of Oak Town 'constructed' the rule that the only possible relationship between a boy and a girl was a romantic (sexual) relationship. The girls had no *friends* who were boys — or, at least, none that they could publicly acknowledge. Some of them did, however, make it clear that they didn't like the system, but that they couldn't seem to find a way around it. Alisa explained: 'Like you always have girl friends. And then it seems like . . . like . . . whenever you say "Can I have a boy over?" they always say, "Oh, you got a *boyfriend*." I just . . . why can't it be for a *friend*?'

Friendships certainly seemed to be more central to the lives of the Oak Town girls than they were to those of the boys. The girls talked about friends and relationships more than the boys did, and seemed to work more at getting and keeping friends. The girls shared and lent books, and sometimes clothes; they wrote each other lengthy notes; they waited for each other when the class had to move from one location to another within the school; and they walked each other home. The boys did none of these things.

This emphasis on friendship was consistent, furthermore, with other attitudes and accomplishments that the girls valued, like cooperation, mutual support, and responsibility to others. In a study of social behavior in an urban Catholic high school, Nancy Lesko (1988) also concluded that the values connected with friendship were related to other social accomplishments. One group of teens, called by others 'the rich and populars', valued individual superiority and individual competitiveness, and based their choice of friends on their desire to establish status and exclusiveness. Another group of teens, called by others 'the burn-outs', valued present pleasures over future successes and chose to put friendships and relationships with others before their own personal advancement. Like the Oak Town girls, Lesko's 'burn-outs' lived by an ethic of community rather than by an ethic of individualism.

This was not to say that just any girl would do for a friend. Friends had to be girls your own age and people you saw every day. Marcia explained:

> Tanis Andrews got to be my friend when we first moved to Oak Town, because they lived near us and we were the same age. I didn't know I was going to stay back, and that she would be a grade ahead of me in school. We're still friends, kinda, but now Tanis's sister Jackie is my friend too, because she's in sixth grade, like me.

Julie agreed that where a girl lived and how old she was were important to her status as a friend. She explained:

> Most of my friends that I like being with, like Sarah, live two doors down from me, like I live here and she lives here. And you know where Alisa lives? She's just two houses away. So all three of us have been friends since we were little, so we play well together . . . And I play with Alisa's sister Anna too. They're only 16 months apart. Anna's one year younger, but she's usually the same age as me. Like in June she'll be 11, and I'm 11 now.

Birthday parties were very important ways of declaring and establishing friendships. Almost all the girls' birthday parties were sleepovers, and that limited the number of people who could be invited to six or seven at the most. A girl could only invite her *best* friends to a birthday sleepover, and the girls thought long and hard about the guest list for a sleepover because it constituted a public declaration of friendship. It also made it very clear which girls one did *not* count among one's closest friends.

As already mentioned, best friends and close friends were such important people that these girls willingly put these friendships with other girls before their romantic relationships with boys. Although these girls did have a few, albeit tenuous relationships with boys to consider, they nonetheless valued the idea that girls' friendships ought to have precedence over relationships with boys. Indeed, at this point in their lives, they saw this as a cultural ideal. Several of the girls, for example, read and loved the book *Dear Sister* , one of the books in the *Sweet Valley High* series. Karen summarized the story: 'You should read *Dear Sister*. Jessica is really nice in that book. Elizabeth gets hurt. Jessica is always by her side and she never thinks about boys any more for a while. Until Elizabeth comes back.'

Samantha had a best friend, Ashley, who also attended the Jehovah's Witness church services in the city on Sundays, but who lived in another town. Samantha had a boyfriend named Kalyn at church too, until Kalyn disappointed her. She said, 'I don't like Kalyn any more. He's fickle. He looks at all the girls. Ashley and me, we used to like him, but no more.' Samantha wanted me to understand that she and Ashley put loyalty to each other above trying to win the affection of a disloyal boy.

At several times during the school year the sixth-grade girls spent considerable time braiding 'friendship bracelets' out of yarn or heavy thread or plastic strips. This practice, and the rituals that surrounded it, demonstrated the girls' ideals of friendship and gender loyalty. If anyone bought material for friendship bracelets and brought it to school, she was expected to share it without hesitation with any girl who asked for some. If one girl knew how to do the braiding while someone else, who wanted to learn, didn't, that girl was expected to help the other girl patiently until she could do it too.

Karen and Julie carefully explained to me the rules surrounding the finished friendship bracelets: you gave them to your friends, and they then wore them for a while before passing them on. If you wore them on your left wrist, it meant you were single and looking. If you wore them on your right wrist, that meant you were taken. Right ankle meant 'party animal' (you just wanted to have fun). Left ankle meant 'mellow' (calm and sweet). If you wrecked a bracelet, you cut it off, made a wish and threw it away. Best friends could keep each others' bracelets and *not* pass them on. The friendship bracelets were used to make statements, more hoped for than real, about one's romantic aspirations. But more importantly, they served as signifiers of a common identity and a common connection between the girls, and as demonstrations of special loyalties between the girls.

Girls also enacted their gender by being 'good'. That is to say, the Oak Town girls appeared to meet the expectations both of their families and of the school. All of the Oak Town parents interviewed felt their daughters were 'good kids' who did their school work and their household chores without much trouble, and rarely gave their parents 'a hard time'. The sixth-grade teachers were not surprised that most of the awards given out at the Awards Assembly on the last day of school went to girls. The children themselves weren't surprised either: it was the girls who served the school — all but one of the members of the School Safety Patrol were girls, and nearly all the members, and certainly all the *active* members, of the Student Council were also girls.

Most of the girls, moreover, were good students. Whereas only 4 of the 21 boys excelled academically, 9 of the girls did. The girls tended to be much more conscientious about getting their work completed and submitted before the deadlines than were the boys. And the girls were more likely to remember to bring their homework back to school. I could see these tendencies reflected in the teachers' daily interactions with children:

> Mrs Gagnon stood at the front of the silent classroom, her arms folded across her chest, glancing around the room at the children who were writing in their journals. Her glance settled on Jake. He was sitting with nothing on his desk, looking into space. She moved to stand in front of his desk.
>
> She asked, 'Where's your journal, Jake?'
>
> 'I lost it.'
>
> 'Have you looked?' (Jake nodded.)
>
> 'Have you looked at home?' (Jake nodded.)
>
> '*Really* looked?' (Jake nodded.)
>
> Mrs Gagnon looked up at the ceiling and sighed. She walked to her desk and came back with a new blank notebook. She tossed it on his desk.
>
> 'Start again. Right now.'
>
> Two minutes later, Nicole approached Mrs Gagnon, who was seated at her desk. Nicole had tears in her eyes. She whispered to Mrs G., who stood and put her hand on Nicole's shoulder.
>
> 'Nicole!' she said, with a look of mock horror. Then she smiled. 'Don't worry. Everybody leaves their journal at home once in a while. You go work on your tissue-paper art for the next few minutes. You can catch up on the journal at home tonight.' Nicole gave her a tremulous smile and returned to her seat.

Mrs Gagnon found that her girls usually met her expectations without a fuss; and the parents interviewed provided a similar picture of their girls' doing household chores, practicing the piano, and generally trying to meet their parents' expectations. Several parents spoke of how well their girls amused themselves and found acceptable ways to fill their time. All those parents interviewed who had sons spoke of how different from their sisters those boys were. These parents reported with amusement and tolerance that their boys were more absent-minded, less interested in schoolwork, less willing to prepare for music lessons, and generally less cooperative.

Walkerdine (1985; 1990) suggests that schoolgirls who strive to be 'good' are suppressing conflicts within themselves, as well as conflicts in their relationships with other people. Compliance with all the demands made upon them wasn't easy, and the Oak Town girls must have sometimes resented the constant pressure to meet those demands. Their own desires must, occasionally, have been in conflict with those of other people. And yet, despite this, they did still comply and cooperate. And moreover, like the girls of Lesko's (1988) 'rich and popular' group, the Oak Town girls also clearly expected *of each other* such 'good' behavior both at home and at school. They had an investment in being accepted, in doing what was expected of them, and in being rewarded for it. One important pay-off for being 'good' was membership in a community of 'good' girls who supported and affirmed each other, rewarding each other in this way for being 'good'.

Constructing Division

It seemed to me that the people of Oak Town acted to position girls and boys as members of 'distinctive, opposing, and sometimes antagonistic groups' (Thorne, 1986). Every day at Oak Town School, grown-ups employed gender as a basic social division. Attendance registers were divided into a Boys section and a Girls section, and the vice-principal filed a monthly report with the provincial government to record how many boys and how many girls of each age had been attending school. Mr Boyle, the school principal, always began the announcements by saying, 'Good morning, boys and girls.' When the Optomist Club had their annual Public Speaking Contest for the school, each teacher was asked to supply a girl contestant and a boy contestant from each class. The Optomists always chose a girl winner and a boy winner.

Like the children, the adults at Oak Town School also used clothes to express their social class, their professional identity, and their gender. Teachers dressed both to express a professional attitude (they tried to be especially well dressed on the day when the area superintendent was coming to visit), and to mark their special status as teachers (while parent volunteers wore jeans and casual clothing to work at the school, teachers almost never did). But most significant was the fact that they dressed to display and mark their gender. Both women and men wore expensive and well-coordinated outfits, but where men's clothing was comfortable, women's was not: Oak Town School's female teachers wore high-heeled shoes and wool dresses that were often snugly fitted at the waist; their hair was carefully cut and curled and colored and styled; and their makeup was painstaking and elaborate.

Adults at school, like the children, also teased each other across gender lines. Mr Peterson complained with a smile that it wasn't safe to eat lunch in the staff room with all those women: they hid things on him and tried to provoke him about little things. Although Mr Peterson and Mrs Gagnon were most often businesslike in their interactions, Mrs Gagnon did giggle at Mr Peterson's occasional failures to keep track of what was happening on a given day. And Mr Peterson teased Mrs Gagnon about manipulating people to get her own way. He would ask in a bantering tone, 'What are you getting Errol to do for you now, Joleen?'

Teasing was demonstrated to the children both at school and at home, and the children had learned to use it to construct the gender division and to maintain gender boundaries. Among the children, the great majority of the teasing that went on had to do with romance, with who liked whom, with who was cute, and with who thought somebody else was cute. Girls instigated this kind of teasing as often as boys did. Most often, this teasing was light-hearted in tone, and was accompanied by smiles or laughter.

Quite often it was flattering to be teased, to be singled out as someone worthy of another's admiration. But the proper pose in response to teasing was one of quiet embarrassment. One didn't want to seem too pleased.

There was always an audience for cross-gender teasing. It took place in public gatherings, during recess, at lunch, or during group work in class. The audience was oriented to teasing as a way of interacting across gender lines and, did not, indeed, expect boys and girls to interact in other, more friendly ways (when they did, the audience teased). The audience expected, and approved, exchanges of words which, although they singled out a person and caused him or her a moment of embarrassment, also served to confirm his or her gender identity before the group.

Sometimes, the teasing had more of an edge to it. Christopher teased Alisa nearly every day. He found insulting things to say. He told her she was naive to think *Flowers in the Attic* might be a true story. He told her she was silly to get scared by a book. Alisa sighed and said, 'My mother says he teases me because he likes me. Do you think that's true?' Marcia pointed out to Alisa that getting teased was a lot better than getting pounded, and that Christopher was better than some of the other boys because he at least teased girls instead of knocking them around.

Teasing was thus the most common mode of interaction across gender lines outside of class time, and one which helped to maintain the idea that boys and girls were members of distinct groups with firm boundaries, groups that defined themselves in opposition to each other.

A second factor that worked to create gender division in Oak Town was the influence of cultural discourses representing girls and women as sexual beings. In Oak Town girls were more sexually 'defined' than the boys were. By this I mean that the girls and the women here were positioned in ways that made male-oriented sexuality an explicit part of what it meant to be female, while the boys and the men were positioned as the 'consumers' of this sexuality. In this way, a gender division was constructed in both opposing and complementary terms.

Children read these discourses early in their lives, and both the girls and the boys of Oak Town used their play to act out the idea that females were essentially different, and sexual, beings. There is evidence that other children elsewhere have done so, too. One sociological study of gender construction in school-playground behavior found that both boys and girls played games that positioned girls as sexual beings. After extensive observations at a Michigan elementary school during the late 1970s, Thorne and Luria (1986) concluded that as early as first-grade, elementary school girls were being positioned as sexual beings through chasing games and ritualized pollution games in which a girl's touch was seen as contaminating. In a different study of urban Black children's play in home neighborhoods, a sociolinguistic analysis of girls' jump rope rhymes revealed strong heterosexual romantic themes (Goodwin, 1985). These games and rhymes were also a part of playground life at Oak Town School, and the sixth grade girls had grown up with them. 'Here comes Love, here comes Marriage, here comes Jodi with a baby carriage,' was chanted by jumpers in Oak Town just as it was chanted by little girls of a different race in the back alleys of Philadelphia. The girls used jump-rope rhymes as one means of representing 'female' as 'sexual', but they had other ways too. During recess, for example, Lacey, Amanda, and Michelle, as mentioned earlier, would stand at the classroom chalkboard and draw figures of curvy, big-bosomed 'ladies' in seductive poses wearing dresses with slits up the sides. They would giggle and point and say, 'Careful. Mrs Cherland's sitting back there.'

The children were not inventing the notion that females were sexual beings. There were many representations of female sexuality in popular culture, and the children encountered these daily. When Joleen asked the children to bring in tapes of their favorite music to use when creating exercise routines for their Physical Education classes, she found herself surprised. She told me she'd had to veto several songs that were too sexually explicit to be appropriate for 11-year-old children in school. We talked about her feelings of shock, and she told me that the worst of it was that it was Alisa and Nicole, not the boys, who had suggested these songs. Joleen could not fully articulate what it was that disturbed her about this, but I came to think that it would have been more acceptable to Joleen to have the boys seeing the girls as the sexual objects referred to in these song lyrics, rather than having the girls *seeing themselves* in this demeaning way.

And demeaning it was. Here again, the girls sensed that like the girls and women they saw on MTV, they were the objects of a 'male gaze', a cultural lens which focused on girls and women as the objects of male sexual pleasure (Kaplan, 1987), as people who could engage in relationships with men only on sexual terms — as, almost, breathing mannequins without other nonsexual, nonphysical dimensions to their humanity. When the children brought in magazine ads for collages, both the girls and the boys brought pictures of women wearing scant clothing, some perched in reclining poses on the top of cars, some posing in front of refrigerators. When the selected songs that Joleen had approved for the exercise routines did, eventually, blare out over the school loudspeaker system, there were still reminders of female sexuality in the lyrics. Joleen accepted 'I don't want your body, baby, I only wanna dance with you,' but that lyric was the exception rather than the rule. The children had already got the message. Knowing that females were sexually defined was an element in the girls' self-consciousness. When Sarah declined to participate in the high jump at the track meet because her loose shirt would expose too much of her body, I found it impossible to imagine a boy making a similar objection.

I want to make a double point here. Firstly, it seems to me that the social system of gender division that the children of Oak Town were growing up with, and which prevailing cultural discourses defined as 'natural', was based upon a compulsory heterosexual identity. A dualistic system which constructed 'man' and 'woman' as both opposite and complementary served the prevailing patriarchy firstly by positioning the woman as the 'other', controlled by sexuality and by the body, and secondly by positioning man as the representative human being, rational, intellectual, and self-controlled. The heterosexual social system worked to legitimate male control of women, firstly by making use of cultural discourses which divided people according to their gender, and then by representing women as helpless sexual beings incapable and unworthy of controlling themselves. The heterosexual social system thus legitimated and naturalized both the marriage institution, on the one hand, and phallocentric sexuality on the other, both of which made it possible for the society in question to exercise control over women's reproductive lives. This, broadly defined, was the social system the Oak Town children lived within.

My second point is that it was essential to the maintenance and reproduction of the social order that the girls of Oak Town (as well as the boys) came to see themselves as sexual beings of a certain type. If the majority of young people had come to see themselves as homosexual, and had refused to participate in the patriarchal structures that shaped reproduction and child-rearing in Oak Town, the social order as they knew it would have been profoundly threatened. It saddens me to think of all the distinguished research which suggests that the maintenance of the social order is not accomplished without damage to the psychological development of girls, who seem to lose, at puberty, their willingness to assert themselves and to speak with confidence (Gilligan, 1989; Rogers, 1993). Neither, however, is it accomplished without damage to the psychological development of boys, who must come to terms with a view of male people as characteristically violent beings (Morgan, 1987; Prothrow-Stith, 1991).

The Oak Town parents, and, to some extent, the teachers, seemed to understand that the heterosexual social system did not operate in the best interests of the girls, since they wanted to protect their girls from this sexual representation for as long as possible. Many of the parents were worried about the girls' reading of romances, and several even prevented their daughters from reading the *Sweet Valley High* books, which centered on relationships with boys. One parent said, 'She's a little too young for the boy stuff. There'll be plenty of time for that in later years.' Errol Boyle, the principal, said that nearly every week, one parent or another called the school to complain about sexual scenes or references in the books that their children had brought home from the school library.

The teachers, too, did some worrying about the consequences of sexual representation, as well as about the consequences, for young girls, of their representing themselves as sexual beings. Pam Smith, the ninth-grade teacher, told me she was 'appalled' to find that some of the ninth-grade girls were doing book reports on library books that included explicit sexual scenes involving young girls. She said that she thought that such books were harmful. And when several of the girls began to wear skin-tight satin-look pants to school, teachers took note, and expressed concern and disapproval in the staffroom. (They did not say anything to the girls who wore them, however.)

It was true that the Young Adult rack in the library held many paperback romances that contained sex scenes. Often, these were written from a young girl's point of view. One that Jerrica read, *A Question of Happiness*, implied that the heroine's younger sisters could no longer understand her now that she had had a sexual experience with a much older man. To this character, in this particular piece of fiction, sex was represented as a profoundly transforming event for young girls.

Parents and teachers in Oak Town acted as if sexual knowledge *was* a transforming thing — as if it were what separated the women from the girls, the latter being mere children, innocent and sexless. Adults acted and spoke as if the girls were always the *victims* of sex, and never sexual agents. Sensitive as they were to the cultural discourses that were shaped by such views, it is not surprising that the adults of Oak Town endeavored to act so as to protect their girls from danger — to deny them knowledge of sex, and of sexual representations, in order to prolong their childhoods. But because sexual messages and sexual representations permeated the discourses transmitted through mass media and advertising, it was simply not possible for individual adults to 'protect' girls from a knowledge of sex for very long.

The girls' active curiosity about sex and their desire to participate in adult sexual life, also worked to make it impossible for them to be denied sexual knowledge. Jerrica, like Karen and Marcia, was quite interested in sex, frequently summarizing the plot of the *Babysitters Club* book *Boy-Crazy Stacey* and other novels in terms of who kissed whom. Jerrica and the other girls teased one another about who would be going to the next school dance with which boy. Not one of them was actually going with any particular boy, but the teasing, touched with a sexual innuendo, made such a thing seem excitingly possible.

Toward the end of the school year, Jerrica wrote out and distributed her own six-point 'permission list' for kissing boys. Other girls recopied theirs to give to friends, and soon nearly every girl in the sixth grade had one. Handwritten on lined notebook paper, it read like this:

> This gives you permission to cuddle anyone, anytime, as long as it is done sweetly!
> 1 Your guy must have his arms around you!
> 2 While kissing, your eyes must be closed.
> 3 Warning! Girls, watch out! Guys hands tend to wander!
> 4 For best results, keep this with you at all times.
> 5 Any boys that see this must kiss you immediately!
> 6 You must copy this out 5 times and send it to five of your friends —
> or you'll have bad luck with boys forever!
> *Good Luck!*
> Jerrica Scott

The 'permission list' above was kept secret and carefully guarded. (It came into my possession when Marcia left a folded copy in the back of her dialogue journal. I returned it without comment. As far as I know, I am the only adult who saw a copy.)

As I have explained earlier in this chapter, refusing to see, and refusing to tolerate, sexual behavior in pre-pubescent children is one way in which adults can personally participate in the social construction of childhood. Childhood is marked as distinct from adulthood insofar as adults are allowed to be more openly sexual beings while children traditionally are not. Generally speaking, the teachers and parents of Oak Town wanted the sixth graders to disregard the attractions of older romantic and sexual identities in favor of being asexual beings and good students (Eisenhart and Holland, 1983). When I discussed this attitude before, I was suggesting that, partly because the adults would not allow children to use sexual behavior as a means both of acting out gender and of distinguishing between genders in the first place, the children were forced to find other means of enacting their gender, and that in Oak Town (where race and class configurations made available both money and time) these means included dress, activities, and demeanor.

Here I want to emphasize a different point: that the construction of children as asexual beings served to distinguish and separate them from adults. The Oak Town adults, privileged by race and class, carried with them notions of childhood constructed in their own youth in the midst of a postwar period of prosperity that allowed for strict distinctions between adults (who worked) and children (who did not). They also carried with them images and texts in which 'child' signified 'purity' — as conveyed in the Christmas nativity story, and in the Laura Ingalls Wilder books that several of the Oak Town mothers purchased for their daughters. They were, however, trying to accomplish this construction of children as asexual in the presence of other conflicting discourses surrounding sexuality and childhood.

It seems clear to me that the ideas reaching Oak Town about the nature of childhood were many and varied. In speaking with me about movies they rented to view at home, several parents mentioned *Taxi*, in which 12-year-old Jodi Foster portrayed a prostitute. During the year of this study Hollywood personality Brooke Shields made the news by suing for possession of nude pictures of her 10-year-old self; Canadian lawyers debated changes to the Young Offenders Act, changes which would have allowed 15-year-old children to be prosecuted as adults in Canadian courts; and the sale of pornography featuring children became an issue in the city nearest Oak Town. Clearly, there were discourses available which suggested that children *were*, indeed, sexual beings.

More than a decade ago, Neil Postman (1981) lamented that childhood innocence was impossible to sustain in the age of television, because television had to violate every taboo in the culture in order to hold its audience, and because it did not segregate its audience: anything an adult could know a child could also know. Now that films of all kinds are available on video and can be shown on home VCRs, it is more than ever the case that images and situations children were once 'protected' from are now available to them. In Oak Town, children were able to watch, at home, the movies their parents had rented for their own entertainment, movies the children would not have been allowed to see if they had been shown at movie theaters in the city. Marcia saw three Freddie Krueger 'slash and burn' videos that her parents rented, while Samantha watched movies like *The Platoon*, rated 'R' (for 'Restricted') because of its graphic violence, with her parents at home. What's more, several of the Oak Town girls picked up and read, in their own homes, adult horror novels that shocked them greatly and disturbed their sleep.

More than one view of childhood existed in Oak Town, and it seemed to me that the children here were continually negotiating their identities in response to the various discourses that surrounded them. They learned to hide their sexual interests from the grown-ups with whom they came in contact. Because these grown-ups had physical and economic control over their children's lives, children usually complied with their commands. In speaking of her own lack of agency in daily life, Cara said, 'I like my brother, but there really isn't much that we could do for each other without my mom and dad.' Cara and her brother did as they were told.

The children of Oak Town hid their sexuality from adults, but their sexuality and their sexual interests still existed. Two messages from two different cultural discourses can be inferred from Jerrica's list. The first is the message that sexual behavior (and having a sexual identity) is physically and emotionally rewarding, and that sex not only brings pleasure but is also an expression of affection or love. Jerrica had read the Young Adult novel *A Question of Happiness*, watched *Dallas* on television with her family, and rented the film *Steel Magnolias* to watch with her friends. Messages about the rewards of sexuality were there to be read.

And yet there was a second message to be inferred from Jerrica's list, the message that sex may be *dangerous* — and in her list, Jerrica had indeed included a 'warning'. The Oak Town children could, after all, see all around them a culture that linked sexuality with violence, and the message was not lost upon them. I choose to examine that message here, at the close of this chapter, because it is an instance of a theme that will recur in later chapters. Sexuality, or perhaps simply being an adult woman, was regarded as a dangerous matter. All the sixth-grade children at Oak Town School had seen Michael Jackson's video 'Thriller'. In fact, most of them had seen it several times. When Mr Peterson suggested that they watch it at their Halloween party in school, they declined. They had seen it too often. 'Thriller' was getting boring.

'Thriller' tells a story, in music, song and dance, about a pretty girl who is pursued by horrible-looking and very threatening creatures on a dark and lonely walk home. For most of the video it appears that the girl will be murdered, and perhaps also raped. The creatures who pursue her are obviously male, and obviously stronger than she. She is small and slim and runs along in her high-heeled shoes while they are tall and broad-shouldered. At the very end of the video, these creatures take off their masks and reveal themselves as Michael Jackson and some of his friends, friendly and charming, and presumably harmless. The girl smiles in relief. But for most of the video, the girl's terror is justifiable and very real.

'Thriller' wasn't the only video delivering the message that being female is a risky business and that the threat of violence is sexy. The programme *Video Hits*, which was broadcast on television every day after school time, ran many such videos. 'White Wedding' by Billy Idol, in which a bride is ripped with barbed wire and later (presumably) murdered, was a particular favorite with some of the Oak Town children.

Miami Vice, a hit television series in which beautiful young women were often the victims of violence, or were mutilated and murdered in crimes that two stylish detectives then proceeded to solve, was another programme that the Oak Town children looked forward to watching each week.

Drug-store racks were full of magazines that displayed photographs of the stars of these rock videos, and that contained posters of the rock groups that made them.

The drug-store racks in question, racks that were accessible to children, also held pornographic magazines. *Maclean's Magazine* (a leading Canadian weekly news publication) has defined pornography as films, videos or photographs of explicit sexual acts, but within this category of materials there are several subgenres (Jenish, 1993). *Maclean's* explains that 'adult only' video stores, such as are usually found in strip malls in major Canadian cities like the one near Oak Town, offer subgenres entitled straight, bisexual, transsexual, gay, stag, all-girls, oral, anal, Asian, big boobs, black-and-white (inter-racial), foreign, and amateur. In February of 1992, the Canadian Supreme Court ruled that explicit sex without violent, degrading, or dehumanizing conduct is acceptable under contemporary Canadian community standards, and that hence these materials are not obscene. Canadian police, however, have pointed out that films, videos and magazines depicting sexual violence, bondage, sado-masochism, bestiality, and necrophilia are also bought and sold by Canadians, despite the fact that the Canadian Criminal Code does not allow such material to be sold at licenced stores in local strip malls.

Certainly, pornographic films and videos of the first type *were* available for rental purposes in the big city near to Oak Town, and the children whispered to each other about parents' or older siblings' renting these. Some of these films may have represented genres of extreme anti-female violence: the 'slice and dice' genre in which a woman is murdered and then dismembered, or the 'stalk and slash' genre in which the camera first devotes a considerable amount of time to the pursuit of the female victim (filmed, of course, from the stalker's point of view), and then dwells upon the victim's eventual death, which is usually by stabbing (Twitchell, 1985). I don't believe that the children ever saw these kinds of video, not, at least, in their entirety. The Oak Town children did have limited access, however, to the pornography available in those magazines that had been purchased for use at home, and that were also displayed in the drug stores in shopping malls. Access was limited, because most adults, acting again to 'protect' the children from sexuality, were unwilling to allow children to read such magazines freely.

I am left with this question: what did these pornographic materials, categorized as nonviolent, and therefore suitable for public sale and consumption, signify for the children who saw them? When I see these magazine and video covers in drug stores, I see photographs of nude and semi-nude women of several different races in undignified and demeaning poses, and I am reminded of Bourdieu's (1991) idea that domination is brought into existence by certain kinds of discourse and by certain kinds of symbols. If symbolic power rests on a foundation of shared belief, and if it presupposes the active complicity of those subjected to it, then it becomes clearer to me how 'nonviolent' pornography plays a part in putting female people and certain racial groups in the position of 'those to be controlled'. There are very few instances of pornographic video-and-magazine-cover art in which men, as well as women, are depicted. Here again, sexuality is seen as inhering exclusively in females. Both men and women are confronted with these photographs of women who appear to be primarily bodies — their faces slack and their eyes vacant or closed. *Maclean's* quotes the remark made by Patricia Herdman, co-founder of a Canadian anti-pornography organization, that these cover photos, and the texts that accompany them, 'present women as insatiable creatures who can't control themselves and who will have sex with anyone' (Jenish, 1993). And the suggestion is that those who can't control themselves need to be controlled by others. The symbolic violence inherent in pornographic magazine covers does not try to tell women and girls what they must do. It tries to tell them *who they are* (Bourdieu, 1991) — namely, people who can be used and exploited. In this way, it predisposes them to accept others' control both of their bodies and of their lives.

Pornography that has been ruled illegal because it is violent, because it involves women and children in degrading and physically painful sexual acts, apparently against their wills, is more explicit than Michael Jackson's 'Thriller' about the link between sex and violence. Such pornography more graphically depicts both the extent of physical domination and the dangers of trying to resist that domination. As a result of such depictions, whenever women and children are presented as the victims of violence and abuse, and whenever violence is linked with sexuality, it can come to feel dangerous to be female or young.

In Oak Town, Jerrica felt this danger, and indeed hinted at female victimization in her 'list'. Female victimization is a strong theme in many sociological, psychological, political, and literary analyses of violence in a postmodern world. Feminist sociological and political studies of wife-assault, incest, rape, sexual harrassment, prostitution, and pornography posit that male sexual abuse of females is a primary social expression of male power (MacKinnon, 1982 and 1983; Edwards, 1987). Violence has become part of our culture's construction of masculinity (Morgan, 1987); and violence and sexual aggression have become significant thematic components of contemporary fiction, rock videos, and horror movies (Twitchell, 1985; Kaplan, 1987). I came to believe that cultural messages linking sex with violence were being received by the Oak Town children, even through the children's fiction that they were reading. I will return to this idea in Chapter 5. Here, I should point out that some children chose to turn their backs on these messages because they seemed to them too painful to be endured. Samantha and Alisa and Cara all refused to read certain books, and avoided seeing certain movies. This is further evidence of the existence of cultural discourses promoting female victimization, but it is also, in a more hopeful light, evidence of female resistance to being positioned as victim.

Resisting Gender

I have just been discussing gender divisions. But there were, of course, important areas of their lives where the Oak Town girls and boys were not divided by gender, areas where they shared the same opportunities and the same restrictions. Both the girls and the boys had time to fill, both were controlled by adults more powerful that they, both loved a good story with lots of action in it, and both girls and boys participated as consumers in the economy that shaped their material lives.

This last point seems an important one. Divided, as they were, by gender, the Oak Town children were *united*, however, by race and class. They were all members of the same privileged racial group, and all members of families with comfortable incomes. The family income enabled these children to use clothing to enact their genders because it allowed them, once they had 'read' the representations given in advertisements, to buy what was necessary to dress as a 'girl' or a 'boy' and to acquire new clothing when fashions changed. The family income gave both children and their parents the necessary leisure time and capital for shopping, which was a way of life in Oak Town (the bumper sticker on Tanya's parents' new van read 'Born to shop'). The Oak Town girls, especially, were positioned as *consumers*, rather than as producers, of income: several of the girls had stickers on their school notebooks that paraphrased the title of a Cyndi Lauper song: 'Girls just wanna go shopping.'

In a similar way, the Oak Town children were also enabled thanks to their social class and their family's income to use certain 'activities' for enacting their genders. Organized hockey leagues for boys and piano lessons for girls required money as well as leisure time, but the money and the time were both available in Oak Town. Parents had the time to drive children back and forth to the city for karate and ballet lessons, for basketball tournaments and synchronized swim classes, and for air-cadet meetings and baton-twirling classes. And they also had the money to pay the registration fees and buy the necessary equipment. The fact that the time and the money were both available meant that both the parents and the children were free to take notice of and respond to representations of gender — as conveyed in the images and texts and discourses that reached them through the media — in ways that people with less time and less money could not. Leisure time for shopping, and for structured activities, was a privilege that money bought. In the inner neighborhoods of the nearby city, sixth-graders were often required to spend their after-school time caring for younger siblings, while the older family members worked. Oak Town mothers, on the other hand, either cared for their small children themselves or hired other women to babysit for them. Oak Town sixth-graders were only just beginning to babysit, and when they did they were paid for it. Other sixth-graders in other communities prepared meals and did the laundry, but the Oak Town sixth-graders had parents who could order out for pizzas, or take them to restaurants when they weren't free to do the cooking themselves. Although the Oak Town girls did help with housework, and the Oak Town boys did participate in yard work, all had the time and the equipment necessary for enjoying the outdoors, video games, television, movies and recreational reading.

These various race and class privileges the children of Oak Town seemed to take for granted, and accept as natural and unproblematic. This was not, however, the case for gender. The prevailing culture's beliefs about gender *were* being reproduced in the Oak Town children's lives, but not without a struggle. There were a number of children who resisted accommodating themselves to the social order. Cara, for one, found it difficult to accept the idea that a girl couldn't be friends with a boy. She named Anthony and John among her friends, but was careful to stress that they were 'only friends'. Julie and Jerrica and Karen, furthermore, were filled with anger over the fact that girls had to do housework while the boys *didn't*, and they planned to subvert the system when they grew up. Cara was less antagonistic, and, in some ways, extremely perceptive: 'Boys are luckier, but it isn't their fault. Grown-ups set it up that way.'

Only occasionally did someone openly and deliberately break the rules for 'doing boy' or 'doing girl', as when Jim refused to join the rest of the sixth-grade boys in a violent attack on Jack. Because Jim otherwise obeyed the rules for 'doing boy', the boys allowed his gesture toward Jack to pass almost unremarked.

Marcia, the only Oak Town girl to openly and purposefully counter the rules for 'doing girl', was a different case. At the beginning of the school year, Marcia was the girl in Mr Peterson's class who was a little different. She had only lived in Oak Town for two years. She had repeated her fifth grade, and as a result was a year older than everyone else in sixth grade. She stayed on the fringe of the group of girls, and seemed to be getting along pretty well.

It was at the beginning of February that people began to notice a change in Marcia. Mr Peterson said she started to get lazy about her schoolwork. She withdrew and wouldn't talk to him, and she changed her appearance: she seemed to stop washing her hair, and now back-combed and sprayed it; and she now wore jeans and black shoes, and the same shirt day after day.

In one interview, in March, Marcia talked for nearly an hour about her passions and her resentments. She resented having homework, as well as classwork that required too much writing. She resented having to do household chores that her brother didn't have to do. She resented 'being pounded and pushed around' by the boys. She resented the pressures of daily life, and chuckled about pretending to be sick and getting to stay home from school. She said her bedroom was such a mess you'd need a map to find anything in it.

After March, Marcia didn't have much to say to the other children in her class. When she did interact with the other girls, she seemed to be trying to shock them. She swore. She wrote on the walls in the girls' bathroom. She lived to watch *Video Hits*, and to read horror novels and *Sweet Valley High* books. She did just enough schoolwork to get by, saying that she didn't want to repeat a grade again.

The other girls were angry. After March, not one would speak willingly to Marcia, and Marcia appeared not to care. The others talked about her in all-girl groups:

> She's so boring! She does bad things. She tries to act so hot. She thinks she's so great. She tries to get people's attention all the time. She writes on the walls and she swears and she says she doesn't care if she gets caught! She used to be so nice, but then she got bad. She's really weird.

Marcia's behavior infuriated the other girls because, for reasons of her own, she was not interested in what they were interested in. She refused to look like they looked. She refused to be a friend. She refused to be 'good'. She was not afraid of authority. She was not afraid of rejection. There was nothing they could do to touch her.

The girls meted out the only punishment they could: They silenced Marcia, and made her invisible. In classroom project groups, and on the playground, they refused to hear anything she said. They tried hard not to respond to any comment she made. She could only get them to respond by attacking and then waiting for a counterattack. They treated her as if she weren't there.

In June, Marcia began to ride bikes after school with Michelle. They lived on the same street, and Michelle was lonely. Perhaps Marcia was too. Marcia gave up reading horror novels and devoted herself to romances. Occasionally, she spoke to another girl in her class, but she got no response. She seemed to accept that. She had resisted meeting the gender expectations of her parents, her teachers, and the other girls, and she continued to pay the price.

An Afterword

In this chapter, I have made the point that the activities that the children chose, and were indeed encouraged to choose, helped to define and create their gender identity. But I should also point out here that the cultural discourses surrounding gender interacted with the cultural discourses concerning *time* in the matter of choosing activities. The connection was this: time was seen by the people of Oak Town as a valuable commodity, something that should not be wasted. It was also seen as an emptiness, an oppressive void, that took on significance and meaning only when filled with an activity. Children, having accepted, to some extent, the prevailing culture's view of time, knew that they were required to fill their time with one or another form of activity. Decisions about which activities to choose were influenced by prevailing gender discourses. In the next chapter, it will become clear that reading fiction was culturally sanctioned for girls, but not for boys.

Notes

1 I realize that it is impossible to truly capture the 'voices' of the people of Oak Town, and misleading to try to combine their many voices into one narrative voice that is actually merely another version of my own. Here, however, because this is in part an interpretive study of the different participants' meanings, I have made some lexical choices that are consistent with what the people of Oak Town said to me, rather than what I might have said myself. For example, in this section I refer to children as 'kids', as they did, and to certain women as 'homemakers', which again is what they called themselves. When I am not attempting to capture the tone of the people's conversation, or conveying information that they gave me about their lives, i.e. when I am, instead, analyzing and theorizing, I will write in a more formal and academic register.
2 The *Babysitters Club* books were one of the fictional series being marketed for preteen girls in the Oak Town area during the year of the study. The babysitters of the series title were a group of 11 and 12-year-old girls who lived within a few blocks

of each other in a small town in Connecticut, and who supported each other in meeting the babysitting needs of the families in their neighborhood. Other series referred to in the chapter include *Sweet Valley Twins* — about 12-year-old twin sisters with contrasting personalities who lived affluent lives in Southern California — and *Satin Slippers* — about a group of teenage ballet dancers. *Archie Comics*, situation comedies, presented in comic book form, with a set cast of stereotypical teenage characters — were also popular with the Oak Town girls.

3 I was angry too, and thought long and hard about whether or not I ought to intervene to protect the girls from the harassment. In the end I reasoned that if I were to interfere, if I were to assert my power as an adult in this situation, the children would no longer treat me as if I were invisible, and as a result my access to their world would disappear. For this reason, I did not intervene. I did, however, talk with the girls about harassment, and encourage them to challenge the boys who used it against them.

4 I believe the pills were probably a form of the drug Ritalin. For the more than 20 years that I have been working in elementary schools, Ritalin has been routinely prescribed for 'hyperactive' children who are unable to conform to the quiet behavior required of them in school. As a teacher, I was told that the drug 'calms and relaxes' children.

Chapter 3

Literacy Practices:
The Reproduction of Gendered Reading

This chapter examines the intersection of two sets of cultural discourses: discourses about gender, and discourses about reading. Cultural constructions of gender shaped the ways in which the parents at Oak Town went about reading, as well as the ways in which they encouraged their own children to read. In turn, those cultural discourses centered on reading became part of the construction of gender. Thus it happened that while many of the sixth-grade girls were reading fiction, many of the boys were not.

This chapter begins with a description of the reading practices of seven Oak Town girls, girls who were all avid readers of fiction. I have constructed this account of reading in the world experienced by these girls both from records of our conversations and from what I recall from the times I spent with each of them. I would like to speak about reading in their lives as they themselves have spoken about it, and although I know that I cannot fully capture the complexity and the multiplicity of each child's many 'voices', I will nonetheless attempt to provide the reader with some impressionistic sense of each child's world as she was experiencing it at the time of the study, and will take care not to intrude, at this point, with my own analysis of their lives. I hope the reader will allow me this interpretive moment in an otherwise largely analytic work. Following these sketches of the girls as readers, I will undertake an examination of the parents' beliefs about gender and reading, together with an analysis of how the girls used their reading practices as to enact both a school culture and a community culture.

Reading for the Girls

Reading for Karen

Sixth grade was the first year in which Karen Andruchuk had done much reading for pleasure. Karen believed that the sixth-grade girls that year were *all* reading for pleasure, both in school and outside of school. Many were carrying copies of one or another of the girls' series books tucked into their notebooks or book bags. Karen said that the series books in question were appealing because they were written specifically for girls of her age, and she knew everyone's favorite series. Leah's favorite one was the *Saddle Club* series, about girls who rode horses. Sarah loved the *Satin Slippers* series, about girls who took ballet lessons. Jerrica was buying books in the *Gymnasts* series, one by one, through the Arrow Book Club. Alisa and Julie and Rene liked *Sweet Valley Twins*, but Jerrica and Marcia and Tanya preferred *Sweet Valley High*. Nearly everybody, however, loved the *Babysitters' Club* books. As Lacey said, 'After you read a few *Babysitters Club* books, you feel like you really *know* those girls. You can't wait to read the next one to see what they're doing.' Karen's own favorite was the *Animal Inn* series. Val Taylor, the girl featured in those books, was a veterinarian's daughter who loved animals and was always doing things to help them. Karen loved animals too, and willingly spent time caring for her pets at home and feeding the animals in the Science lab at school. In October of her sixth-grade year, Karen read three *Animal Inn* books, and she knew that she wanted to go on to read them all.

Karen had read and enjoyed a few of the *Babysitters Club* books, too, but she had experienced a feeling of vague dissatisfaction in connection with them. She had decided that she wanted to start at the very beginning and read all of them all the way through so that she would know everything about the girls in the *Babysitters Club* books. That way, she'd have no difficulty understanding everything that was happening in those stories. Karen also thought it would be fun to keep a list of all the books she read, and to write down a little of what they were about, so that she could look back at the list some day, as if it were a diary. Karen kept a diary.

Because there were so many distractions and so many demands on her time, Karen was never able to read as many books as she had planned to, or wanted to read. For one thing, she found that she couldn't read in school at all. Even during the silent reading time organized by Mr Peterson, she found it difficult to read, especially after he had rearranged the seating and put Karen's desk into a group of four where the other three people were boys. The boys poked her, and each other, and talked when they were supposed to be reading. Karen explained to me that boys just weren't serious about reading.

Sometimes, Karen took an interest in those library books that the other girls were reading. She would ask about the book, wait until the girl reading it had finished with it, take it out herself, and carefully keep track of when it had to go back to the school library so that she could check it out. Often, however, she didn't find time to read the book after she had taken it out. The library-loan period was only seven days, and that was never long enough for Karen.

The days went by so quickly. Karen read at bedtime in the winter, after she had finished her homework. She told me she had a disappointed feeling at nighttime when she had too much homework and it grew too late to read: lying on the bed at night and reading without worrying about the time was a real pleasure, provided, of course, the book was a satisfying one. Karen also liked to retreat to her room to read when one of her brothers annoyed her — no matter what the time of day. Everyone left her alone when she did. At night, her dad would come in at around 9.30 p.m. to tell her to go to sleep, but she didn't usually stop reading until 10.30 p.m. or until whenever he started to get angry. Sometimes, the book was so absorbing that it was difficult to stop reading. Then, Karen felt she wouldn't be able to sleep without knowing what was going to happen next.

Karen said she didn't find much time to read on weekends, either. On Saturday and Sunday mornings, she liked to sleep in, and then, she admitted with a smile, she still liked to watch the cartoons. The cartoons changed from time to time, but the ritual didn't: Karen enjoyed eating cereal in her pajamas in front of the television set with no obligation to be anywhere at a certain time. Saturday afternoons, she and Renee had their gymnastics lessons, and then they went shopping. Their mothers took turns driving them. Sunday afternoons, Karen's family had company, or sometimes, in winter, her parents took them ice-skating or cross-country-skiing. Sometimes, Karen went over to somebody else's house, or she had someone over to *her* house. Most Friday and Saturday nights, Karen explained, she could have a friend come for a sleepover, something she really enjoyed.

Karen read books she had heard about from the girls at school, and either she borrowed them from friends, or she took them home from the school library. When I lent her *Julie of the Wolves* and asked her to read it for a book-talk group, she accepted the loan casually as a friendly gesture. I was delighted by her subsequent response: she made me feel I had given her a lovely gift. She said *Julie of the Wolves* was the best book she had ever read. 'It was excellent, and I felt like I *couldn't* stop reading it. Something wonderful was always happening in it.' But Karen wasn't interested in my suggestion that she try something else by the same author. Some of the girls had favorite authors and tried to read everything by that person, but Karen said she never thought about the author when she chose a book. She only cared about whether or not the book was a good one.

In May and June, Karen told me, she played softball, and that meant that there wasn't any time at all for reading. She had either a real game or just a practice every night, and then she had to do her homework after that. Playing outdoors was exhausting, and as a result she couldn't stay awake to read.

Reading for Jerrica

Jerrica enjoyed her reputation for being smart. She confided that she and Tracey were the most popular girls in Mrs Gagnon's class, explaining that while Tracey was popular because she was so athletic and because she played Ringette (girls' hockey), Jerrica was popular both for being athletic and for being the best at schoolwork. Jerrica seemed to me to carry with her a sense of being special. She received an invitation to every birthday party given during the sixth-grade year, and this was a reliable indication of the other girls' regard.

Jerrica let me know that there were some uncomfortable things associated with being smart. Her worst problem was that she regularly finished her work early and then had empty time on her hands. She believed that that was why she had made reading so much a part of her life: she used reading to fill her time in school, and from there it became a habit. She pointed out to me that reading was 'safe' because the teachers didn't object to her reading — as long as she read during work time, was quiet and had already completed the classwork. In fact, Jerrica sensed that her teachers even liked to have her reading. Mrs Gagnon, for example, allowed Jerrica to leave class and go out to the library, without asking permission, whenever she finished the book she was reading before the period was over.

Sometimes, Jerrica didn't wait for work time. If a teacher were talking, and she felt bored, she would sneak her book open in her desk, pull it out a little into her lap and look down at it. She could read pretty well that way, and she had never been caught. It seemed a little risky to Jerrica, but she knew the teachers all thought of her as a good girl who would never intentionally do anything wrong, and after all, the alternative to sneaking in a little reading was painful boredom. Jerrica assured me that nearly everybody read when they weren't supposed to.

Reading filled in her extra time at home, too. Jerrica didn't have homework because she finished it in school. She liked to watch *Family Ties* and *Silver Spoons* on television after school, but she still had time to fill before and after supper. She said she would sit on the living-room couch, with her blanket over her, 'and read and read'. After supper, there were a few other things Jerrica liked to do in her room. She wrote in her diary, she wrote to her pen pals, she sent away for mail-order goods, and she listened to the local rock radio station. Then, she usually read until after bedtime. When she felt sleepy, she finished off her reading with an *Archie* comic, then went to sleep. Jerrica said that her parents, like her teachers, seemed to approve of her reading. She explained that her mother would rather read than do anything else. Sometimes, when Jerrica didn't have to babysit, she read all day and night on Saturday or Sunday, and no one suggested that she stop.

Jerrica did not, however, read when she had a chance to be with other people. During recess, she preferred to play computer games with her friends. Jerrica was involved in nearly every activity at school, including sports, drama and band activities. She explained that she joined everything so that she could spend more time with the other children and more time outside the classroom. She especially liked Track, because there were so many older boys in Track. In sixth-grade, Jerrica was very interested in the boys in the seventh, eighth, and ninth grades. She looked forward to school dances with excitement, seeing them as chances to see and talk to these older boys, and she envied her friend Karen because she had two older brothers. Jerrica told me she couldn't wait to be a little older herself. She had been reading the *Sweet Valley High* books, and they had a lot of information to offer about boyfriends and dating and relationships. In fifth grade, she had also read *Sweet Valley Twins*, but they no longer seemed interesting. In sixth grade she looked for the new *Sweet Valley High* when she went to the mall. She had collected over 30 books in this series, buying them with her babysitting money.

Jerrica made it clear to me that while she liked older boys, she didn't care much for the sixth-grade boys. Most of them were unimpressive, and some were very difficult to live with. James was the worst of them, whispering dirty things to her and patting her bum. Jerrica said that she and the other girls hated James, but she had worked out a strategy for dealing with him. She had decided never to let James see her upset. When he bothered her, she would tell him to leave her alone, and would be sure to sound like she meant it. She wanted to sound tough. She thought a girl did better with boys if she didn't complain when the boys got rough in soccer games, and she would never let a boy or anyone else see her cry over a book. Jerrica thought her mother looked ridiculous when she was watching a sad movie or reading a sad book with tears in her eyes. She would have been embarrassed to death to be seen in such a state.

In sixth grade, Jerrica also began reading the books on the Young Adult rack in the school library. These books, as far as she knew, were intended for ninth graders, but no one prevented her from taking them out. She told me that while some of them were 'stupid' (and those were the ones she returned) others, like the Christopher Pike mysteries, were great stories, and others still were sexy. *Weekend* and *Slumber Party*, which were full of suspense, were probably, as far as Jerrica was concerned, the best books she had read since she first discovered Judy Blume.

Reading for Julie

Julie Dallas told me she was both the youngest person and the best girl athlete in her sixth-grade class. She was also the best girl at Math, and getting high grades gave her great satisfaction. Many things felt satisfying to Julie: playing outdoors was her favorite thing to do, but she also loved playing the flute in the sixth-grade band, doing crafts, and reading. Those were her pastimes. Alisa and Sarah were her best friends, and they liked to do the same kinds of things.

Julie read a lot, but unlike the other sixth-grade girls, she didn't read the series books. Julie explained to me that they were expensive, and that it seemed a shame to spend money on books when there were other ways of getting them. Julie and her mother exchanged books with her cousins and her aunts, traded at the Book Exchange in the city, and borrowed books from both the town library and the school library. In October of her sixth-grade year, Julie's grandmother sent her two *Nancy Drew* books for her birthday, and Julie enjoyed them. She hadn't bothered to read *Nancy Drew* books before that, even though they were in the library, because the covers looked 'awful'. Julie explained that the cover usually had a picture of Nancy Drew standing there with a strange man in the background 'just *looking* at her, like he wanted to kill her or something. It gives me the creeps.' But she had, however, enjoyed the two books that her grandmother had sent to her. She had found an order form in the back of one book, and thought seriously about sending away for two more.

Julie told me that she appreciated the classroom library I had set up because there were some *Babysitters Club* books available there, and she was pleased to have a chance to try them. She had thought they might be boring, but when she tried them she found that she enjoyed them. She did not intend to buy any, however. Her parents would never let her spend money on them, she said. Nor did they approve of ordering books through the Arrow Book Club. Julie explained that she understood how her parents felt about the money, and that she was satisfied not to own a lot of books. She preferred to spend what money she had on clothes. Sometimes, the girls lent each other books, and Julie felt it was a problem that she didn't really own many books to lend. Instead, she *recommended* the good books she had read in the library. When she read *I, Trissy*, for example, she enjoyed it so much that she told Alisa about it. Alisa then read it, and told Sarah about it, and the book thus passed on from hand to hand. Julie guessed that 10 or 11 girls had read it within the space of a month or two.

Julie loved the *Anne of Green Gables* books, and all the Jean Little books. She explained to me that she liked anything 'sad' and anything 'scary'. But a book could be *too* frightening. *Flowers in the Attic* Julie described as 'sad, and kind of gross. It made you feel sort of shivery,' and to be a little frightened, in this way, was enjoyable for Julie. But once, she said, she had picked up one of her Mom's Stephen King books at home and read the first chapter, and that had been *too* frightening. A story about something horrible hiding in the closet at night, it had given her bad dreams, and her mother had told her not to read any more of it.

Julie read quite a bit in school, after she had finished her work and during silent reading time. Many of the girls, she thought, read during the silent reading time, while most of the boys did not. The boys seemed to spend that time cleaning out their desks or simply turning over pages, especially if Mr Peterson hadn't yet returned from recess. Like Jerrica, Julie read surreptitiously in class when she felt bored. But she had decided never to read at lunch time. During that period, there were too many people for her to talk to, and reading would have absorbed too much of her attention. She knew that if she began reading when she went home for lunch, her food would grow cold, and she would be late returning to school.

Julie thought the best time for reading at home was bedtime. She explained that she liked to go to bed at about 9.00 or 9.30 p.m. and then read until 10.30 or so. Her parents became upset if she had the light on any later than that. Sometimes, if the book was very good, she would put her biggest pillow over her head and over the light in such a way that, although she could still see to read, her mother would think her light was out. Sometimes Julie read in the evening too; or if not, she sat at the dining-room table and worked on crafts at that time. But she preferred to be outside playing whenever possible. She looked forward to the May–June softball season all year, and on winter evenings after supper she could go skating over at the rink in the schoolyard whenever she liked. The lights remained on over there until 9.30 p.m. During sixth grade, there were even a few ski trips out to Mission Ridge at night, and Julie relished these opportunities to be active outdoors.

In summer, Julie spent every weekend, and as much of her other spare time as she could manage, at her family's beloved lake cottage. During the summer before sixth grade, she had started taking books along for rainy days, and since then, Julie had taken a book along with her everywhere. She always took a book along to the mall, in case she had to wait while her mother shopped for something, and she even took one along to school assemblies in her jacket pocket. No one was allowed to talk during an assembly, and when the assembly became boring, Julie could always read instead. Once, when Julie was rereading *Anne of Green Gables*, she had kept one copy at home and one copy in her desk at school, so that she could move further ahead in the book whenever she had a few minutes, no matter where she was. That arrangement had worked well, and Julie had continued to do that whenever she could get two copies of the book she was reading.

Reading for Alisa

Most of the time, Alisa Weiss was, as she herself stated, a happy person. She knew that being happy required the ability to get along with other people, and fortunately, she *had* that ability. Her only unhappy times occurred when she was angry with someone, or when someone was angry with her.

In Alisa's view, it wasn't difficult to get along with teachers. She was fairly sure that teachers assigned people different grades according both to how neat and tidy they were and to how well they behaved. Alisa explained to me that her grades were good, even those for Phys Ed, because she was reliable and always did her work. Schoolwork was usually enjoyable, she thought. Even reading *The Lord of the Rings* had been all right after they'd finished the section on the history of the Council of Elrond. Fractions had been a problem for Alisa in sixth grade, however. On one occasion, Alisa did an entire page of problems wrong, and had to do them all over again. Fractions were one of the several things that Alisa found stressful in sixth grade. Another was the fact that she was left-handed, and found it difficult to write neatly without smearing the pages. Still another was the requirement of frequent group work since, as Alisa complained, she always seemed to be put in the group where no one else wanted to do any work.

After school, Alisa was usually exhausted, and didn't feel capable of doing very much. She described her time after 4.00 p.m. as follows: 'Most days I just bum around and watch TV. I have to feed the dog, but that's my only chore. Once a week I have my Creative Writing class at the university, but most days I can rest.' In good weather, Alisa and Julie sometimes played outdoors after school. In May and June, when they played softball, she saw Julie nearly every weekend — and sometimes, other friends too.

Every day, however, Alisa did find some time to read. She read in the car on the way into the city; or during recess or lunch, especially when she was too tired to talk to people; or during silent reading time, because that was what she was supposed to do then; and finally, at bedtime. The *Archie* comics were the best read at bedtime because they helped her to fall asleep. She bought one every time she went to Safeway or Bi-Rite, and had now accumulated a big stack of them under her bed. At bedtime, Alisa just reached under her bed and pulled one out — it didn't matter which one.

Annoyed that her mother had said that she only read *Archie* comics and *Sweet Valley Twins* books, Alisa protested that this wasn't true. Once in a while, she also read a library book. One month, she found an excellent mystery there, called *A Deadly Rhyme*, about strange happenings at a girls' boarding school. She had started it during silent reading time, and then brought it home to read all afternoon after school. She couldn't put it down, because it was 'scary'. It didn't frighten her badly but it was eerie. She was so curious about what was going to happen next that she had kept on reading until she had finished the book.

However, most of the time, Alisa chose to read a *Sweet Valley Twins* book. These books were about two twin sisters, Jessica and Elizabeth Wakefield, both in sixth grade, who had all the latest clothes and hairstyles, as well as a lot of interesting problems with their friends which they always managed to solve. Alisa collected that series, and had bought every one of them with her own money. Recently, the price of each book in the series had been raised to $3.50 — the same price as a *Sweet Valley High* book. This price increase seemed unfair to Alisa — since the *Sweet Valley High* books were twice as thick as *The Sweet Valley Twins* — and she felt she had to stop lending her books out because they cost too much. Once, her friend Tanya came grocery shopping with Alisa and her mother, and Tanya had left one of Alisa's *Sweet Valley Twins* books in the grocery cart. They never did get it back. It was *#17*, and Alisa had to buy that one again.

Whenever Alisa went to the Eastside Mall she checked the bookstores for the new *Sweet Valley Twins* book. A new one came out every two months or so, but Alisa found it difficult to wait that long for the next one. While she waited, she read the old ones over again, because she wasn't anxious to try a lot of different kinds of books. When everybody at school was talking about *Flowers in the Attic*, Alisa borrowed Tanya's mother's copy, but she only read the first chapter. She told me, 'That is such a stupid book. Boring and dumb and gross. I couldn't stand reading it.'

Alisa thought that reading should help her forget her troubles. She liked reading because teachers and parents approved of it, and because it was soothing to watch Jessica and Elizabeth Wakefield manage their complicated lives and make everything turn out the way they wanted it to in the end.

Reading for Marcia

I thought Marcia sounded relieved to be able to talk. She said she had the feeling that life had been deteriorating during sixth grade. Some days, she felt as if she were fighting with everyone, and that there wasn't a soul in the world who understood her. Her mother, for instance, was cranky all the time, always pressing Marcia to do her chores and to clean up her messy room. The teachers were never happy either, even when she *did* do the stupid homework. At school, she felt on the edges of things. Phys Ed was the worst because they played dodge ball so often — a frightening and dangerous game. But most of school, however, was boring rather than dangerous. Math was boring, she said, because she didn't understand it, and writing out all the answers to questions in Reading and Social Studies and Science was also tedious.

Sometimes, it seemed to Marcia that *real* life only happened *outside* of school. At home, she could sit in her room alone and not think about herself. Her problems seemed to disappear when she was watching *Video Hits* on television, or listening to her favorite music on the radio. Marcia had a huge poster of Jon Bon Jovi on her bedroom wall, and she knew all the words to the Bon Jovi songs.

For Marcia, reading was relaxing, as was watching *Video Hits* or listening to the radio. Lately, the *Sweet Valley High* books had been her favorites. The *Sweet Valley Twins* girls were younger than she was, only 12, but in *Sweet Valley High* the girls were 16, and it was so interesting to see what older girls did, how they talked, and how they acted. Marcia never found those latter books boring, even when she read them again. Although there were 53 of them, Marcia only owned two since she had borrowed quite a few from her friend Jackie (who owned *all* of them).

Marcia explained that she was definitely *not* interested in boys' books. The boys in Mr Peterson's room, she said, liked reading about dogs or about wars or adventures. There weren't enough girls included in their books. Boys' books weren't about people really, not in the way that girls' and women's books were. Marcia was, however, attracted to the horror books her mother brought into the house, and she read them all, over her mother's objections. Marcia thought the Stephen King books were wonderful, creepy and horrifying, and asked if I had read any. She and Jackie had read Jackie's mother's set of the *Flowers in the Attic* series, starting with *Garden of Shadows* and reading every other book in turn. The stories as told in the books were complicated and absorbing, and Marcia found that she didn't like the movie of *Flowers in the Attic* half as much.

Usually, Marcia said, horror books were better than horror movies. Once, her parents had rented the three Freddy Krueger movies, and Marcia had watched them all. It was awful. People had burned him and he came back, like a ghost, with razor blades for fingers. He chopped girls up or killed them under a broiler, and he grew into a person's dreams. Marcia admitted to me that although she hadn't wanted to watch all three of those movies, at the same time she *had*. She hadn't been able to turn away from them. However, she had vomited after she saw the third one, and she had slept on the couch for two weeks after that, afraid to be alone in her room. No, Marcia felt the horror books were a lot better than the horror movies, because they were interesting, not just sickening.

Marcia read her share of school library books too, and she usually had two in her desk for silent-reading or free time. Some were fine, but others were too short. Marcia appreciated the fact that the horror books she read at home were long. In sixth grade, the *Sweet Valley High* books were beginning to seem too short. Something around 300 pages now satisfied Marcia. She read for at least two hours a night, and she liked to have a book last three nights. She was disappointed if she finished a book too quickly. Reading a good ·book was like watching a good rock video, in a way. It seemed as if you were sharing a secret that was in the music, or in the book. You had to listen carefully, or read closely, to find the secret . . . and then you knew the secret too.

Reading for Cara

Cara was thoroughly satisfied with reading in school. She enjoyed the novels her teachers chose for the sixth graders to read, she enjoyed the stories in the basal reader, and she even enjoyed *The Lord of the Rings* when there was something happening in it. She didn't mind writing answers to questions about the stories they read, but she did prefer the assignments that required them, instead, to draw a picture about a story. She enjoyed the activity cards that went with the novel studies, and she also enjoyed the discussions: she found that she always had something to say about a story. When the sixth graders were asked to write a 'Tolkien journal', pretending to be one of the characters in *The Lord of the Rings* and writing from that point of view, Cara undertook the assignment with enthusiasm.

Cara especially enjoyed school when they were asked to *do* things: when Mrs Johns had them making nutritious snacks in the Health class, when they were learning to make something new in Art, or when they were out on the playground illustrating the sizes of the galaxies for Science class, Cara was a happy girl. Sometimes, she even thought she might be *too* enthusiastic about

Science. Whenever she asked Mr Peterson questions in Science, he often didn't answer her, and she sensed his displeasure.

Occasionally, school felt like a struggle for Cara. Usually, she was able to get the good grades she desired, but in sixth grade Math had proved very difficult. She had begun the year in the group that worked through individual contracts, but she didn't learn much by working alone. Then, Mrs Gagnon had placed her in the other group that worked under the teacher's supervision, and Cara had suffered great embarrassment about being placed with the slower students. She worked very hard, and asked Mrs Gagnon several times if she would put her back in the contract group — which, in the end, she *did* do. Since then, she'd been worried that she might not be doing well enough in Math to stay in this upper group.

Cara's biggest complaint about school was that occasionally she worked very hard on something only to get a small reward at the end of it. She spent a lot of time, for example, preparing her project for the Science Fair — spending every single night for two weeks in her dad's workshop constructing some gyroscopes. When she took the project to school, looking forward to giving clear demonstrations of how these gyroscopes worked, people walked by her table at the Fair, and it was all over in a couple of hours. She had received very little in return for all that work.

At home, Cara was writing a book about a girl her age, making entries in a special notebook at night before she went to bed. Cara also kept *two* diaries, having found that one alone didn't provide enough room for writing everything she wanted to say about her experiences at school, and about what happened to her after school. Cara liked also to read, as well as write, at home, but she saved reading until after she'd done some other things first. She had figure-skating lessons twice a week after school in the winter, and having earned all the figure-skating badges, she was about to begin learning to do solos. She took swimming lessons in the fall and in the spring, and every day she practiced her piano for half an hour after supper. When the weather was nice, she spent time outdoors with her friend Renee. In the springtime, especially, they liked to go out in their rubberboots to squish around on the edges of the big pasture, and to climb the trees.

Sometimes, Cara watched television after school. After she had fed the rabbits, the birds and fish, she could sit on the living-room couch and relax. After supper, however, she preferred to read.

Cara's books came to her in a number of ways. Firstly, she read books from the school library, one every day or two. Secondly, she used her allowance money, plus the money her grandmother gave her, to buy *Sweet Valley Twins* books at the mall whenever they went shopping. And finally, her aunt, who was a teacher-librarian, sometimes sent her books from

Chicago that had been autographed by the author. Cara had an autographed picture of Auntie Jane with Betsy Byars, and another of her with Jean Little.

Cara usually enjoyed a quiet period of time for reading after supper. Her father and her brother would be down in the workshop, and her mother would be in the kitchen doing things, and Cara found that she could read until about 8.30 p.m. Then, she'd get ready for bed and read in her room. She was supposed to have her light off at 9.00 p.m., but she found ways of getting round that. From March onwards, it was light outside late enough for her not to need her reading light on in her room: her room was painted white, and she had a west window that caught the last little rays of light.

Cara read on weekends, too, and always took a book along with her when they went anywhere in the car. Time passed more quickly when she read. Occasionally, it felt as if she went somewhere entirely different when she read, so that it was hard to come back. That happened when she read at the skating rink, while her brother played hockey. When Cara stopped reading, it was hard for her to remember where she was. She laughed when she saw the same thing happening to another girl, with comic results, at the music festival. This girl, who had already played her piece in the competition, was reading while waiting to hear the adjudicator's comments. The official had called her name and the adjudicator had started reading his notes, but the girl hadn't even looked up from her book. The girl's mother had to go over and shake her to get her back from the book, so that she could listen to what the judge had to say.

It took a very good book for Cara to lose herself in it like that. Jerrica had recommended some very good books that made that happen, like *Locked in Time*, *Weekend*, and the latter's sequel, *Slumber Party*. Those were mystery books from the Young Adult rack, and Cara had been able to get lost in all of them. But the very best books for Cara were *sad* books. Cara's favorite authors were Judy Blume and Jean Little because they wrote books that made her feel sad, and yet that made her feel good too.

Reading for Samantha

Two years ago, Samantha had loved the *Nancy Drew* books, but now she read books from the Young Adult rack instead. The Public Library lady had told her they were 'problem-realism' novels, but Samantha thought of them simply as books about girls her own age.

It had been fun collecting those *Nancy Drew* books. At one time, Samantha had made her parents carry around in their wallets a list of the

Nancy Drew books she didn't have yet so that they could buy her the missing ones if they came across them in a store. Samantha still kept them all together on a bookshelf in her room, looking through them often, and rereading one once in a while. However, they were no longer as absorbing as they used to be.

Samantha was writing a book of her own, little by little each night, in a notebook she kept in her room, a book about a girl her own age and the problems she faced. Samantha planned to be a professional author some day. In sixth grade, her favorite authors were Lois Lowry, Dorothy Harris, Paula Danziger, and Judy Blume. Samantha loved Judy Blume especially, and hoped some day to meet her.

But Samantha found that sixth grade left her with little time to think about the future. She was good with her schoolwork, and usually managed to leave school without any homework to do, but she had to keep up with her chores at home, and she had to be careful to get enough sleep. When things bothered her, she got sick and missed school, and then the work piled up. Her father was out of work, and her mother had headaches, so Samantha had plenty to worry about.

She had her worries at school too. Most of the time she got along with the other girls all right, but she was aware of the differences between them. Samantha and her family went to church every Sunday, and it seemed to her that no one else in Oak Town did. Samantha's best friend and a boy she liked were both people she had met at church on Sundays. The kids at school were all right, but Samantha stood apart from them a little. Sometimes, at lunch, she would sit and read instead of socializing with the others. She would have liked, in fact, to sit and read through *all* of school time, instead of having to do her regular schoolwork. That was what Anthony did, whenever he could get away with it. Samantha admired him for doing that, but she wasn't willing to try it herself for fear of getting caught.

The part of the day Samantha liked best came after supper when she could spend some time in her room. She would call her best friend Ashley — who lived in the city — every day on the pink telephone she had saved up for and bought herself. She listened to the radio her parents had given her. She enjoyed rock and country music, and the contests where people called in with the right answers to questions they asked. Once, there had been a contest where the prize was some living-room furniture. Samantha had called in every evening, but the radio announcer had always said that they'd take the *sixth* call, and she had never called at the right time. She thought it would be wonderful to win something like that.

And after supper Samantha also read. When she read, she felt as if she *were* the character she was reading about, and she saw herself as solving that character's problems. For Samantha, the Young Adult novels were the best choices. *Sweet Valley Twins* books were about girls with problems, but the problems weren't very significant or important. The library books were better because the girls in them had more serious problems to overcome. Sometimes, Samantha would read a book with a sad ending, where somebody died or the girl didn't solve her problem and didn't feel really happy and satisfied at the end. But there weren't too many of those, and Samantha never intentionally chose a book like that. When Samantha was reading she was conscious of her own desire to understand what would happen next, and she felt satisfied when everything turned out all right in the end.

Parents and Reading

Michelle Scott sat at her kitchen table and reminisced:

> I don't remember my own mother reading all that much, although I know she liked to read. She didn't have time. After all, she had eight children. I think our family's reading goes back a long, long way. Cuz my grandmother, that's Jerrica's great-grandmother, was a horrendous reader. My mother's mother. She read a lot. We always saw her reading.
>
> I was always encouraged to read. Nobody ever discouraged me from it. My mother was patient with it. I've talked to her about it, and she says that when I was a child sometimes she'd talk to me for about ten minutes and I wouldn't hear her. I was just lost in the book.
>
> Jerrica's 12 now. She's always seen me read. I seem to read no matter what else I'm doing. Like, if I'm baking, I'll read while things are in the oven. Sometimes, I'll use my book as a reward, I think, I'll just do this one thing I have to do, and then I'll read for a while. Jerrica does that too, I think. It doesn't surprise me that she's such a reader.

The Oak Town parents, like their children and the rest of the people in Oak Town, behaved according to North American culture's tacit 'rules' for constructing gender: 'male' and 'female' were seen in terms of binary categories, and defined in contrasting relation to each other; men were seen as more physically assertive than women, and their sphere of influence as the public world, while women were seen as having responsibility for maintaining human relationships, and their sphere of influence was seen as the private world. These same rules have been identified in other studies of contemporary Western cultures (Anyon, 1984; Christian-Smith, 1987; French, 1985; Henley, 1977). Although everyone knew people who were exceptions to these cultural 'rules', the rules were still unconscously accepted. This chapter provides a detailed analysis of the gendered nature of the girls' reading practices. First, however, it seems appropriate to examine one important way in which the girls' reading had come to be 'constructed' the way it was. Beliefs about reading and gender had been, and were still being, transmitted from one generation to the next. The Oak Town parents' beliefs about the gendered nature of the practice of reading had helped to shape their children's lives.

Fathers and Sons and Reading

The statements made by the Oak Town parents in their interviews reflect the tacit beliefs about men and their reading habits that the parents were transmsitting to their children: men read for utilitarian purposes. They did not read fiction, and they did not regard reading as an acceptable pastime. When asked to talk about reading, Julie's father made it clear that he did not see reading as something useful or valuable in his life.

> I'm the first to admit it. I was never a reader, and I'm still not. I like working on woodworking and stuff like that. Working on the vehicles. I don't know. I like to be doing something with my hands instead of sitting and reading. I'm an outdoor person. I like to skidoo. I like yard work. I think that's why I never got into books. It's kind of like sleeping. It's a waste of time. Doesn't seem productive for me.

Karen's father, on the other hand, *did* value reading, but only as it related to his work.

> I read every moment of spare time, things that have to do with our business, investment portfolios, and magazines that have to do with real estate and financial planning. *Fortune Magazine* or *The Financial Post*. Once or twice a year I read something like this. [He showed me a copy of *The Power of Positive Thinking* by Dr Norman Vincent Peale.] I read *Iacocca*. No, I don't read very much in the way of fiction.

Jerrica's father, who worked as a computer programmer, said that he read computer magazines and computer manuals in his spare time. Alisa's father, who worked as a firefighter and did not have work-related reasons for reading, said that he did not read at all.

Several fathers spoke of checking out 'how-to' books during family trips to the public library. Books on carpentry, woodworking, and electrical wiring were popular choices. The values that informed these reading choices were clear: reading, if it was to be done at all, had to be 'useful'.

Furthermore, no one believed that men read fiction, and very often, the Oak Town fathers were themselves careful to explain that they did not read fiction. Marcia's father, for example, who worked as a crane operator, said that he collected and read history books as a hobby. 'Most of the books I read are true to life. War books usually. I like history. I don't read fiction.' Julie's father also said that he valued realistic and factual material, and even when he did read fiction, this preference still applied:

> When I do read, like at the lake in the summer, it's relaxing. The last Stephen King book was a good one. I like the suspense in Stephen King, and the facts. It's not far-fetched. It seems it could happen . . . A guy was telling me about *Iacocca*, and how interesting it was. Like, I don't know if I could make it through a book like that. A biography. It sounds interesting enough that I could get through it, though. Because it's fact.

Other fathers, too, clearly preferred nonfiction:

> Jim likes reading magazines. He's not into novels or anything. Anything to do with health. Fitness magazines. The newspaper, too. But not novels.
>
> (Mrs Ulrich, Samantha's mother)

> I don't read books. No novels. I read magazines. I like the hobby magazines on radio control and model airplanes. And I like the 'how-to' books from the library.
>
> (Mr Alexander, Cara's father)

Others pointed out that while their daughters read fiction, their sons, on the other hand, did not. Of the five girls who had brothers old enough to read, each had a parent who distinguished the girl's reading of fiction from the reading that her brother(s) did. Karen's father's statement is representative:

> Our daughter reads fiction, but our sons would both rather read about sports. They both read the newspaper, and sometimes *Heavy*

Metal, the music magazine. Billy likes to do things with his hands more . . .

But in spite of this disavowal of the value and use of fiction among men, there are signs that these men *do* read fiction. The transcripts of the interviews with the parents of Oak Town contain many references both to Stephen King novels and to *Readers' Digest* condensed novels that fathers had recently read. Two fathers mentioned science fiction as a favorite genre. One father recalled his enjoyment of *The Incredible Journey* when his class had read it in grade school.

But these men did not want to admit to reading fiction: they did not want to be known as readers of fiction. When asked if they read fiction, they all denied it. When asked, also, if their sons read fiction, they denied this too. They 'did gender' by appearing to conform to one of the tacit rules of the culture at large: men do not read fiction.

> No, I wouldn't choose reading. I usually find something else to do. I like playing computer games. Hacking, too. And I coach Jason's hockey. That keeps me busy.
>
> (Mr Scott, Jerrica's father)

> I've always detested reading. The only book I ever read as a kid was *Treasure Island*. It took me over a year to read it. I liked it when I was reading it, but picking it up to read was always a last resort for something to do. Reading has never been a pastime for me . . . Jeremy (my son) is just like me. He's not very fond of reading. It's a last resort. He's not interested in reading. He'd rather play hockey. Or baseball, or soccer.
>
> (Mr Alexander)

In summary, these interviews with the parents of Oak Town made it clear, in several ways, that these people did not view reading as an appropriate pastime for men. Firstly, the parents stressed the utilitarian aspects of men's reading; secondly, the fathers themselves vehemently declared that they did not read fiction; thirdly, the parents denied that their sons read fiction; and finally, the sons involved also denied that their fathers read fiction:

> My mother was a reader, but my Dad wasn't. He didn't read. I'm a mold of my Dad that way. Basically, I'd rather putter or do something. Alice's Dad doesn't read either. Alice's sisters gave him

novels for Christmas, because he's just retired. But he hasn't even opened them.

(Mr Dallas, Julie's father)

Of the five families with school-age *sons* as well as daughters, all five believed that the girls read fiction while the boys did not. And all five felt, moreover, that this was acceptable, and not a cause for worry. Fiction was a privilege for girls only.

Mothers and Daughters and Reading

Here are some other tacit beliefs about reading that the Oak Town parents were transmitting to their children: the practice of reading fiction is a valuable, pleasurable part of a girl's childhood; the reading of fiction is a pastime that women friends *share* with each other; and finally, the reading of fiction is something a girl can be proud of — an appropriate time-filler for girls.

Nearly all the Oak Town mothers interviewed remembered their mothers and grandmothers reading. Several spoke of their sisters as readers, and remembered themselves also as reading, whether alone or with other girls, during their own childhoods. The Oak Town mothers remembered reading series books during their elementary-school years: the *Bobbsey Twins* books, the *Nancy Drew* series, and the *Donna Parker* books were each mentioned by four or more of the seven mothers. Four mothers had actually saved cardboard boxes full of their old books for their daughters to read; and two had encouraged their daughters to put aside their *Sweet Valley Twins* books for their younger sisters. Actions like these, combined with a general consensus that they were pleased with their daughters' reading, showed that the Oak Town mothers valued the role that reading played in their daughters' lives.

Three of the women spoke of their own joy in reading, and even said that they were afraid to begin reading a book on a day when they had many household responsibilities to fulfil: Charlene Weiss, Alisa's mother, said she'd be afraid the family would come home and find that supper hadn't even been started; Alice Dallas, Julie's mother, said that she tried to make herself wait until the evening to read, because it was easier not to start than it was to put the book down; and Michelle Scott said in the interview quoted above that she used reading to get herself through the household chores. Reading was clearly an intense pleasure for all these women. Six of the seven women interviewed identified themselves, as *avid* readers, and again spoke of the joys of reading as an activity. All the mothers and fathers interviewed said that they were pleased that their daughters read so much. Four sets of parents explicitly connected reading at home with their daughter's academic success. As Michelle Scott said:

> Jerrica's reading has made it so easy for her in school. I guess I hear of others who can't get their children to pick up a book, and they're struggling with this and they're struggling with that. It just seems like such an asset to be a reader.

Mrs Dallas, furthermore, made it clear that reading is something she had always shared with her sisters:

> My two sisters, and my husband's two sisters, we're all readers. When we get together we each bring a shopping bag full of paperbacks, so we can talk them over and exchange them.

On a similar note, Mrs Scott said that she gave away books she had read to her friends when they came for coffee. Mrs Thomas, Marcia's mother, also spoke of exchanging books with 'girlfriends', and Mrs Weiss closed her interview by lending *me* two novels.

Although the Oak Town parents did not seem to be aware of it, the field notes and the children's interviews for the larger study together showed that those Oak Town girls who were avid readers of novels were also busy at school sharing their reading with other girls. On any given day, a group of 6 to 10 girls could be seen seated around a table in the lunch room at noon, discussing, recommending, lending, and exchanging books. The boys, however, did not openly engage in this kind of activity; and it would appear that the girls had learnt from their mothers that the sharing of reading matter is something that women do.

It was clear to the Oak Town parents that being a reader is something a girl can be proud of. Seven sets of parents were asked for permission for their daughters to participate in this study. All seven gave that permission without hesitation. (All seven also asked for the names of the other girls who had been 'chosen'.) All assumed that being an avid reader was an individual achievement of which their daughters could be proud. Being a reader seemed to mean being smart.

By contrast, none of these parents admitted to having a son who was an avid reader of novels, and all said that they were unconcerned about their sons not reading fiction.

Only two mothers said that they were concerned about the quality of the books their daughters were reading. Alisa's mother said that she'd like to see

Alisa read something more challenging that the *Sweet Valley Twins* books once in a while. And Marcia's mother said that she hoped the horror novels that Marcia was reading wouldn't be upsetting for her. But these were the only reservations that were voiced. All the other indications were that the parents saw reading as an accomplishment — something to be proud of.

Reading was also seen as an appropriate *time-filler* for girls. Cara's mother made the point clearly: 'I like her reading. It keeps her occupied.' Alisa's mother put it in a different way: 'I encourage Alisa to spend her allowance on books. If you spend your money on a book, that's three or four hours of entertainment.'

Samantha's mother pointed out that there were always unfilled hours in the day that needed filling: 'Samantha doesn't care for television. She doesn't watch TV after she gets her homework done. She reads instead. Even if we're driving into town for something, she takes a book with her and reads while we're driving.' Other parents commented that their daughters also brought books along to the mall, to swimming lessons, to grandma's house, and to the lake. The girls read in the car, and at any other time which needed to be filled.

Parents approved of this. They knew that reading was enjoyable for their daughters. It was a feminine activity, one their mothers engaged in. And it was educational. For all three reasons, it was a highly appropriate time-filler for these girls.

Gender, Time and Reading

Reading was a feminine activity, and the Oak Town children knew this. Of the 21 boys and 21 girls in sixth grade during the Oak Town study, 15 of the girls made extensive use of reading to fill their extra time, while only 7 of the boys admitted that they ever read in order to fill time. Parents encouraged their daughters to read, but did not, on the other hand, encourage their sons to read. As already indicated, this happened in part because these parents lived within a culture in which meanings were often encoded in the form of binary oppositions, and gender categories were no exception (Weedon, 1987). Living as they did in a culture that saw girls and boys as opposites, the parents believed that the girls and boys *naturally* preferred different kinds of activity.

The Oak Town parents saw reading as an activity that benefited the reader, strengthening the reader's mind the way exercise strengthens the body, and for this reason they would have liked to see their sons reading more often, just as, conversely, they would have liked to see their daughters *get* exercise more often. But having said that, they chose not to intervene when the children responded to cultural cues that led them to spend their time in gender-appropriate ways. Cara's mother put it this way: 'I guess I'd like Jeremy to read more than he does. But it's not really that important. I'd like him to read more, say, if he was bored and looking for things to do . . . But he has other interests. He's different from his sister.'

> Cara and Daddy and Jeremy climbed out of the car at the rink in Bergen. Jeremy carried his skates and his hockey stick. Cara had her library book clutched in her mittened hand. The book was *Locked in Time* by Lois Duncan. Cara had signed it out that day and had read the first three chapters before supper. She couldn't wait to get back to it. It had been too dark in the car to read on the way here, and the 10-minute ride seemed longer and colder than usual. Their footsteps crunched across the snow. Daddy pulled open the heavy wooden door and they entered the rink. Jeremy headed away toward the brightly lit ice, Daddy moved toward the other parents standing in a group at the railing, and Cara hurried up seven rows into the stands, high enough to be by herself and close enough to the ice to benefit from the light. She settled herself on the wooden bench, turned up her quilted collar, and took her mitten off long enough to find the right page. When Cara took her mitten off again to turn the second page, she forgot to put it back on. By that time she was conscious only of the world of summer in Louisiana, a world of humidity and mist and lush green forest. She imagined Nore, the beautiful teenager in the white dress, exploring the old mansion and beginning to solve the mystery. She was there, dealing with the sinister Lisette. She was there, dancing in the hot, noisy disco with Gabe and Josie. Daddy had to put his hand on her shoulder to get her attention. Cara looked up at him, disoriented. It took her a moment to remember where she was. The cold, cavernous rink seemed strange. Jeremy and the other eight-year-olds, taking their skates off after the game, seemed unfamiliar. Her mitten fell to the floor as she stood up to follow her father out to the car.

Cara read in order to leave the pressures of the world behind her. In the world around her, the card shops were full of notecards, birthday cards and greeting cards carrying images of girls and women reading. These were idealized images, chosen for duplication and for mass marketing because they represented a cultural ideal. And it was clear from the white ruffled dresses of the women on the greeting cards that reading was a quiet activity. Readers did not engage in physical exercise, noisy leadership, or competition. Readers sat and dreamed. In this cultural discourse, reading provided a compatible and appropriate image of femininity[1].

Of course, there is more to the Oak Town girls' practice of reading than just the fact that their parents approved of it. Reading also met the girls' own needs in matters of managing time: they used it to fill the void of time; they use it to cope with the pressures of time; and, as Cara did at the hockey rink, they used reading to create a sense of escaping time altogether.

It was nearly 4.00 p.m. Marcia and her younger sister and brother trudged up the street from the bus stop to their home. Marcia had the key. The snow had been shovelled off the front deck and away from the pretty blue and brass door, but the kids tramped around to the back entry. Jason headed next door to play with his friend Kevin. The girls left their boots and snow gear in the back hall, padding into the family room in their stockinged feet. Mom and Dad wouldn't get home for another hour yet.

Megan turned on the TV. Marcia grabbed a can of pop from the kitchen and went into her bedroom to find the *Sweet Valley High* book she had started last night. When she returned to the family room, Megan was settled with a snack in front of *Silver Spoons*. Marcia stretched out on the couch and opened her book. She didn't care for *Silver Spoons* and *Family Ties*, the programs that were on every weekday at this time.

At 5.00 p.m. Marcia's mother got home. Marcia said 'hi' and went into her bedroom to watch *Video Hits*. This was her favorite program. On Fridays, it was on for a whole hour, but Monday through Thursday it was only on from 5.00 to 5.30 p.m. Marcia watched it intently, trying to catch everything in the flickering images and trying to understand and memorize the words to each song. When *Video Hits* was over, she went out into the kitchen. Her mom and the kids were eating plates of chilli in front of the TV. Marcia took a plate and helped herself from the pot on the stove.

When she had finished eating, she went back to her room to finish the *Sweet Valley High* book. She read slowly, with the radio on, stopping occasionally to think about the events of the school day, but she'd finished with the book before 7.00 p.m. That was disappointing. She had hoped it would last longer. Now she remembered that she was supposed to have *Summer of the Swans* by Betsy Byars read for a literature response group tomorrow. In fact, it had been due for today, but she'd forgotten. She went to the back entry to find it in her school bag. Her mom was in the kitchen and Megan was still in front of the TV. Jason must be at hockey. Leaving the radio on, she stretched out on her bed to read. For the next two hours, Marcia read, listened to the radio, daydreamed and yawned. The book was all right in places, but slow. Kind of a boring book, she thought to herself. She pushed through it. She skipped parts. It got better in the second half when Sara got to be friends with Joe Melby, a boy in her class, and they were able to find Charlie. But then the book ended, right when Sara was getting ready to go to that party. That wasn't fair! Marcia wanted to know what happened at the party.

It was 9.30 p.m. Marcia wandered out into the family room. Her parents were watching a movie, and the younger kids were in bed. She sat and watched for a few minutes, but the movie didn't interest her. She picked up the Stephen King novel her mother had left on the end table, got some cookies from the kitchen, and returned to her room.

Jackpot! Stephen King was great. Marcia's scalp crawled with delicious terror as she read and munched. At 10.15 p.m. her mom came in to say it was bedtime. Marcia got ready for bed, turned out the light, and crawled under the covers with the Stephen King book and the flashlight she kept hidden. She read secretly, with the lights out, for another two hours.

Reading for a Girl's Purposes

Children enacted 'girl' and enacted 'boy' in their daily lives in Oak Town. They were acting both in response to directions from the adults in their lives, and in response to cultural messages about gender. Some of them, some of the time, resisted acting in expected ways, but, as a group, the children nonetheless 'did' gender in ways that were approved by the generation preceding them. Let me say this in another way: because the practice of reading served both as a means of doing gender and as a way of responding to other family members, it became a powerful site of cultural reproduction.

I would like to close this chapter with a consideration of a double point: not only was reading, for the Oak Town girls, a site for the enactment of culture, it was also woven into the fabric of their relationships with each other and with other people. My message is this: the cultural discourses which positioned girls to read in certain ways were both personal and powerful. The Oak Town children were experiencing these discourses in a context of aesthetic pleasure and familial love, so that their spiritual as well as their intellectual lives were involved. In Chapter 5, I will examine more closely the girls' construction of their own identities — of their senses of themselves — in response to these discourses. Here, I want to give the reader a sense of the power of the cultural, textual and interpersonal suggestions that surrounded them by describing these 'suggestions' as they operate in their daily lives. To that end, I will be examining two discourses in particular that surrounded the girls: one through which a community offered instruction in how to 'do girl', and another through which a culture awarded girls with the prerogative to *feel freely.*

Reading Fiction to Learn Gender

Just as Michelle Scott had learned from her mother and her grandmother that women read, so Jerrica Scott was now learning the same thing from *her* mother, Michelle. And other girls were having similar experiences. Of the seven girls at the center of this study, six, as already mentioned, had mothers who were avid readers. Mrs Dallas (Julie's mother) and Mrs Weiss (Alisa's mother) both said that they had been avid readers all their lives, and that reading was their favorite entertainment. Mrs Thomas (Marcia's mother) read several novels a month, and exchanged them via a network of friends — as did other women. Mrs Ulrich (Samantha's mother) and Mrs Alexander (Cara's mother) also spoke of how much they enjoyed reading, and said that they would choose to read more than they did if they had fewer household responsibilities.

Mrs Andruchuk (Karen's mother), however, said she didn't read much, and never had. 'I've always been more interested in sewing and embroidery and crafts.' She had learned these as a child from her mother, and had already taught Karen to do some sewing. Karen herself hadn't developed an interest in reading until she was in fifth grade. Her mother said Karen began to read more then because her friends were reading so much.

The other sixth-grade girls who read 8 or 10 novels a month *did*, however, have mothers who enjoyed reading, and because these mothers provided living examples of what it meant to be women in Oak Town, their daughters learned a good deal about gender from them. There were two ways in which girls learned gender through the reading of fiction. Firstly, the girls learned gender by reading fiction to *emulate their mothers*: when mother liked to read, it was very likely that her daughter would like to read too. And there was evidence to show that the boys of Oak Town similarly tended to take an interest in those activities that their *fathers* liked best: Cara's brother

Jeremy spent hours beside his father in the basement workshop, and flew model airplanes with him on summer Saturdays; Jerrica's brothers played computer games with their father; and Samantha's 10-year-old brother assisted his father in both carpentry and woodworking projects. Secondly, the daughters took a keen interest in *what* it was that their mothers read. When several of the Oak Town mothers bought copies of *Flowers in the Attic* at the Bi-Rite drugstore, the girls discussed the matter at lunch. Tanya reported that the book had made her mother cry. Nicole and Stephanie said their mothers had read *all* the V. C Andrews books. Alisa and Amanda said their mothers had labeled the book 'sick' and had forbidden them to read it. But the girls had wanted to read it anyway, or at least see the movie.

Marcia began to read V. C Andrews novels because her mother was reading them, and because they were distinctly different from what she had already been reading, attractively adult, and, in that way, a challenge. She said:

> I sort of admire my mother because she reads such good books. She likes horror books, and I do too. I mean I really don't like mysteries as much as I do *Sweet Valley High* and stuff like that. I like kids' books. You can understand them better. But my mother's books, they're really fun to read because they're different.

The girls saw their mothers exchanging books with their friends and they emulated *this* activity too. When Alisa's mother lent me *The Crimson Chalice* (a thick paperback retelling the Arthurian legends), Alisa began, also, to look for books in the school library that she thought I might enjoy. And similarly, Marcia, having noted with interest the fact that her mother had exchanged several horror novels with a friend on Sunday afternoon, told Amanda that she'd like to read the book Amanda had when Amanda had finished reading it.

Just as the girls, seeing that their mothers were well groomed and carefully dressed, watched and noted the details of how this was accomplished and tried to emulate their mothers, taking great care with their own dress and appearance, so, in a similar way, they watched their mothers reading, and were moved to read themselves. This happened in part because the girls were actively *guided by* their mothers in the reading of fiction: the mothers talked with the girls both about what they ought to read, and about *how* they ought to read, and in this way they were actively teaching their daughters to read like women.

Charlene Weiss, for example, found and saved articles both from the newspaper and from *The National Inquirer* that she thought her two daughters ought to read.

Some days, the girls'll come home from school and they'll read something that I've read, like in *People Magazine*. And they love the *National Inquirer*. They love to read about the movie stars, or if there's something in the newspaper, like an article on drugs or a human-interest story about heroism or whatever, I'll point it out and say, 'You guys should read this', and they'll read it.

Other mothers similarly chose reading material for their daughters. Mrs Dallas brought Julie books from the city's Book Exchange, often trading in a book that Julie had already read. Leah's mother would bring her back three or four books in a given series, like the *Satin Slippers* books, after a shopping trip to the Eastside Mall. Michelle Scott recommended books to Jerrica that she had enjoyed as a child, and encouraged Jerrica to try to find them in the school library; Jerrica came to read *Girl of the Limberlost* in this way. Marcia's mother and Lacey's mother both read the book *Sunshine* and recommended it to their daughters. Charlene Weiss, however, told Alisa that *Sunshine* was very sad, and for that reason Alisa chose not to read it, explaining 'I don't want to bawl my eyes out.'

The girls' mothers also took a keen interest in the books that their daughters chose for themselves. Samantha said she would talk to her mother about the stories she was reading, and often, if one of her books happened to intrigue Mrs Ulrich, she would read it too. Similarly, Julie said that she and her mother talked about the books they read, and 'tried to put a value' on each one. Mrs Dallas would also read some of Julie's books, and Mrs Scott and Mrs Thomas also occasionally picked up and read one of their daughter's books. Several of the girls, moreover, brought their dialogue journals home, so that they could show their mothers what they had written about the books they were reading, and how I had responded.

Sometimes, the girls' mothers used their adult authority to forbid a book or a movie, or to discourage the reading of a book that they considered inappropriate. Leah's mom, Cara's mom and Amanda's mom all asked their daughters not to read any V. C. Andrews books. And Julie's mother outlawed Stephen King novels, saying:

Stephen King's my favorite author, but when Julie picked up one of his books, it bothered her a lot. She couldn't sleep. I told her to leave the Stephen King books alone. She's just too young for that.

Although, for the most part, the girls accepted these restrictions without complaint, there was some degree of resistance to this kind of 'guidance'. No one nagged her mother to rent a forbidden movie, but if an opportunity arose to see a forbidden movie at someone else's house, no one hesitated to take it. Jerrica, for one, found all her mother's restrictions infuriating, and often assumed an angry stance in relation to her. She was angry when her mother told her that her nail polish was an awful color; when her mother said that she had to learn to cook; and when her mother told her she shouldn't read *Flowers in the Attic*.

The girls, thus, learned gender from their mothers by emulating their mothers' reading of fiction as a feminine activity; and in addition they learned *what* was appropriate for them to read, how to incorporate reading into their daily lives, and how to share their reading with a network of other women. Entering into delicate networks of suggestion and control, they were guided by their mothers in the selection of fiction, and they often learned to like what their mothers liked, and to feel what their mothers felt in response to certain books. They thus learned to choose and value books in gender-appropriate ways.

But the girls did not learn gender *only* from their mothers. The reading of fiction provided the girls with access to *textual* constructions of gender and these constructions were also positioning the girls to grow into certain kinds of women. Adolescent romance novels, like for example the *Sweet Valley High* books, offered both 'visions of what constitutes young womanhood' (Christian-Smith, 1987) and constructions of femininity which were shaped by configurations of power and control. Such romances involved women who were 'getting along' with men in ways that did not favor feminine strength and initiative, ways that required female characters to compromise and change; and they textually interpreted gender relations as primarily a *site of struggle*. As a result, the Oak Town girls, no matter what kind of gender relations they experienced at home, came into contact with discourses that promoted, through the novels they were reading, a *conflict* between the two genders (Christian-Smith, 1987).

I should also point out that such romances make use of a narrative structure, involving binary oppositions, which produces meaning in part by contrasting such qualities as 'good' and 'bad', or 'weak' and 'strong', and that these contrasts positioned the girls of Oak Town to think of gender in *oppositional* terms. Jessica and Elizabeth Wakefield, the fictional twins at the center of the *Sweet Valley* books, embody the characters of sinner and saint respectively, and their presentation as 'opposite' personalities shadows the plot's own machinations with *opposite* gender meanings. Where the female characters (both the saint and the sinner) had to be more indirect by nature and inclined to concern themselves more with the managing of *people* rather than with the managing of events, male characters, on the other hand, had to be more direct in their approach, and to concern themselves more with the managing of *events* rather than with the managing of people.

The *Sweet Valley* books, very popular with the Oak Town girls, were thus offering them suggestions for constructing gender in essentially oppositional terms. But this process was not entirely a straightforward one. The 'visions of young womanhood' offered in the fiction they were reading did not always closely correpond to the lives they actually lived, and the characters, moreover, did not necessarily seem like real people that the girls knew. The girls were aware of this, however. Marcia, for example, in commenting on the *Sweet Valley* world, suggested that perhaps things were a little different in California. The books represented gender relations in ways that worked to produce certain suggested subject positions for the readers to adopt, and those subject positions, in turn, worked to preserve the unjust gender-divided social order. At the same time, while they were incorporating those gender values that served the dominant society, they were also incorporating values that not only proved more appealing to their young female readers but were also in conflict with traditional gender roles. The Jessica Wakefield character, for example, who never worried about her own personal safety, chose to ride in cars with strangers and attend late-night parties with people she hardly knew, and this was behavior the Oak Town girls said they admired. The ways in which the girls dealt with these contradictions will be made clearer in Chapter 5, when we look more closely at how the girls constructed their own identities in response to these discourses. For now, I will simply point out that the books that the girls read provided models of womanhood which both complemented and added to the models of womanhood that their mothers provided. The Oak Town girls seemed to accept the *Sweet Valley* world as a *possible* contemporary world. That world, which entertained and educated its readers with a presentation of a possible life, constituted its own cultural discourse about gender relations.

The Oak Town girls were open about the fact that they read series books in part to learn about how to live and how to act, and about how life was *supposed* to go. Marcia, in her interview, spoke in the same breath about watching rock videos and reading *Sweet Valley High* books:

> I just like watching them [rock videos] to see how they sing and how they act. I always wanted to learn how to play the drums and stuff. You just see them doing drums and you just watch them, and you listen to them. Then you remember what they do. And the *Sweet Valley Highs*, they're fun to read, because it's sort of interesting to read about girls your age. Well, the *Sweet Valley Twins* are 12 and I'm 13, but in *Sweet Valley High* they're 16. It's just interesting to see what other girls do. Even if it's not true, it's so close to life. You can imagine that there's twins doing that. I never find those books boring when I read them again.

Marcia read her *Sweet Valley High* books to see how the people of the books talked to each other, and to see how they acted in order to be successful members of this teenage culture. Rereading the books and imagining herself there, she took in information about what kinds of behavior, on the part of teenage girls and boys, were valued by the culture in which they lived. This is not to say that Marcia simply drank in information without weighing and questioning it, without criticising and analyzing it, first. She knew that the *Sweet Valley High* world of California was different from her own. Other children also challenged the textual constructions of gender given in such books. Christopher, for example, when discussing *Bridge to Terabithia*, said that he had read several books in which the girl ran a race against the boy and won. This he found hard to accept: 'Most books, they show that girls are equal to boys *constantly*.'

Having said that, I also saw several instances of children first discussing and then *accepting* the gender messages that they received from a text. The morning after the showing of a television movie called *Those She Left Behind*, five of the girls talked at length about the behavior of the characters involved. The story concerned a young woman dying in childbirth. Alisa said, 'I liked it so much when the baby's father and the secretary got married. That was good.' Jerrica added 'Yeah, I was worried when he wanted to give the baby up because he didn't think he could take care of it. But he learned to love it.' The other girls nodded in agreement and satisfaction.

On another occasion, Jerrica expressed her fascination with a detail in *Mamma's Going to Buy You a Mockingbird*. In that novel, the character Tess lost a button on her blouse during a fight with some bullies. After the fight, she held her blouse together, and stood embarrassed in front of Jeremy, another character in the novel. Jerrica showed the other girls how she thought Tess must have sood, held her head and spoken. In acting out her interpretation, Jerrica was also expressing her approval of the way Tess had handled the situation.

But again, the girls *did* sometimes question the gender messages they received from a text. For instance, Marcia felt that Sara, in *Summer of the Swans*, was not interested enough in her peers. She thought that this character certainly ought to have shown more interest in Joe Melby, and, furthermore, that she ought to have worked harder at establishing a wider circle of friends. Sara, in Marcia's opinion, was not doing all that a girl ought to do in managing her life.

In these examples, we can see the children reflecting upon the texts in ways that involved the 'construction' of gender. The Oak Town children were considering gender possibilities through the reading of fiction and other texts. They accepted some of the messages they received, and they questioned others. And they used fiction as a source of information, about gender, that was based in a wider world.

When we consider that their other important sources of information about gender were their interactions with the adults who inhabited their daily worlds, we gain some sense of the *power* of the various discourses with which they came in contact. The girls learned different ways of 'doing' gender both in an aesthetic context and in a context of familial relationships and familial love. How easy could it have been for the girls to distance themselves from these messages within either context? Not easy at all. Can we be surprised that, in spite of all the questions they raised, the Oak Town girls were growing up to read the way their mothers read and to live the way their mothers lived?

In order to strengthen the reader's appreciation of the power of these discourses, and of the intensity with which the Oak Town girls experienced them, I will go on to look more closely at one particular aspect of their use of reading as a way of 'doing girl'. 'Doing girl', as we saw, required accepting the responsibility for maintaining human relationships, and as we also saw, the practice of reading, because it played a part in initiating and sustaining friendships, thus helped the girls in question to fulfil this 'duty'. Friendships with other girls were important for the girls' emotional lives and served to bind the Oak Town girls even more strongly to culturally approved ways of 'doing' gender.

Reading Fiction to do Friendship

In Oak Town, being a friend was both a girl's obligation and a girl's prerogative. It was an *obligation* in that being a friend was one of the required aspects of 'being a girl': girls who refused to put time and energy into friendships were punished with social isolation (one such case was described at the end of Chapter 2). And it was a *prerogative*, a satisfying way both of fighting loneliness, and of sharing the joy of living that was a girl's special privilege. Boys, by contrast, were not expected to 'be friends' in the way that girls were.

Although, in Oak Town, the activity of reading fiction did provide one means for 'being a friend', the children seemed to think of reading more as an individual and isolating activity. One study of teenagers' attitudes toward reading found that the young people interviewed felt that the best thing school offered was companionship, but that reading, by contrast, was a *solitary* and *lonely* activity (Eidman-Aadahl, 1988). The Oak Town girls felt this way too. Cara pointed out that reading was something she did only when she was alone. Friends always came before reading, and a girl would never avoid her friends in order to stay home and read instead. The focal girls in this present study, with the exception of Marcia, all agreed that friends came before reading.

However, what was also clear was that one became a member of a community by having read the *same* books, and that one remained active in that community by lending and borrowing books, by recommending books to each other, by looking for books for each other, and by talking about books together.

> Michelle hovered around the edge of the group of girls talking about *Babysitters Club* books. She listened and watched. When the other girls moved away, she approached me. 'I've never read a Babysitters Club book', she said wistfully. 'I tried one once, but I only read a few pages. I think I'll try one again. They must be really good.'

Michelle wanted to be a member of the community of girls that lent and borrowed and discussed *Babysitters Club* books. The sixth-grade girls of Oak Town lent and borrowed books on a daily basis, and not to participate meant exclusion. Nicole kept a supply of *Sweet Valley High* books in her desk, to lend out to people; Alisa handed the latest *Sweet Valley Twins* book to Julie in homeroom; Jerrica exchanged a stock of books with her cousin over the weekend; Karen borrowed *The Haunting at Cliff House* from Julie during recess; and Marcia waited for Amanda to finish *The Diary of Anne Frank* so that she could borrow it and read it.

Sometimes, the girls actually borrowed books in order to lend them to other people. Samantha searched the classroom and the school library for Enid Blyton books in order to lend them to a friend; Cara and Alisa borrowed books from other girls in order to lend them to me; and Samantha looked for books in the library that she hoped would interest her brother.

> Jade stood at the book counter and smiled and nodded. 'Yup. I've been bringing these *Narnia* books home one at a time for my Dad to read. He really likes them. I don't read them myself, but he reads them and tells me a little about them. Then I bring them back and get him another one. It's fun.'

I saw only one instance of a *boy's* borrowing a book for someone else; boys, as mentioned, did not engage in these activities to the extent that girls did, nor were they ever encouraged to.

Marcia's father spoke reflectively; 'I love books about history, you know. I collect them. I really like books about war and war equipment and battles the best. Anyway, Jason knows that. The other day he came home with a couple of library books. One was on tanks. It was just a kid's book. I got a million books like that. He showed me, and I told him I didn't want to look at it . . . You think he brought that book home for me? I don't know.'

In addition to lending and borrowing books, the girls also *recommended* books to each other. Samantha had enjoyed reading two Marilyn Halvorson books so much that she recommended them both to her mother and — because they were about boys, and she thought, therefore, that he would enjoy them — to her brother too; Cara said gratefully that the best books she had ever read were the ones that Jerrica had recommended to her; and when Julie said she'd like to read Madeline L'Engle's *A Wrinkle in Time*, Alisa searched the library shelves to find a copy for her. The girls also saved books for each other, and remembered which books to buy as birthday presents for each other. These incidents show that books amounted to items of emotional currency: the girls were taking some trouble, and expending a certain amount of emotional energy, to please other people via the books they were recommending and offering, and their efforts were appreciated.

The sharing of books through lending and borrowing often happened in the course of conversation about books, which is not surprising since book conversations formed part of the girls' social organization for 'doing friendship'. I began to understand this when Alisa reacted with delight to the suggestion that the girls and I start literature-response groups for the purpose of talking together about a book we had all read. Alisa said 'I can't wait to start! That's fun! We do it all the time!' Reading fiction and then sharing it through talk was one way in which the girls could demonstrate their concern and affection for their friends and relatives. The lending and borrowing of books provided opportunities for acts of giving and receiving of the kind that nurture human relationships.

Before I finish discussing the ways in which the Oak Town girls learned and enacted their gender through literacy, and before I bring to a conclusion my efforts to demonstrate the powerful influence of various cultural discourses on the girls' reading I would like first to discuss briefly a number of cultural demands, imposed upon the girls, that required them to 'be' a certain kind of person. Powerful discourses offering ways of 'doing' gender existed side by side with discourses that attempted to tell the girls 'who they *are*', to use Bourdieu's (1991) phrase. One such powerful discourse offered girls the pleasures of emotional indulgence and release while at the same time positioning them as people who were more emotional and less logical than male people. The next section offers a detailed portrait of that particular discourse as seen at work in Oak Town.

Reading Fiction to Feel

If being a friend was a girl's prerogative, so too was being free to express her feelings. Girls had the culture's permission to feel freely and deeply, and to show their feelings as they chose. The boys in sixth grade were unlikely to display any emotions (other than anger), but it was not uncommon for a girl to be seen crying in school. When Alisa cried with frustration during group work, or when Julie cried in school over a sad part in a book, no one harassed them about it. In contrast, it was highly unusual for a boy to cry in school, and any tears coming from a boy were treated as a disgrace. When Jack was attacked by a group of boys on the playground, and when Anthony had a model volcano explode in his face at the Science Fair, both boys, in both cases, struggled hard not to cry.

The girls did not hestitate to benefit from this permission to feel in their responses to fiction. They enjoyed feeling deeply as they read a story, and they valued those books that provoked a strong feeling — especially that of sadness. Samantha explained in her dialogue journal that she loved books that told about feelings. '(I like to read about) feelings of wanting to help another person, and feelings about being a teenager. Like another book was *The Trouble With Thirteen*. I loved it. I cried so much. It was excellent.' Jerrica wrote to Julie, in her dialogue journal, as follows: '*Bridge to Terabithia* was an excellent book. The characters seemed really real. I could feel what they were feeling. It was so sad.' Entries like these made me wonder what it was that the girls meant by the word 'sad', because such entries seemed to imply a variety of different senses. I began to comb all my data for instances of their use of the word 'sad', and to analyze the meanings given to it. I found many. When writing in their dialogue journals about those books that they had enjoyed reading, the girls used the word 'sad' to refer to any strong feeling.

Julie seemed to mean *grief*. She reported crying both over the father's death in *Mama's Going to Buy You a Mocking-bird* and over the death of the dog Louie in the *Babysitters Club* book *Kristy and the Snobs*. 'I cried and I laughed, but mostly I felt sad because of Louie dying and then all the snobs treating her so badly. If my dog died and the people in my neighborhood were treating me so badly, I would feel awful!' Cara, for her part, said she felt 'sad' when Nore was almost killed in *Locked in Time*. And similarly, she thought that *Flowers in the Attic* was neither horrifying nor frightening but again just 'sad'.

Alisa was often reluctant to read 'sad' books. She didn't seem to enjoy sadness and seek it out the way the others did. She also avoided dog stories because, as she explained, she felt so awful, and she cried, if the dog got hurt or died. And furthermore, she chose not to read *You Shouldn't Have to Say Goodbye* and *Sunshine*, again because they sounded so sad. The feeling of sadness that came with the reading of these pieces of fiction may, for Alisa, have been *too real* to be pleasurable.

In contrast, Cara took great pleasure in the feelings of sadness associated with such books. She wrote in her dialogue journal about her feeling of sadness about Julie's loneliness in *Julie of the Wolves*, about Anne Frank's persecution, and about the father's death from cancer in *Mama's Going to Buy You a Mocking-bird*. During one interview, I asked Cara how she felt when she read a good book. She replied:

> I don't know . . . I feel into the story . . . I feel happy for the person or I feel sad . . . I feel sad when something happens that makes a person sad. Or, if that person has something done to them that isn't nice. Like in *So Far From the Bamboo Grove*, because that was mean when they knocked the girl, like the policeman kicked her in the ribs when she fell. And when . . . the mom died. And . . . how they happened to be so cruel, like when they were on the train? And they had to sit with all those people . . . [Here Cara had a sharp intake of breath.] . . . And the saddest thing was when the pregnant lady had a baby . . . then there was a day go by and she was saying how good the baby was being. She goes 'Wake up, it's time for your feeding.' and it won't wake up and she started crying and crying . . . and one of the nurses grabbed the baby and threw it off the train and the mom jumped off the train and she died. That was *sad*.

The girls loved sad books, but they also loved 'scary' books too, and they recommended the best mysteries to each other. Some still read the *Nancy Drew* mysteries, but they did not find these as satisfying as they had a year or two before. They said they enjoyed the 'spooky' feeling that came with a good mystery book. The feelings the girls associated with being frightened were pleasurable, like their feelings of 'sadness', but the girls did not express them as freely. 'Scary books' were part of another cultural discourse which positioned girls as victims of violence, played with their desires, and offered different views of what it meant to be female. Only Alisa did not allow herself either to read 'sad' books widely or to feel freely in response to such books; but there were also several other girls who would similarly not allow themselves to read or respond to certain 'scary' kinds of book. These self-imposed limits were, I believe, a form of self-protection, as well as a response to a complicated cultural milieu in which violence against women was a fact of daily life. This milieu, and the girls' responses, will be considered in detail in Chapter 5.

For now, I will conclude this chapter on gender in literacy practices by asking the reader again to imagine the power of the cultural discourses at work in the Oak Town girls' lives. Loving parents, familiar contexts, and compelling texts all pressed the Oak Town girls to connect their gender with reading as an activity. It is not surprising, then, that the reading of fiction played a part in the cultural reproduction of gender ideology in Oak Town. Within a culture that placed girls and boys in opposite categories, and then granted them different rights and privileges, the Oak Town girls read more than boys did for at least two reasons: firstly, the reading and sharing of fiction were culturally approved ways of 'doing girl'; and secondly, such reading allowed the girls to exercise two of their cultural prerogatives, namely those of enjoying friendship and feeling freely. In confronting these powerful cultural discourses, the girls sometimes found the strength to question and resist, but most often they accepted and cooperated and acted as they were expected to act. The ethnographic evidence shows that, externally at least, they conformed.

But there is more to the story of how they became the people they were, since there is *another* way of looking at cultural reproduction, one which complements not only this ethnographic data but also our examination of the children's lives. Chapter 5 turns away from outer positionings and looks more closely instead at *inner workings* — at how the girls thought about and dealt with the cultural discourses surrounding their reading practices, and at how they worked at constructing themselves.

Note

1 Certainly, cultural beliefs about class and race are also relevant to the images on these greetings cards. These beliefs will be discussed in Chapter 6.

Chapter 4

Instructional Practices: Gender and Reading at School

It was 11.10 a.m. and Mr Peterson's class was beginning Language Arts. He had just distributed blue paper charts to the children, who were pasting them into their Literature notebooks. Everyone had a pencil and was beginning to fill them out. On every desk I saw a copy of *The Mixed Up Files of Mrs Basil E. Frankweiler*

Mr Peterson said, 'Okay everybody, the first one says to make a list of Claudia's characteristics. What are they? Alisa?'

Alisa hesitated, then asked, 'Claudia doesn't like inconvenience?'

'Good point! Everybody write that down.' Alisa sighed and smiled with satisfaction as she wrote.

'Okay,' said Mr Peterson, 'Here's another characteristic. In order to run away, Claudia liked to . . . I'm looking for one word.'

Most of the children looked up at him. No one had an answer. Silence. Finally, Karen raised her hand. 'Plan?'

'Right!' said Mr Peterson. 'Claudia likes to *plan*. Make sure you get *that* down.'

The children wrote on their blue sheets. Mr Peterson continued: 'For number two, look for events that will change Claudia's character. We have a column for those events on the blue sheet, and at the end we'll be coming back to look at how Claudia's character has changed and what events have caused that. I hope to collect your notebooks and grade them on Friday.'

In this scene, we see a teacher and his pupils interacting around a book that is an established part of the children's literature curriculum for many Canadian schools. I sat on a chair at the back of the classroom and watched this scene as it happened, lulled by its familiarity and feeling faintly bored. I wondered why it seemed so familiar, and decided that I had seen this pattern of teacher–student interaction many times before: the teacher had something in his mind, and the children were guessing what it was. The teacher controlled both what was said and, to a certain extent, what was *thought* about the book.

I wondered why it seemed boring to me. Then it occurred to me that Mr Peterson, too, seemed faintly bored, and that the children also were experiencing boredom, in spite of the fact that we had all enjoyed the preliminary reading of the book. I thought about the pleasure that many of the sixth-grade girls derived from their reading outside of class, and I wondered at the different emotional tone I now sensed in this classroom. I knew what boredom felt like, but I wondered what boredom meant in school, and where it came from.

I will not attempt to explain boredom until Chapter 4, but I will, in this chapter, explore several other dimensions of, and possible meanings for, the scene above. It begins with some tentative explanations of why sensitive and concerned adults might choose to teach literature the way it was being taught here. I will attempt to represent, for the reader, the ideas and the attitudes both of the two sixth-grade teachers and of their principal, as I came to discern these over time. I will try to make explicit their assumptions both about literature and about teaching, and to reflect upon what I believe to be the personal and political consequences of their thinking.

This chapter will also present and analyze the ways in which the sixth-grade children themselves experienced and responded to the teaching of literature at Oak Town School. I am going to argue that the cultural norms and values for reading which the parents were demonstrating and teaching at home, and which children were then bringing to school, were not a good match for the ways in which reading and literature were being taught at Oak Town School; and, furthermore, that the way in which literature was taught at school was consistent with cultural discourses which positioned the children not only as members of a certain social class but also as compliant citizens of the state. I want to make visible the 'hidden curriculum' (Jackson, 1968) — the unstated values and ideas that were embedded in the routines that made up classroom life, and which were repeatedly being demonstrated to the children.

In another part of this chapter, I will return to the idea of 'doing gender' (West and Zimmerman, 1987) and examine the ways in which the children used both literature itself and the literature curriculum to 'do gender' in school. The children were using their talks about books, and displaying their attitudes toward literature and literary study, in the same way that they used everything else that came to hand, namely to 'do' gender and to demonstrate to others that they were 'boy' or 'girl'. Processes I have discussed before, like the use of teasing to mark gender boundaries, and the gendered division of the emotional 'work' required for maintaining human relationships, are all visible within the frame of literary study in the classroom.

Finally, lest the 'doing' of gender through the reading of fiction in school seem idiosyncratic or harmless, I will offer some commentary upon the ways in which gendered forms of literacy may work against the best interests of the children. If one considers the nature and role of existing forms of literacy within established patterns of structural power (Lankshear and Lawler, 1987), and then examines the ways in which certain forms of literacy serve some human interests but not others, it becomes clearer just how powerful is the role of literacy in the reproduction of culture.

Reading and Literature at Oak Town School

The Principal's View

Erroll Boyle, the principal of Oak Town School, was always pleased to chat with me about curricular innovations. Proud of his school, and anxious to show that it had the latest and the best, he was careful to explain why Oak Town School was not a Whole Language school.

> I wouldn't dream of insisting that all my teachers use a Whole Language approach. Some of them choose to do Whole Language, and that's fine, but Whole Language takes a teacher's Whole Life, and I can't really ask that. Besides, there are problems with Whole Language. A lot of the time teachers work so hard and have nothing to show for it. And what about the slower kids who need more structure? I encourage my teachers who want to do Whole Language to use some structured things with the slower kids. That way they have something to show parents that parents can understand, and that way the kids know what's expected of them.

But if Oak Town School wasn't a Whole Language School, it *was* known in the district as 'the literature school'. Erroll was proud of that nickname. Several years ago, he had attended a workshop by Dr Tom Penner, Professor of Children's Literature at a well-known university, who had explained his 'structured tales curriculum' for Grades K-8. This curriculum identified the types of literature and literary themes that Penner felt ought to be taught in elementary schools. It also listed specific types and themes for teaching at each individual grade level. Erroll thought the curriculum was beautifully laid-out, and especially appreciated its explanations of 'how literature is structured.'

Erroll liked Penner's literature curriculum so much, in fact, that he decided to use it whenever he was covering for other teachers during their preparation time. He had worked out a system for taking the two classes at a certain grade level *together* for two periods each during the week. He would teach this large group something from the structured tales curriculum, and that was when the two teachers for that grade would have their released time for preparation. Occasionally, I went with him to these large-group literature lessons. Often, he would read a novel aloud during those periods, teaching the children its structure as outlined in Penner's guide.

But Erroll was not content to offer the Penner curriculum as a supplement to the regular program. For several years before I had come to Oak Town School, he told me, he had been speaking to each teacher about Penner's 'structured tales' idea, and encouraging anyone who wanted to abandon the basal-reader to buy classroom sets of the novels Penner suggested and teach Reading through those instead. Erroll had made it easy for those teachers who were interested in Penner's plan to attend his workshops in the city twice a year, and he had made sure that the school library purchased those books that Penner had identified in his curriculum. Not all the teachers had chosen to use the Penner program, but Erroll had certainly, at least, raised the staff's consciousness about literature. I could see this change reflected in the library, which was well-stocked, well-used, and decorated with displays about special authors and their books. Nearly every teacher read aloud to children daily, and daily silent-reading time was also a common event. The Arts Education teacher, furthermore, often built her music and drama lessons around those picture books which had won the Caldicott medal; and the Art teacher for the upper grades often designed art projects for the children that were inspired by the novels they were reading.

The sixth-grade teachers had been especially responsive to Erroll's suggestions for the Literature curriculum, and this seemed to please him very much. For example, Erroll loved Tolkien, and Matt Peterson and Joleen Gagnon had both come to share his enthusiasm. During the year of the study, he and Matt and Joleen read aloud, to the sixth grade, excerpts from Tolkien's *The Fellowship of the Ring*. (Erroll told me that he had also read *The Hobbit* to the same children when they were in fourth grade.) In September and October, Erroll and the two teachers would put the sixth graders together in one of the classrooms during the Language Arts period every morning, and during this period each adult would take a part and play that role as they read aloud. (Occasionally, they assigned me a role and insisted that I join them.) They changed their voices, and tried to act out the story convincingly, taking turns to fill in the narration, obviously enjoying themselves. For Frodo's birthday (22 September) Erroll, Matt, Joleen and I stayed on after school to bake and decorate an elaborate dragon cake for the children, and in October, Erroll made a papier-maché map of Middle Earth that the children then painted and decorated.

After 1 November, Erroll continued to read the novel aloud to the sixth graders during his two Literature periods every week.

> The point of reading them *The Fellowship of the Ring* is to teach them something about character development. I want them to know that early in their development characters depend on *luck* to save them. Later, they depend on *courage,* and in the final stages of their development they depend on *w sdom.* Penner says that. It's really clear in *The Lord of the Rings,* and you do find that type of character development in a lot of novels. I really enjoy knowing that kind of thing. That Penner book is wonderful.

Matt Peterson's View

Matt Peterson had been teaching the sixth grade for seven years when I met him, and he had no difficulty in explaining why he taught Language Arts the way he did.

> Well, I think we *could* move in another direction if we wanted to, but right now Joleen and I feel comfortable centering our Language Arts Program on literature. I've been able to incorporate all those things that seem to go with Language Arts teaching — like punctuation, spelling, paragraph writing, and letter writing — into the novel approach. The novels make the program cohesive. I can really do a lot with plot and character, and it all seems to mean more to the kids. Even the slower kids can see how characters change and develop. And they *enjoy* it. That's very important.

After several months of getting to know him, I felt I understood why Matt Peterson felt confident about centering his Language Arts program around children's literature. He had told me that during his first year of teaching he depended heavily on both the workbook and the reader, because he felt that he didn't have enough background in elementary Language Arts to work independently. But in his second year, he began looking for something that would be *more interesting*, both for him and for the children, and he found it in the Penner curriculum his principal was promoting. 'Erroll was pretty instrumental. He was the driving force in getting us to look at novel studies as a means of teaching Language Arts.' Matt tried working with a novel study based on Lloyd Alexander's *The Book of Three* during his second year of teaching at Oak Town, and found he enjoyed it. After that, he did more such novel studies each year.

One year, Erroll had made it possible for Matt to attend one of Tom Penner's workshops, and he remembered it as a wonderful experience. He told me about it:

> It was one of the best workshops I ever went to. Just a one-day session. But for me it was so pertinent to what I wanted to be doing in my classroom. Like everything, I was hanging on every word he was talking about, and it was great. Penner got me to see what was right there in the literature to be taught, and what I could do in the classroom to teach it.

When Matt did a novel study, every student was assigned a copy of the book and allowed to read most of it in class. Matt read aloud regularly, the children took turns reading aloud, and there was time for silent reading. Matt explained:

> I like to discuss the novel in class, to go over the plot events and look at the characters' motivations, so that everybody understands. The kids have booklets to do their comprehension questions in, and then there are these laminated Activity Cards for skills practice. Some of the things we do are fun things, like writing a letter to a certain character. Sometimes, we learn new vocabulary words or find metaphors and similes, or things like that. Some of the Activity Cards help them learn their literature terms, like 'protagonist' and 'antagonist', 'foreshadowing', 'climax', and things like that.

Matt and Joleen also tried to tie writing instruction to the actual study of the literature. They asked the children to keep 'Tolkien journals' and assigned each child a character, giving more complex characters to the better writers and the simpler characters to the poorer writers. They asked the children both to write about events in the story as if they *were* the character assigned to them and to show how that character felt about those events. The children would first do a rough draft, checking it for errors themselves as well as asking a friend to check it. Then, they would do a 'good rough' draft, which a teacher checked, and then finally, a recopying, before the work was graded. The two teachers supported the journal writing by asking the children to help them list the story's events on chart paper, for easy-reference purposes.

Matt and Joleen were not pleased with the journal-writing assignment for two reasons. Firstly, it took some of the children a very long time to complete the journal entries, and the teachers found themselves having to keep track of which draft each child was working on and then push the children to finish. And secondly, the children didn't seem to want to apply the knowledge they were supposed to have acquired about good handwriting and spelling to the writing they produced in their journals.

Matt drew well, and he had been able to make some large illustrations of various scenes found in the different novels that the class had studied. He laminated these pictures and put them up around the classroom 'for atmosphere'. He also had the *children* doing art work related to the novels: they seemed to enjoy it and he thought that it kept their interest up. The children also enjoyed the 10 minutes of silent reading time that he allowed them every day after recess, although they often complained that 10 minutes was not enough. Matt said he wished he could give them more time to read, but either Phys Ed or Science or Language Arts came after this reading peirod, and he didn't feel that he could take time away from those subjects.

Matt liked to include a few 'fun' Language Arts activities in his program — that didn't have anything to do with literature — just because the children liked them. One day, we all watched a video clip of the bar scene from *Star Wars*, and the children then chose one of the creatures we had seen and wrote a character sketch for it. On another day, Matt assigned the children to work in groups and design a product, together with an advertising campaign to sell it, and in October he asked them to produce a Halloween play that they had written. But these things were 'extras': the novel studies were the heart of the Language Arts program.

Matt appreciated Erroll's suggestions about which novels made good studies, and he also appreciated Erroll's support in finding the money to buy the class sets of the novels that he chose to teach. In the year that I was with them, Matt's class read *The Black Cauldron* and *The Book of Three*, *The Mixed Up Files of Mrs Basil E. Frankweiler*, and *Mrs Frisbee and the Rats of NIMH*. (Matt had also wanted to do *Call It Courage*, but what with the canoe trips scheduled for June, there really wasn't enough time.) And of course, they continued to study Tolkien. After October, Erroll did *The Lord of the Rings* with the sixth graders for two periods a week in his Literature class — an arrangement that continued for the rest of the school year.

Joleen Gagnon's View

Joleen told me that although the year that I had spent at Oak Town School was her first year at teaching Grade Six, she had taught *fifth* grade for several years prior to moving on to sixth grade.

Although she'd always used the basal-reading series with the fifth graders, she explained:

> I'd been getting really sick of it, and when I switched to sixth grade I thought, if *I'm* sick of the reader, think how the *kids* must feel about it! Matt had been doing novel studies with the Grade Sixes, and I thought I'd like to try that too.

Erroll had encouraged her to make the change. As part of her transition to novel studies, she had agreed to work on the Tolkien novel with Erroll and Matt and his class, although at the same time she had also gone through all the old sixth-grade readers and chosen from these a few units with themes that matched some of the things she wanted to do during the year. One was a unit called *Strange Creatures,* and she thought that that would go well with the Tolkien book. Joleen told me that she first wanted to be sure that she was covering the right skills, even if she wasn't using the reader. Then, she said, she planned to fill in the program with various novel studies. As it happened, however, she only found time for two novel studies: *Mrs Frisbee and the Rats of NIMH,* which seemed to take forever, and *The House of Sixty Fathers,* which they managed to do in the space of only four weeks during May and June.

For most of the school year, Joleen complained, she felt that her Language Arts time kept disappearing on her. Even though they had time for Language Arts at the beginning and the end of every day, there was just so much to do. At the start of the year, reading the Tolkien book aloud had taken a lot of time, and later on, they were always struggling to get those journals done. When they were doing *Mrs Frisbee and the Rats of NIMH* some of the children had raced ahead both with their reading and with their questions, and she felt that she had to wait for a few of the slower ones to finish their questions and catch up. She said that when she taught the book again, she would try using an activity center, so that the children could work at their own speeds.

After Christmas, I noted that Joleen started to write a schedule on the board for every Language Arts period. When I asked her why she did this, she explained that the schedule helped her to get to some of the things she really wanted to include. She scheduled 15-minute handwriting practices to be done three times a week; she had the children write several different kinds of poem; and she assigned a folk-tale unit in the reader for seatwork. Joleen also saw that her class did regular spelling studies and post tests, as well as regular studies of vocabulary words, homonyms, antonyms and synonyms, and some of the literature Activity Cards both for the Tolkien book and for the *Mrs Frisbee and the Rats of NIMH* book. And that was really all there was time for. She found that she could only fit in silent reading for half the class at a time, i.e. when the other half went out for computer-keyboarding practice on even-numbered days.

Joleen said that although she felt she had handled the time well, she wasn't really happy with her class's performance in Language Arts. She seemed confused and dissatisfied:

> Most of the kids don't show a very good attitude, you know. They work as slowly as they possibly can, except for a few of the brighter girls. I do everything I can think of to make it fun for them and to help them. I have them illustrate their work and I put it up on the walls on display. I give them lists of adjectives that might help them in their writing. But it almost seems they do as little as possible . . . Maybe another year I can fit in more novel studies. I hope so, because there are so many good books for sixth graders to read, and I do want to give them some choices.

The Children's Views

We were waiting for Mr Boyle. There were 42 sixth graders sitting on the floor in the library in front of the big relief map of Middle Earth. This was Day 3 of the six-day timetable, which meant that this was a day for Literature Class. Mr Boyle would be reading from J. R. R. Tolkien's *The Lord of the Rings*.

Mr Boyle came in. He walked past the children and took a chair beside the map, facing them. The talking subsided to silence. We all waited for a full three minutes while Mr Boyle found his place in the book. It was 9.12 a.m. by the library clock when Mr Boyle began reading aloud.

The children sat cross-legged, girls in front and closest to Mr Boyle, boys ranged across the back of the group. Many sat with their elbows on their knees, chin in hand. They stared at the floor. A few of the girls against the side wall had back support. They pulled their knees to their chests.

9.20 a.m.: Mr Boyle read on.

Marcia was to his right, surreptitiously reading a *Sweet Valley High*, glancing at Mr Boyle every few seconds. . . .

9.25 a.m.: Mr Boyle read on. We heard a stifled yawn in his voice. He paused to remind us that we were reading Tolkien in order to learn about character development. We needed to watch for evidence that Frodo was growing wiser, he said.

Marcia and Lacey had a game going. They were scraping a small yellow sticker off the back of Michelle's hooded sweatshirt while Michelle sat on the floor in front of them. They were trying not to let her feel anything. Cara watched them.

The other girls studied their fingernails and the weave of the carpet. They retied their shoelaces. . . .

9.30 a.m.: Mr Boyle read on. Anthony closed his eyes. Alisa closed hers. Tom closed his. No one was smiling. Foreheads were creased.

Nick leaned back against a chair turned upside down on one of the library tables. It shifted and started to fall. He fixed it quietly and sat up. Five minutes later it happened again. Marcia's movements attracted Mr Boyle's attention. He said, 'Listen, please, Marcia.' When he looked away from her, Marcia smiled off to her right toward the group. Only a few were looking up. . . .

9.37 a.m.: Mr Boyle read on. People were restless, shifting from side to side. Several in the front turned around to glance at the clock on the wall behind them. Class was over at 9.45.

Mr Boyle had been reading for 24 minutes. No one else had spoken in that time.

Eight minutes later he closed the book. 'You may go.' The children rose and moved away. 'Next time, we'll find out who *she* is,' said Mr Boyle. The library was empty.

Very few of the sixth graders admitted to enjoying *The Lord of the Rings*. Many of them said that they liked *The Hobbit*, but did not like *The Lord of the Rings* because it was an adult book, full of history and without much action. Julie, for her part, said that the book *was* okay, but she hated sitting still for so long. Mr Boyle let them answer his questions once in a while, but he didn't like it when *he*, in turn, was asked questions.

Alisa said, '*The Lord of the Rings* is the most boring book in the world. It was okay at the beginning of the school year, but now I feel like crying when it's time for Literature Class. It's like Mr Boyle reads it to the wall.'

Mr Peterson's class was in general agreement that the novel studies they did with Mr Peterson were much better than *The Lord of the Rings*. Everybody really liked *The Black Cauldron* and *The Book of Three*. Karen said that she really got attached to the characters, especially those of Taran and Eilonwy, and when Mr Peterson asked them to think of a gift to give each character at the end of the second book, she enjoyed doing that as well. Karen, like many of the sixth graders, thought that Mr Peterson chose excellent books for the novel studies. 'I like reading the stories. I don't even mind answering the questions, but I do think it's hard to finish the 12 activity cards we have to do for each book. They take so long!'

Sarah liked the novel-study books too, but she was impatient at having to answer all the questions. She said: 'I wish we could just read those books for fun. All those questions just ruin it, and some day I'll tell Mr Peterson that!'

Most of the sixth graders enjoyed doing the art projects for the novel studies, and they admired the pictures that Mr Peterson did himself. Several found that the books had such good stories that they read them *again* outside of class. There were only a few complaints: Karen said, 'I'd like to have books with a few more girls in them,' and Marcia added: 'The books we read are boys' books.' And sometimes, also, the children complained that they had read the books before. But on the whole, the novel studies were seen as a pleasant and acceptable part of the school's curriculum.

There was one exception: Mrs Gagnon's class did not like *Mrs Frisbee and the Rats of NIMH* very much. Jerrica said: 'It was a pretty good book, but I read it in Grade Three, and the books I read now are a lot more interesting.' Everyone, however, had seen the video, and that, at least, helped. Many of the children also complained that doing both the questions and the activities took forever, especially if the child involved was a slow reader. On the whole, the children seemed to prefer *The House of Sixty Fathers*, perhaps because they went through that particular novel study at a faster rate. There were nine chapters to this novel. Mrs Gagnon got them to read the first three chapters and do the relevant activities, then read the second three chapters and do the activities, and finally read the last three chapters and do the activities. They had finished it in only four weeks. The story took place in China, and Mrs Gagnon had told the children that she wanted to do this particular story because China was close to Korea and the children were already studying Korea both for Social Studies and as their particular country for the Multicultural Fair.

For many of the children, *Mrs Frisbee and the Rats of NIMH* and *The House of Sixty Fathers* were the only books they read all year because they had so much other work to finish. Those who finished their work during school time, such as Jerrica, Cara and Samantha and a few others, had free time to read. Most people, however, didn't. It seemed to the children that they hardly ever had silent-reading time, and as a result some of them took matters into their own hands: some would find a good book in the library and try to read it when the class became boring. A few became very good at sneaking reading and the teachers rarely guessed when they weren't paying attention. I would see Anthony, for example, hiding the book he was reading inside his Math book during Math class — or inside his notebook when he was supposed to be finishing his Tolkien journal. Mrs Gagnon caught him twice, so he had to stop it for a while — but he didn't give up. He persevered where other children resigned themselves and accepted the fact that it was nearly impossible to read in school.

The Hidden Curriculum

Erroll Boyle, Matt Peterson and Joleen Gagnon knew that they were teaching more than just literature when they taught Literature. They were aware that they were using the school subject 'Literature' to teach a number of other things besides, and they had even made conscious decisions to do so. When I asked them to clarify, for me, what they were intentionally teaching through Literature, both teachers began to answer by saying 'skills'. By 'skills' they seemed to be referring chiefly to the mechanical aspects of writing, spelling, handwriting, and punctuation. They were also clear about teaching 'good study habits': keeping neat notebooks, completing assignments on time, and being willing to revise and improve one's writing.

They had chosen to teach these particular 'skills' and attitudes as a result of certain beliefs which they shared — I assume they believed these things because they acted in accordance with them, during their time at school, day after day and month after month — and it seemed to me that these shared beliefs lay just below the surface of consciousness, informing almost every curricular decision. Erroll, Matt and Joleen. for example, believed that knowledge and the curriculum were things created by an external authority. They believed that teachers transmitted knowledge and delivered the curriculum, but that *someone else* provided both these components in the first instance. They accepted the responsibility for making intelligent choices among the different curricular alternatives — choices based both on their experiences with the children and on their own talents and preferences — but they did not expect to create the actual knowledge or the curriculum used themselves, nor did they expect the children to do so. These Oak Town adults acted as if children could not be trusted to choose for themselves what they should learn; as far as they were concerned the *teachers* had to be in control of what was to be studied. The idea was that skills had to be taught, or the children would not learn them at all.

Because they assumed that knowledge had to be created by an external authority, Matt and Joleen did not feel free to leave the basal reader behind them without substituting another printed program, such as Tom Penner's 'Structured Tales Curriculum'. They accepted a number of views: that knowledge existed both in a literary work and in someone else's commentary on it; that knowledge was there to be explained and understood; and that their task, when teaching, was to uncover and present it, while the children's task, in turn, was to memorize and retain it. I want to note here, however, that the Oak Town teachers did not *always* accept the authority of a text, or the idea that knowledge resides in the text. Resistance to those ideas would, sometimes, occur when Matt Peterson encouraged a student to construct his or her own answer to a question about a novel, or asked a student, 'What do *you* think?'

For the most part, however, because they felt that they were responsible for transmitting a codified body of knowledge, the teachers did not feel free to neglect the traditional 'skills' instruction which they themselves had received in school as children. Because they believed that knowledge had to be *taught* if it were to be learnt, they did not often imagine curricular possibilities that would have called for the children to *create* the knowledge of a literary text. Knowing that this codified and externally created knowledge did not belong to the children, they also sensed intuitively that the children, for this very reason, would learn it only under duress, in tightly controlled classroom situations. They saw that the children would not accomplish the adults' agenda unless they were *made* to do so. The literature curriculum and the actual teaching of literature in Oak Town therefore became, for the adults involved, the means to several ends. Literature as a school subject gave the children 'training' and practice in reading and writing 'skills' — i.e. what the teachers saw as the real business of the Language Arts curriculum — and it also provided the children with a knowledge of literary structures and terms. These latter elements are what comprised the 'content' of literature which had been identified for all concerned by an external authority.

One other aspect of the teachers' views of Literature teaching deserves a brief mention here, although it will also be described more fully later in this chapter. A knowledge of the elements of literature amounted to *socially prestigious* knowledge, i.e. to the kind of cultural 'capital' that could one day be exchanged for a place at university, or for professional work (Anyon, 1981); and for this reason, teachers seemed to believe that Literature was somehow 'good for' their students. Because the Oak Town community similarly saw a knowledge of literature as *prestigious* knowledge, the school's distinctive Literature program was regarded as enriching the school's other offerings, and as a contribution to Oak Town School's reputation as a place where the curriculum was of a high quality and up-to-date in its approach.

Thus far, I have been discussing matters that the Oak Town adults were often conscious of and taught explicitly, and I have also been discussing the assumptions and beliefs which informed their Literature teaching — or at least, those they would probably have deemed acceptable if I had articulated them for their approval. However, in addition, I believe that Erroll and Matt and Joleen were also teaching and demonstrating *other* things which they were not quite as aware of, matters that existed beneath the level of conscious thought. It seems to me, therefore, that they were also teaching a 'hidden curriculum' (Jackson, 1968): the children were learning from *how* they were taught, as well as from *what* they were taught. Eisner (1982) puts it this way:

> What pupils learn is not only a function of the formal and explicit content that is selected; it is also a function of the manner in which it is taught. The characteristics of the tasks and the tacit expectations that are a part of the structured program become themselves a part of the content.

For more than 20 years, reproduction theorists have been referring to a 'hidden curriculum' in studies which directly implicate the school in the social reproduction of society (Althusser, 1971; Bowles and Gintis, 1976; Anyon, 1984; Spender and Sarah, 1980). The 'hidden curriculum' has been defined as the unstated norms, values, and beliefs that are transmitted to students through the underlying rules that structure the routines and social relationships that make up school and classroom life (Giroux and Purpel, 1982, as quoted in Simon, 1983, p. 238). Such an underlying curriculum is bound to have an influence on the academic curriculum being taught, because the norms, values and beliefs that it represents will serve to shape decisions both about *what* will be taught and about *how* it will be taught. What is taught and how it is taught will then, in turn, serve to demonstrate and convey, themselves, these underlying values and beliefs, and it is in this way that the academic curriculum becomes an important vehicle for the *transmission of culture*. The literature curriculum at Oak Town School provides an example of these processes at work.

Simon suggests (1983) that all knowing can be understood as an ideological process (p. 245), and that the process of asking certain critical questions about what is taught in schools and how it is taught can help us to understand the ideologies that shape a given curriculum. Some of the critical questions that Simon poses are these: What counts as knowledge? How is such knowledge produced and distributed? Whose interests are served by the forms of knowledge taught? What types of questions is it possible for students to ask in response to these forms of knowledge? What types of questions, on the other hand, is it *impossible* to ask? It is worthwhile considering each of these critical questions in connection with the literature curriculum at Oak Town School.

What counts as knowledge?

What counted as proper knowledge, when it came to the curriculum for novel studies at Oak Town School, was a knowledge of the particular literary text that was being studied. Children received such knowledge from their teachers, who used an instructional process of transmission which involved posing questions about a text and then directing the children to guess the answers, almost as if they were prizes to be won. The teacher had the authority to declare an answer right or wrong. This is the process described in the scene that opens this chapter. It was clear to the children that there *was* a pre-existing correct answer which they had to guess, because occasionally someone would guess *incorrectly*, and the answer would be judged not acceptable. I never heard a child ask *why* an answer was correct, or *where* the teacher's knowledge of the text had come from (in this case, of course, it had come from Dr Tom Penner).

The teacher's copy of 'The Structured Tales Curriculum' pointed to a way of identifying and legitimating the 'facts' about character development in the novel *The Mixed Up Files of Mrs Basil E. Frankweiler* — 'facts' which the children, in this chapter's opening scene, were being directed to list on blue worksheets. Because of the 'factual', reified form it took, such knowledge was again regarded as *legitimate* knowledge. Knowledge that was taught and tested was knowledge that could be committed to memory, and about which there was no disagreement. Such forms of knowledge included: a knowledge of plot events, and of the terms that described and labeled the structure of the plot; a knowledge of character, of changes in character, and of the events that caused changes in character; a knowledge of the setting; and finally, a knowledge of certain stylistic devices. What counted as knowledge could most often be traced to a particular page in the text, or to certain words on the page.

I came to think that what counted as knowledge of literature was strongly influenced by an 'ideology of individualism', an ideology which had broad and profound effects on many aspects of life in Oak Town. The term comes from Apple's (1982) observation that the North American capitalist economy requires both an ideology of individual consumption and a belief that the individual's worth is determined by the possession of material goods. Acting out this ideology in their daily lives, the people of Oak Town devoted themselves to the acquisition and display of material possessions, and made competition a way of life. The point being made here is that even the school's literature curriculum was influenced by this ideology of individualism, since it served to position children as 'consumers' of knowledge (what counted as knowledge was something which could be 'consumed'). A knowledge of plot and character appeared as most important to those people who were living in a culture that emphasized time and gender and individualism; and the focus on *character*, as the key to understanding literature, was also consistent with the belief in the importance of the individual. What therefore counted as knowledge of literature, for the people of Oak Town, was information in the text about individuals and the events in their lives.

The Oak Town children were not always entirely willing to accept the definition of literary knowledge as 'facts to be consumed', or even to see this kind of knowledge as at all worthwhile. Sarah's anger at the fact that having to answer the study questions was coming before her own enjoyment of the book was a challenge both to the authority of the teacher and to the teacher's view of what counts as knowledge. When the children of Mrs Gagnon's class took too much time to complete the exercises that were required after the reading of *Mrs Frisbee and the Rats of NIMH*, they were resisting her position as the determiner of what counted as knowledge. Such acts of resistance did not, however, serve to transform the situation, in part because, at the same time, the children were assigned a report-card grade that was based upon their performance in tests and activities which required them to write down what the teacher had told them was acceptable knowledge about a given text. This report-card grade was seen as important currency to be used in the exchanges involved in acquiring and displaying, and in *competing for*, the 'possessions' which marked the worth of the individual. What counted as a knowledge of literature was thus also part of a cultural system for constructing status.

I might also say that what counted as knowledge of literature in Oak Town also had something to do with social class. There are identifiable and socially meaningful differences between the various forms of educational knowledge that are made available to different social classes (Anyon, 1981; Apple, 1993), and it is possible to look at what counts as a knowledge of literature and see the *class conflicts* which shape the nature and distribution of educational knowledge. For the children of those people — comprising the *upper classes* — who had accumulated money and attained the highest educational levels, people whom Anyon refers to (1981) both as 'affluent professionals' and as 'the executive elite', the field of Literature (and indeed of History, Mathematics, Science, and Art) becomes an arena for creativity, a place where children are encouraged to think for themselves, to solve problems, and to create meaning. Unfortunately this was not the case in

Oak Town. In Oak Town, the way in which Literature was studied did *not* serve to produce conceptual and critical forms of understanding that might have enabled the children to wield political power, or to manipulate economic situations to their own advantage. The people of Oak Town seemed to see, in literature, a kind of 'prestigious knowledge' (Anyon, 1981) — the kind of knowledge which they associated with the advantages of the upper classes, and which they viewed as a kind of 'cultural capital' that would be valuable later in life. But I think they were mistaken in their assumption that it was information, facts and dates that comprised the kind of knowledge that could be exchanged for good grades, college, a job, and economic success in life. In my view they were mistaken both about the nature of the knowledge involved, and about the directness of the exchange. The knowledge of literature that worked as cultural capital required the learner to generate critical conceptions about a given piece of work, and although I believe that these critical conceptions were not original but rather constructed in response to dominant cultural discourses, I believe that these conceptions did, however, contribute to the construction of individual identities that were secure both in feelings of self-worth and in knowledge of how to rule. The Oak Town children were growing up secure in the knowledge of their ability both to memorize information and to produce a right answer. The view that knowledge was there *in* the text served to support a view of knowledge as something external to people, while at the same time obscuring the idea that knowledge might instead be socially constructed *by* people. This view asserted the authority of the text over the authority of the reader. Unfortunately, in a world where *leaders* made more money than followers, and had better chances for self-actualization, the Oak Town children's beliefs about legitimate knowledge worked *against* their best interests.

How is such knowledge produced and distributed?

Knowledge reified in the curriculum for Literature study at Oak Town School had, as has already been mentioned, been produced by an authority external to the school — namely, Dr Tom Penner. Supported by a long tradition of literary analysis and criticism, Penner had described, in writing, the structure of plots, the motivations of different characters, and the various acceptable themes which together constituted an approved body of knowledge for certain selected texts. Occasionally, the teachers who had been trained in the tradition of Tom Penner would decide for *themselves* what would count as knowledge, and would use their own past experiences, in connection with plot and character and style to 'generate' the knowledge of the text that they expected their students to acquire. But rarely did the *students* of Oak Town produce any knowledge about the text, and rarely, moreover, did they *share* with each other their knowledge about the text. Knowledge was handed from the curriculum expert to the school administrator, from the administrator to the classroom teacher, and from the classroom teacher to the student.

This 'handing on' of knowledge happened in several ways. Tom Penner had sold his curriculum to a publishing firm which was successfully marketing it to school divisions right across Canada. The school divisions that bought the curriculum then distributed copies of it to individual schools and teachers, giving varying degrees of direction as to its use. Penner also distributed the curriculum himself, traveling to cities across Canada for a period of several months each year, and conducting workshops for teachers which explained and expanded upon his work. Teachers came to the workshops and listened — taking notes also, and attempting, for the most part, to see in the text what Penner himself saw.

Penner had produced his collections of literary knowledge by centering on certain texts, but it is not enough to describe his method of knowledge-production simply as a 'text-centered' one. It is also possible to *collaboratively construct* knowledge about a given text. (Chapter 6 will suggest pedagogies that call for this kind of activity.) But Penner had constructed the knowledge of the text which he was marketing by applying certain rules and traditions that governed what constituted acceptable knowledge and acceptable literature; and he was advocating the passive acceptance of this knowledge through the very way in which he was *distributing* it.

Penner's curriculum dealt with a limited number of texts, namely those which had been selected as worthy of a place in his literary canon because they embodied traditional social values. These texts included many 'traditional tales' and Newbery Award winning children's novels. Raymond Williams, in explaining (1977) how it is that certain works come to be selected as literature, argues that it is not the qualities of imagination or beauty or worth inherent in the works themselves which are responsible for their selection as literature, but rather those qualities of the works which define them as part of a 'tradition'. The development of such a concept of tradition, he further explains, 'drew on all the positive forces of cultural nationalism' (page 51), and as a result, the literary value of a work came to be defined by the extent to which a work endorses or supports beliefs that the people of a certain nation and the structure of that nation's society are inherently worthy and natural and beautiful. Christian-Smith (1989) has suggested that just as there is a 'selective tradition' operating in relation to the canon of adult English literature, so there is also a 'selective tradition' operating via the Newbery Awards, insofar as most of the winners of this award present the status quo as something natural, and do not challenge existing social arrangements. In the same way the canon of children's literature, like the canon of adult literature, has valued some works over others because they represent certain gender and class interests.

In answering questions about how literary knowledge is produced, it is thus helpful to consider the forces at work in the selection of the texts through which such knowledge is generated.

Whose interests are served by the forms of knowledge taught?

Thus far, I have argued that the people of Oak Town acted in accordance with the assumption that 'prestigious' knowledge resided in literary texts, and that some texts were inherently more 'worthy' than others. Here I want to go on to argue that the acceptance of the authority of the text and the acceptance of the authority of the whole literary canon served to maintain the class and gender interests of the groups in power. This is because both the individual texts selected and the canon as a whole serve to represent the unequal structures of society as if they were *natural* forms of social life, and present male experience as if it amounted to the *whole* of human experience.

I will begin by pointing out, again, that what counts as knowledge in schools, in terms of structure and content, often depends on the particular social class that is being served by the school (Anyon, 1981; Simon, 1983; Wieler, 1988). Where knowledge for working-class children may often take the form of isolated facts and simple skills and procedures, and where knowledge for the children of the wealthy may take the form of concepts generated through discovery and direct experience (Anyon, 1981), knowledge for the Oak Town children, on the other hand, seemed to take the form of generally accepted statements, about human experience, which had been generated by experts: in Science, the children learned the names of the planets and their distances from the sun; in History, they learned a version of the settlement of the Canadian Prairie West that did not hint at conquest; and in Literature, the teaching emphasis was on both the structure of the plot and the main characters' stages of development. The various forms of knowledge passed on to the children served to encourage certain ways of thinking which, whether they were resisted or not, made it more likely that working-class children, on the one hand, would end up carrying out mechanical tasks while the children of the wealthy, on the other hand, would learn extreme forms of individualism that would allow them both to separate their own affluence from the poverty of others, and to serve a world capitalist economy. Although inspiring stories about individual teachers who have worked to change the nature of school knowledge for their own groups of children certainly do exist (Ashton-Warner, 1967; Conroy, 1972; Herndan, 1970; Kozol, 1969), the idea is nonetheless well-established that the great majority of school knowledge acts as a *reproductive* force which 'contributes directly to the legitimation and perpetuation of ideologies, practices, and privileges constitutive of present economic and political structures' (Anyon, 1981, p. 31). In this way, we can see that certain forms of knowledge actively serve the interests of those social classes with the greatest accumulations of wealth and power insofar as these forms of knowledge work to encourage the people found in these classes to keep their places within the social order into which they have been born.

It is the idea that the prevailing structure of society is something natural and acceptable that is the most dangerous feature of the children's literary canon as made available in school libraries, and as taught in school Literature classes. The canon serves the interests of those at the top insofar as it undermines resistance, and makes one's place in society seem inevitable — and therefore not to be questioned. Older Newbery winners like *Onion John* and *Blue Willow* serve both to *naturalize* poverty, and to assign the responsibility for the relief of such poverty to kind individuals rather than to social programs. More recent Newbery winners have treated racism as something caused by the attitudes of the *individual* (*Maniac McGee*, for example), and poverty as the result of individual bad luck (*Shiloh*). Class relations, furthermore, are presented as involving the *individual's* struggle, and the *individual's* sense of responsibility, and class restrictions are often presented, in these narratives, as being overcome through an *individual's* perspicacity or an *individual's* effort. The children who read these texts but resist these messages, may still, unfortunately, be discouraged from collectively organizing because of the sheer power of those cultural discourses, valorizing the effort of the individual, to which they have been exposed.

Particular kinds of gender relations, also, are commonly naturalized by the children's literary canon, and more often than not, as already mentioned, male experience is presented as if it amounted to the *whole* of human experience. All the Oak Town sixth graders, for exampe, were expected to identify with Taran, the central (male) character of Lloyd Alexander's *Prydain Chronicles*, and to learn from Taran's 'development' toward manhood. Similarly, they were all expected to identify with the problems that were faced by the main *male* characters in *Call It Courage* and *Shadow of a Bull*, both of whose stories centered on their struggles against society's expectations for adult *men*. Comparable stories of female experience were noticeably absent from the school curriculum. When I suggested two such possibile stories, they were not accepted for study, on the assumption that the boys would not be interested in 'a girl's book'. The perpetuation, within the school's Literature curriculum, of the idea that male experience equates with human experience will be discussed at greater length later in this chapter. My point here is simply that the forms of knowledge presented through the school's Literature curriculum served, on the one hand, to validate only man's experience of the world and, on the other hand, to position female people as outsiders — in Kate Millet's words, as 'the Ladies' Auxiliary to the human race'.

These, then, were the patterns, the messages implicit in the cultural discourses embodied in their Literature curriculum and elsewhere, which positioned the Oak Town children to accept the structure of the society in which they lived — to accept, in other words, the authority of the text, the authority of the literary canon, the authority of the classroom teacher, and the authority of the literature expert. If a literary expert with authority over the teacher produces the knowledge, and if a teacher with authority over the students then imparts that same knowledge, the hierarchy of unequal social relations, on the one hand, and the particular interests of those groups in power, on the other hand, both receive considerable support.

What kinds of questions is it possible for students to ask in response to these forms of knowledge? What types of questions is it impossible to ask?

Students and teachers can ask only certain types of questions if it is assumed that knowledge resides in a literary text. To begin with, they can ask 'recall questions' that can be answered by reference to certain 'facts' recorded in the text (e.g. 'What did Claudia take with her in her suitcase when she left home?', or 'Where in Prydain did Gwydion lead the companions to meet the golden ships?'). But it is also possible to ask either questions that involve recounting the plot (for example, 'What happened after Tien Pao lost control of the sampan?', or 'How did Karana come to leave the island?'), or questions concerning a character's motivation that are based on a common view both of the world in general and of social relations (for example, 'Why didn't Winnie drink the water of immortality right away?', or 'Why was Miyax so angry with her father?'). Finally, other questions could ask the student to seek out instances (as identified by experts) of certain literary devices (for example, 'Explain the extended metaphor used in the Prologue of *Tuck Everlasting*', or 'Identify four symbols in Chapter 10').

Students and teachers who assume that knowledge resides in the text are not able to ask questions that can only be answered by the creation of new knowledge. They cannot ask critical questions about the assumptions that underlie a work of literature (for example, 'What is Lloyd Alexander's attitude toward war as it is expressed in *The Chronicles of Prydain?*', or 'After reading *Maniac McGee*, explain Jerry Spinelli's beliefs about racial violence and racial harmony.'). These kinds of questions cannot even be asked, because students and teachers do not feel free to question or challenge the views of an author or a character — they feel that they do not have the authority to do so.

The reason such critical questions cannot be asked is that the ideologies that are communicated to the teachers through the literature curriculum, and hence to children via those teachers, signify ideologies of authority, shaped in part by those discourses of individualism which support a capitalist economy (Apple, 1982). Arising from the economic 'necessity' of individual acquisition, these discourses serve to separate one person from another by making even the pursuit of knowledge an enterprise whose success is judged by the *individual's* level of achievement. These ideologies of authority, however, are rooted not in a belief in the worth of the individual, but in an acceptance of the particular relations of power and authority that exist in society today. The Literature curriculum at Oak Town School brought children and teachers into contact, in an immediate and powerful way, with cultural discourses which helped to *reproduce* social relations of power and authority.

Children, Gender and Literature at Oak Town School

Using Literature to 'Do Gender'

But if the literature curriculum at Oak Town School was a reproductive force because of the hidden curriculum it embodied, it also became a reproductive force by virtue of the purposes for which the children themselves used it. As I have shown, it was possible to see these children 'doing gender' in soccer games, in their play during recess, in their journal-writing activies, and in nearly everything else they did. Because gender was a routine accomplishment embedded in everyday interaction, gender could, and did, appear both in conversations about any subject and in the performance of any partiular activity (West and Zimmerman, 1987). It is not surprising, then, that children 'did gender' both during their reading of fiction and during their talk about fiction at school.

> Alisa was talking to Amanda about the plot of *The Egypt Game*. She said in a hushed and horrified tone, 'Do you know what the murderer did? He grabbed April around the neck and tried to choke her!'

Christopher overheard. His tone was sarcastic. 'Ooooo, that's so *scary*, Alisa.' Alisa turned toward him. 'It *is* scary, Christopher. That could be a true story, you know.'

Christopher glanced up at the ceiling and then looked back at Alisa with a tired and resigned expression on his face. He sighed. 'Alisa, that's so silly and gullible. It's *not* a true story. You're like most people. You believe everything you read.'

When I witnessed the conversation related above, I felt, as I watched, that this was yet another instance of children enacting their gender. In Oak Town, Christopher knew, it was not considered manly to be scared, and only a female child would have felt free to use the word 'scary' to describe a book. Being frightened was acceptable only as a female pose, and for this reason Christopher was putting on a show of disdain in order to distance himself from Alisa's stance, to define his own masculinity, and to assert his own superiority. The response to a piece of fiction here became the vehicle for establishing gender hierarchy.

I also saw children enacting their understandings of gender during the *literature-response* groups organized for this study[1]. When they met for the self-directed discussion of a book they had all read, they again 'did gender'. For example, cross-gender *teasing* was used in the groups to mark and maintain gender boundaries (just as, indeed, this tactic was used elsewhere). The reader may recall from the discussion in Chapter 2 that I made a distinction between 'teasing', on the one hand, and 'harassment', or 'bugging' on the other, and that by 'teasing' I mean the act of speaking in a group in such a way as to intentionally provoke or irritate another person about something that is not of significance to the larger work of the group as a whole.

I discerned certain patterns inherent in the various instances of teasing that were recorded in the transcripts of the literature-response groups in which some of the sixth graders participated; these patterns, I felt, were again related to gender. Where only 2 instances of teasing occurred in 9 of the same-gender groups, 13 instances of teasing, on the other hand, took place in 5 of the mixed-gender groups; and only one instance of teasing occurred in an *all-boys* group (when Christopher teased *me* about the fact that the boys were 'getting out of class work'). In the all-girls groups, teasing occurred only *once*, and that was during a discussion of *Mama's Going to Buy You a Mockingbird*, one that also happened to take place during Marcia's two-month period of gender resistance. The girls were ignoring Marcia, and she managed to get Julie's attention twice by teasing her about being eaten by bugs when she died.

The teasing that occurred during a mixed-gender discussion of *Frozen Fire* had to do with something that was closely related to the content of this particular text. Michael teased Julie and Alisa both for missing details in the text and for giggling about reindeer when they were mentioned. When the same two girls expressed disgust at the fact that the boys in the novel were forced to eat raw rabbit meat to stop themselves from starving, Aaron and Michael teased them about eating sushi, and later on Michael ridiculed Alisa's interpretation of the polar bear as a 'symbol'.

West and Zimmerman, in 'Doing Gender' (1987), cite Goffman's (1976) remark that gender is displayed 'as highly conventionalized behaviors structured as two-part exchanges of the "statement-reply" type in which the presence or absence of symmetry can establish deference or dominance'. Although the 'behaviors' that Goffman refers to do not necessarily involve talk, it *is* possible, nonetheless, that teasing may figure as one of these 'highly conventionalized behaviors'. If so, the fact that more teasing went on in the mixed-gender groups now becomes significant because it may indicate that the establishment of a relation of deference or dominance was more relevant when both genders were present in a group. The fact that teasing interactions almost always involved *both* genders may indicate that teasing was being used as a strategy for *establishing dominance*. The act of teasing delivered a message: 'I have the power to provoke or annoy or belittle or scorn or laugh at *you*.' In this light, silence in response to a tease may be seen as 'a reply slot noticeably filled with silence' (Schlegloff, 1974) — one perhaps indicating deference — while answering one tease with another tease, on the other hand, may be seen as a way of preventing a dominance relation from being established in the first place. Most of the cross-gender teasing in the Oak Town literature-response groups was, as it turned out, greeted with *silence* from the party being teased. Here is one example:

> Julie   (to Alisa): 'See, I got two heart stickers in my journal.'
> Alisa   (to Julie): 'I got three fish stickers in mine!'
> Michael   (Looking at the ceiling in exasperation, then back at the girls): 'Come on, silly girls, this isn't the time for you to be doing your sticker book collections.'
> Silence. The girls look down at the table top. Julie turns her book over in her lap. There is a three-second pause.
> Michael   (to the group at large): 'I liked the book. It was more adventurous than the other books we read.'

Cross-gender teasing in literature-response groups, like cross-gender teasing in the course of other classroom interactions, worked to maintain gender boundaries by enacting, and even *producing*, a relation of antagonism between the two gender groups. At the same time, however, teasing, as an activity, also provided a *socially acceptable* way of interacting across such gender lines. A *contradiction*, on the other hand, was something quite different. A contradiction was any statement that disagreed with, and that went against the meaning of, the previous speaker's statement. And again we find that, as with teasing, much more contradicting went on in *mixed-gender* literature response groups than went on in *same-gender* groups, with almost all the instances of contradicting occurring in *cross-gender* interactions. Like teasing, contradicting most often placed the genders in opposition to each other, creating antagonism between the two gender groups.

Contradicting may also be seen as a conversational technique for establishing and 'contesting' the kinds of power relations that are constituted in talk (Fairclough, 1992). The control of a conversation through certain conversational practices such as contradicting amounts to 'a powerful covert mechanism of domination' (p. 9) — an activity which may work first to give one person control of the present situation and then to help shape a particular kind of relationship in which that person remains the dominant individual. In the example that follows, Alisa worked to place Michael in the position of being incorrect, and therefore 'one down'. (They are discussing the beginning of the novel *Frozen Fire* in which an Inuit boy and a white boy become friends, and confront their cultural differences, while attempting a rescue in the frozen Arctic.)

Michael: 'Well, Kayak was the first boy Matthew saw there in the North. Like he and his dad went to the airport to meet them.'

Aaron: 'Yeah, he was the only boy Matthew knew in his class, the only boy he ever talked to in the book.'

Alisa: 'No, they met each other on the plane.'

Michael: 'In the airport.'

Alisa: 'Yeah, I know, but like they weren't supposed to meet. They just met.'

Michael: 'I know. That's what I mean . . .'

Marla (contradicting): 'You said that they were there to meet them.'

Michael (laughing): 'Whatever.'

The distribution pattern for contradictions in these groups was very similar to the distribution pattern for teasing. There were no contradictions made in the all-boy groups, and those few contradictions that *were* made in the *all-girl* groups served other, quite different purposes (Marcia contradicted Julie repeatedly in order to sustain an interaction with her, while Alisa defended Samantha and Mr Boyle by contradicting when slighting remarks were being made about them). The contradictions made in mixed-gender groups occurred even when *only one boy* was present. (On an occasion when only one *girl* was present, that particular girl remained silent throughout the discussion, and no contradictions occurred.) Christopher was responsible for seven of the nine contradictions that took place during one discussion of *Bridge to Terabithia*, while Michael, on his part, repeatedly contradicted Alisa and Julie during a discussion of *Frozen Fire*. Alisa was the girl who was contradicted most often, and she was also the girl who *spoke* most often. In these instances, I suspect, the contradictions in question may have amounted to another way of enacting a relation of dominance — another way, indeed, of using fiction to 'do gender'.

This excerpt from one of the literature-response-group transcripts, in which the children are, at first, discussing Tolkien's *The Lord of the Rings*, may give the reader a better sense of the uses of contradiction, as well as a feeling for *another* feature of these group conversations, namely the fact that the boys did *more* talking than the girls.

Alisa:	'It never gets good.'
Girls:	'No. No.'
Christopher:	'The only time I found it at all good when I read it was when they were in those mines of Morely [Moria]. Everything else was just so boring.'
Alisa:	'I liked *The Hobbit* when they killed the dragon.'
Karen:	'*The Hobbit* was much better.'
Christopher:	'*The Hobbit* is a kids' book. This isn't.'
Karen:	'He's [Mr. Boyle] gonna read this to us again next year, I think.'
Alisa:	'*The Hobbit* was a good book. It was easier to understand . . . I liked the Byorn guy.'
Karen:	'And then we saw the movie so we understood it.'
Christopher:	'*The Hobbit* didn't have so much history behind it.'
Girls:	'Yeah.'
Jerrica:	'It was so much easier to follow the adventure or whatever. Are we getting near the end?'
Christopher:	'Of this first book, okay? But this book just leaves you hanging. There's that big Byorn guy? And he [Boromir] dies between the first book and the second. In the first book he starts to die. The Orks start shooting at him. And then the second book, like he actually dies. So it just leaves you hanging if you don't read the other ones.'
Me:	'Have you read all three of them?'
Christopher:	'I've read the first two on my own. It gets so boring. They have 10 pages on this guy just walking around fighting with other armies.'

Jerrica: 'They have too much fighting in that book.'

Christopher: 'Not enough! Not a fraction of enough!'

Alisa: 'I know what your kind of action is, Christopher. It's arms falling off people every minute.'

Christopher: 'No. The actual *action* they don't talk about. Like in the book I'm reading now there's action *constantly*. It's a really good book.'

Alisa: 'They [the Tolkien books] talk more about family history.'

Christopher: 'Like Aaron said he read the third Tolkien book. And the main dude is beat up by a little hobbit. Before the book, five of the best wizards couldn't even beat him, and in the third book he's whipped by this little wimp. It was Sam or Frodo. Frodo gets all beat up in the third book and Sam carries him around.'

Jerrica: 'It was probably Sam, because he was such a little wimp in all the other books.'

Me: 'What other books are you kids reading now?'

Christopher: 'I'm reading one called *The Legend of Huma* and it's based on these chronicles.'

Alisa: 'Is it the one with the two dragons?'

Christopher: 'It's about this guy, he's a knight, and he goes out adventuring. His group gets split up. He finds a minotaur and he saves him and they become friends. And they are attacked by a bunch of red dragons. And a silver dragon comes down and helps him. And later on there's this really good-looking girl who cures him [the girls giggle here] and it ends up that the girl is the dragon, but she won't tell him, right? She keeps switching behind his back, because he keeps thinking the dragon is male. And it happens that she falls in love with him and at the end of the book she has to choose being either human or a dragon? I don't know which she does.

'And there's these dragon lances that they got and they go out. They forged 20 of these things, and they have to go out against 500 dragons with 20 lances. All of a sudden they find out this one guy had forged three or four hundred of them. So they go out in this big battle and they win, and then they go to this one place and they take on a wizard and he summons this big demon, a big five-headed dragon, he summons her, and right now I'm at the part

Table 4.1   Girls' Mean Length of Turn

	Girls' groups	Mixed-gender groups
Karen	14.7	12.2
Alisa	9.5	9.0
Jerrica	11.7	10.4
Julie	11.2	9.8
Cara	11.6	4.5
Samantha	5.4	4.3
Marcia	10.7	8.7

Note: All the girls averaged shorter turns in the mixed-gender groups.

	where he has to fight with the dragon. It's a good book. It's got lots of action.'
Jerrica:	'What's the name of it?'
Christopher:	'The second one is *Terricus and the 500 Dragons*[2].'
Alisa:	'Is that the one I got you for Christmas when I was your 'secret admirer' or whatever?'
Christopher:	'No.'

It was this section of transcript, in which Christopher was the only boy present, and seemed to do more talking than the other members of the group, which first led me to wonder whether the Oak Town boys might also be asserting themselves by talking more than the girls did during the literature-response groups. In order to discover how much each of the children actually spoke in the 14 literature-response groups conducted, I calculated a 'mean length of turn' for each participant by first totalling the number of words a person spoke in each day's discussion and then dividing by the number of turns that person took that day. I began with the girls, calculating a mean length of turn for each and every one of the girls involved in both the all-girl groups and the mixed-gender groups. As shown in Table 1, every girl averaged *shorter* turns in the mixed-gender groups than she did in the all-girl groups.

I also figured a mean length of turn for each and every one of the boys who participated in both the all-boy and the mixed-gender groups. With the exception of Carl, a boy who participated in only two of the groups, and who took fewer turns to speak than any other child in the study, every boy averaged *longer* turns in mixed-gender groups than he did in the all-boy groups (see Table 2). What's more, *all* the boys in the mixed-gender groups attained averages that were *higher* than the *highest* average that was attained by a girl (in this case, Karen) in these same mixed-gender groups. Conversely, all the girls had averages lower than the *lowest boy's average* — if Carl is

Table 4.2 Boys' Mean Length of Turn

	Boys' groups	Mixed-gender groups
Michael	14.1	15.6
Aaron	10.5	13.0
Christopher	13.9	23.1
Carl	7.3	5.5

not considered (I should point out that Samantha and Cara had lower mixed-group averages even than Carl).

When I calculated the mean length of turn for the section of transcript quoted above, I found that Christopher averaged 40.5 words, Jerrica averaged 11.5 words, Alisa 10.9 words, and Karen 8.6 words. This pattern held for the entire transcript from which this excerpt was taken.

Let me say this in another way. All the girls took their greatest number of turns in the *all-girl* groups. Furthermore, in every mixed-gender group, the person with the highest mean length of turn was a boy, even in the group where only one boy was present. And finally, in every mixed-gender group, the person with the shortest mean length of turn was a girl. I thus concluded that when the Oak Town boys and girls discussed literature together, the boys 'did gender' by taking *longer* turns, and the girls, on the other hand, 'did gender' by taking *fewer* turns and *shorter* turns.

The Discourse of Feeling and the Discourse of Action

The transcripts of the literature-response groups conducted for this study showed the Oak Town children 'doing gender' in other ways too. The girls produced what might be called a 'discourse of feeling' in their talk about literature. This discourse involved a focus on *emotion* in literary texts. It dealt with human relationships, it valued loving kindness, and it attached a positive value to 'caring'. Furthermore, it looked at the plot in question in terms of the light that the plot's details could throw on character development. This excerpt from the transcript of an all-girl group that was discussing *Summer of the Swans* by Betsy Byars provides one example of this 'discourse of feeling'. The story recounts a few days in the life of a 13-year-old girl whose troubles in growing up include caring for her younger retarded brother.

> Cara: 'It was kinda sad. I feel sorry for Charlie. And it was exciting too. Like when he was lost. I thought he wasn't going to be found. But . . .'

Jerrica: 'It's sad, because when he leaves, he kept on running because he didn't understand things that well, and people teased him and called him 'retard' and stuff like that.'

Karen: 'Yeah, I kinda liked Charlie . . . I wonder why . . . why can't a person talk?'

Jerrica: 'Well, either he can't talk or he doesn't *want* to talk.'

Karen: 'Yeah, cuz he was okay until he was 3 or something. Then all of a sudden he stopped talking.'

Jerrica: 'He didn't want to talk after that. Something happened to his brain.'

Karen: 'Oh yeah.'

Jerrica: 'He had an illness or something and then it said something happened to his brain and he couldn't talk any more.'

Cara: 'That's real sad. It sounds like he wasn't born retarded. It sounds like he got a fever and it made him retarded, you know? That seems extra sad to me.'

Karen: 'His sister, she really . . . like at the beginning she always wanted him to leave her alone so that she could play with her friends, but she really cared about him at the end? And she kept on walking and walking and walking . . .'

Jerrica: 'And she made friends with that Joe guy. She was always saying he was such an idiot.'

Cara: 'Yeah. He didn't seem like such an idiot to me.'

Karen: 'For being enemies for a while, he sure cared about Charlie a lot to go out and look for him. Cuz not very many people, they'd say, "Wait till I finish this baseball game and then I'll come look," or something like that, but he just leaves his baseball game and comes and looks.'

Jerrica: 'Yeah. That was nice. A lot of guys might not care at all.'

The same set of transcripts, in contrast to this 'discourse of feeling', also showed that the Oak Town boys tended to participate in what might be called a 'discourse of action', a discourse concerned with logic and legality, a discourse that valued reason and credibility, and that sought meaning in the plot and in the action. This discourse of action reflected an inclination to define characters by what they *did* rather than by what they *felt*. The following excerpt from a transcript of two boys discussing *Shane* provides one example of this discourse of action. (*Shane* is the story of a gunfighter who enters into an intense friendship with a farm family in Wyoming at the time of the range wars of the 1880s, and sides with them against the cattle ranchers who are trying to drive them off their land. *Tuck Everlasting* is the story of 10-year-old Winnie Foster and the Tuck family —

four people who have become immortal by drinking water from a certain magic stream.)

Aaron: 'This book was a lot more interesting than *Tuck Everlasting.*'

Michael: 'It had more action. The other book, like in some places you couldn't understand it, some stuff, but in this book I could understand everything. In *Tuck Everlasting* we were wondering how she got there, how it went into the future all of a sudden at the end there.'

Aaron: 'This one didn't do that. It was sort of like a realistic story. Like *Tuck Everlasting*, it was sort of on the verge of not being, like it couldn't really happen. But it was pretty close, like they sort of *lived* like some people. So it was realistic in the way they lived, but not quite realistic. Not the way *Shane* is.'

Michael: 'Yeah. Like this could really happen. And the time thing. Like *Shane* takes a summer. He comes in the beginning of a summer. Yeah, he comes in '89, I think.'

Aaron: 'So this story happened a 100 years ago. In 1889.'

Michael: 'Yeah. He was just riding by on his horse, and he went there for something.'

Aaron: 'For a drink.'

Michael: 'For a drink or something. And he was looking for work, and Joe who was living there, he was looking for a hand, because it was a rough time with the people who were taking the farms away?'

Aaron: 'Because he had another helper, I think his name was Morely. He got beat up by Fletcher's men, so he left.'

Michael: 'Then Shane worked there and they had supper, and then they just told about how he was working, like with that stump?'

Aaron: 'Yeah. But . . .'

Michael: 'Like with the axes.'

Aaron: 'I found that strange. That part of it.'

Michael: 'Well, for two pages or more they were doing that.'

Aaron: 'Mmm . . . Maybe they did that to show their strength, how much strength they have.'

Michael: 'Something like that. Or maybe just to show Shane's strength. Because Joe wanted that stump out a long time ago. He was trying to get that out for a long time. Then Shane came.'

Aaron: 'He couldn't do it alone.'

Michael: 'Maybe they put that in to show how well they could work together.'

It may be that these different modes of talking about literature reflected the different forms of moral understanding in girls and in boys of the kind that Carol Gilligan has described (1982). Gilligan analyzed the responses on the part of an 11-year-old boy and an 11-year-old girl (both in sixth grade) to a moral dilemna devised by Lawrence Kohlberg. In this dilemna, a man named Heinz was considering whether or not to steal a drug, a drug which he could not afford to buy, in order to save the life of his wife. The druggist had refused to lower his price.

Gilligan's boy (Jake) was clear from the outset that Heinz should steal the drug. He told the interviewer that the situation was like a math problem but with humans instead. He used *logic* to analyze the situation. On the other hand, Gilligan's girl (Amy) saw in the dilemma not a math problem involving humans but a narrative of relationships that extended over time. She saw a world that cohered through *human connections*, rather than through a system of rules. She felt that the druggist *had* to lower his price. The druggist, she felt, had to relate to the wife. Gilligan summarizes: 'Jake sees a conflict between life and property that can only be resolved by logical deduction, Amy a fracture of human relationship that must be mended with its own thread (p. 31).' Jake and Amy seemed to be operating according to the gender–appropriate cultural values that also guided the children of Oak Town. Perhaps, like the girls of Oak Town, Amy had been taught how to work at maintaining human relationships. Perhaps she knew she had the culture's permission to feel.

I want to use the term 'discourse of feeling' here as a descriptive term for a way of talking about literature, a way of signifying, through language, a concern with the *feelings* both of the reader of the text and of the characters portrayed in the text in question. The example from the transcript of the girls' discussion of *Summer of the Swans* illustrates some of the character-istics of this style: much of the time, the readers used it in order to speak of their own emotional responses to a text. Such responses began with state-ments of feeling: 'I liked . . .', 'I wanted . . .', 'I knew . . .', 'I wish . . .', 'I didn't appreciate . . .', 'I hated . . .', 'I felt sorry for . . .'. The conversation did not always name *specific* feelings, but tended instead sometimes to center on more general emotional and physical states: disgust, depression, fear, shyness, embarrassment, loneliness, and wonder. Some of this can be seen especially in Karen's responses to the novel *Julie of the Wolves*, the story of the 13-year-old Inuit girl Miyax who spends an Arctic winter living with a wolf pack, and learning to live with the cultural conflict between traditional and 'white' lifestyles:

> Karen: 'I admire Miyax. I mean she's very independent. She really had nerve to run away from home.'

Jerrica: 'Yeah, she was brave. I wouldn't be afraid of a wolf pup, but I'd be afraid of a wolf!'

Karen: 'But I felt just awful when they shot Amaroq [the wolf] from the plane. And later it was weird when she found her dad. I was depressed, like she was too, when she found out he killed people from a plane. I mean wolves.'

Cara: 'Well, I didn't get it though. Like, why was the bird dying, of old age or something?'

Karen: 'Tornait, do you mean?'

Cara: 'Yeah.'

Karen: 'Maybe it was cold. He dies, and she buries him in the snow. I think that's when she knows she isn't going to San Francisco. She says the pink room that Amy was going to give her was filled with Amaroq's blood. She felt awful. She didn't want to go there any more.'

Jerrica: 'She's an Eskimo at the end.'

Karen: 'The wolves. That was her real home. In the whole book, I felt like her real home was with the wolves.'

Here, Karen distinguished between her *own* feelings, on the one hand, and those of the main character on the other. At other times, the 'discourse of feeling' was used to compare the reader's feelings with the feelings of a particular character, as in the example above when Jerrica compared her own fear of wolves with Julie's courage. Alisa and Jerrica and Karen were all sure that they hated Sunday School just as much as Jess hated church in *Bridge to Terabithia*. Karen said she couldn't love her brothers the way Sara loved Charlie in *Summer of the Swans* because her brothers wouldn't accept her love. And Alisa, in responding to descriptions of the family's first Christmas after the father's death in *Mama's Going to Buy You a Mockingbird*, expressed her empathy and understanding: 'And when he gave Hoot, the little stone owl, to his Mom, he must have wanted to keep it. But his Mom was really sad, so he did that. I would have done that too.'

The children also used the 'discourse of feeling' to name the particular emotional states of the characters ('That bothered her,' 'He was worried,' 'She cared.'), or alternatively to analyze certain characters and describe what they might have been feeling. *Bridge to Terabithia*, Katherine Patterson's novel of the friendship of a 10-year-old boy and girl which ends with the accidental death of the girl, inspired this kind of talk. 'That really surprised me at the end when Mrs Meyers, the home-room teacher, took Jess outside and then she started crying,' said Karen. 'It didn't really seem like *she* would cry, you know? But she must have been sad that Leslie died, even though she was mean before.'

As in the examples above, the discourse of feeling used the particular details of the plot to throw light on certain characters and their motivations. In *Bridge to Terabithia*, Mrs Meyers' taking Jess outside and crying was something of interest because it served to reveal her emotional state. In *Mama's Going to Buy You a Mockingbird*, which told the story of a family coping with the father's cancer and subsequent death, Jeremy's Christmas gift to his mother of a treasured keepsake given to him by his father was of interest because it made it clear that Jeremy could sympathize with someone else and feel her pain. In a related way, Alisa pointed out that one result of Sarah's overhearing remarks about her father's 50–50 chance to live was that Jeremy felt compassion for her, while Julie remarked that the fight that Tess and Jeremy had had with the bullies had led to Tess and Jeremy liking each other. In another discussion, Karen reflected that the invention of Terabithia occurred because of Leslie and Jess's yearning for activity and friendship: 'So they *had* to go out and make up an imaginary land. Like at first I thought like it doesn't sound like something Grade Five kids would do, but they'd *have* to make up something and pretend something around there, because they were alone, and you can't just walk five miles to ask somebody if they want to play.' The question the girls asked themselves therefore seemed to be: how does the plot help us to understand what the characters are *feeling*?

The 'discourse of feeling' often dealt with human relationships, which were always of great interest to the girls involved. When we discussed *Tuck Everlasting*, Cara was surprised and interested when I pointed out that the grandmother of the man with the yellow suit was the friend of Miles's wife, and the girls speculated frequently and at length about Winnie Foster's children. Alisa said that she liked the opening of *Mama's Going to Buy You a Mockingbird* because it showed the nature of a relationship between a brother and a sister, and 'I can relate to that.' (On the other hand, Alisa told me that she did *not* like the opening of *Tuck Everlasting*, because there was no feeling and no relationships evident in the Prologue.) In another group, Cara pointed out the two contrasting dimensions of Sara's relationship with her brother Charlie in *Summer of the Swans*: Sara felt resentful about having to take care of him, but on the other hand she also loved him. And the girls also discussed at length the missing father's relationship to his children in *Summer of the Swans*:

> Cara: 'Especially when they called him, the father he just said, "Well I'll call you back later." . . . Like, even though Aunt Willie said it wouldn't be any sense for him to come right out then but wait till night time to see if they found him, I still think he could comfort them. He should be rushing out there in a way, he should call them himself and find out all the details.'

Jerrica: 'It depended on where he lived, because if I was gonna come and I lived three hours away or something, I doubt I'd come. That would be a long way.'

Cara: 'So? It's your *son!*'

Jerrica: 'Well, if he didn't even live with them, then why should he . . . If he doesn't even care about them then, why should he come, see?'

Karen: 'But still, I would come, even if I lived eight hours away! I would come, just in case they couldn't find him, I would be there. And if they *did* find him, like he could still be happy with all of them, cuz that's his son, you know.'

Cara: 'I think he should have come. It's his son, even if he doesn't see him very often.'

Karen: 'I think it kinda made Sara sad. I think Sara had already catched on that he wasn't very nice, and he wasn't really a father to them, like she's sorta smart mouthing Aunt Willie, saying "Why should he come? He doesn't even care about us at all." But Aunt Willie kept on saying, "Well, he'll come, he'll come," and in the end he doesn't come. It's sad.'

It seemed to me that the girls were speculating here both about the father's feelings and about the nature of his relationship with his children, and that this was one more instance of the girls' choosing to make *human relation- ships* the focus of their discussion.

There were a few instances of the discourse of feeling which did not, however, fall into the categories that I have been describing. Marcia, for example, used the discourse of feeling to express *anti-social* sentiments, and to distance herself from the group by intentionally expressing feelings that the others did not feel themselves or attribute to the text. She said that she didn't care that Winnie died at the end of *Tuck Everlasting*; she said she found it 'funny when Leslie and Jess were making fun of that fat teacher' in *Bridge to Terabithia*; and she teased Julie by talking with relish about the horrible aspects of death.

There were also two instances of the discourse of feeling that had to do with the *stylistic devices* of a piece, rather than with characters portrayed. Jerrica pointed out that the song 'Papa's Going to Buy You a Mockingbird' contributed to the sad mood of the story. And Karen, on her part, suggested that the two different points of view in *Summer of the Swans* helped us to know *both* characters' feelings. But for the most part, those who used the discourse of feeling were valuing loving kindness, and attaching a positive value to those characters 'who cared'. They were looking for meaning in the *feelings* a story portrayed or engendered, and were seeing the events of the plot, on the other hand, as mere clues to an understanding of the different characters and their motivation.

In contrast, the Oak Town boys tended to use a 'discourse of action' in literature response groups. 'The discourse of action' is a cover term for a different style of talking about literature, a style that reflected a concern more with the plot, or with what *happened* in the story. It thus reflected a desire to find meaning in the *action* occuring in a story rather than in any of the story's human relationships or literary stylistic devices. The 'discourse of action' had six characteristics:

1 It appealed to a reader's sense of *logic* by seeking to clarify the logical progression of the plot, and it worked both to put events in chronological order, and to make the cause-and-effect relationships very clear. Because it was concerned both with clarifying events in times past, and with matters such as the characters' relative ages, this kind of discourse was characterized by words like 'because', 'when . . . then', and 'either . . . or', 'what if . . .' or 'why did . . .?'. People using the discourse of action reasoned logically about how it had happened that the man in the yellow suit came to know the Tucks' secret, and about what exactly the boys in *Frozen Fire* might have seen when they found gold frozen in water. They used clues from the text to determine how long Jeremy's father was ill in *Mama's Going to Buy You a Mockingbird*, and how old Winnie Foster was when she died:

   Christopher: 'So the tombstone says 1870–1948.'
   Aaron: 'So how old would she be if she was born in 1870 and she died in 1948?'
   Christopher: '78. She was 10 when the story happened, so 68 years. 68 years have gone by, and like Aaron said, the gas stations and the trucks and things tell you that it's modern times. Like when would this story have taken place?'
   Michael: 'About the 1880s. If Winnie was born in 1870 and she was 10 when the story took place, then it was about 1880.'

   Using the logic of time to understand the story, the boys were thus working with one aspect of the 'discourse of action'.

2 It was also a language of *legality*. It included talk about how the Tucks could have continued to get jobs in the twentieth century without birth certificates and social-insurance numbers. And it spoke of what the law would say about who drew a gun first at the climax of *Shane*.

Aaron: 'Shane, it took him two shots to get Stark Wilson. Cuz he
            hit him in the arm once, I think.'

Michael: 'Yeah.'

Aaron: 'And then second in the chest.'

Michael: 'And Wilson had two guns, right?'

Aaron: 'Yeah. And I think he drew one, and he missed.'

Michael: 'And he missed, and Shane got him in the arm. And he
            pulled a second shot with the other gun and that's when
            Shane killed him. And Fletcher had shot first at Shane.
            Fletcher shot from the balcony behind him. He was gonna
            shoot him in the back, but he missed.'

Aaron: 'That's how he was up there, and Shane just spun around
            and got him.'

Michael: 'So that's sort of a good part too, that Shane didn't go for
            the fight first, like it shows that he's a decenter man. And to
            shoot him in the back, that's a coward. Especially when
            there's one there and one there, he's gotta pretty well shoot
            that guy first.'

Aaron: 'Shane said he wanted to talk with Fletcher, and Stark
            wouldn't let him. And so Stark actually picked the fight cuz
            he wouldn't let Shane speak to Fletcher. It was in self-
            defense that Shane killed both of them. Sure it was.'

Working through the *legal* aspects of the situation, the boys then
engaged in another aspect of the 'discourse of action'.

3 It defined characters in terms of what they *did*, not by what they
felt. In the excerpt quoted above, Michael drew conclusions about
the characters from their *actions*. That fact that Shane didn't draw
his gun showed his decency, while Fletcher's attempt to shoot him
in the back marked Fletcher as a coward. In an earlier excerpt, we
heard Aaron and Michael speculate that Joe and Shane had pushed
over the big stump to show that they were friends and that they
worked well together. And Michael analyzed the character of the
wild man in *Frozen Fire* again by primarily examining his
actions: 'I sort of wondered about the wild man, too, like if he was
really crazy, like cuz I felt if he was crazy he wouldn't have let them
in. I'm surprised he did. Because he gave them the bow and
everything, even though he knew it would break. That shows he's
crazy. Like giving them a plastic bow.' Similarly, in the boys'
Tuck Everlasting group, Michael did not say, 'Winnie felt
lonely,' or 'Winnie missed the Tucks.' Instead, he said, 'She was
abandoned by them.' The discourse of action spoke of the external

circumstances that motivated characters to act, not of their *internal motivations*. Here is one example:

Aaron: 'See, this Chris was standing at the bar, then he dumped his beer onto Shane. And then later Shane walked in and he spilled something onto him (Chris). That's why they got into another fight.'

In describing the motivation for the bar fight in *Shane*, Aaron did not consider either their *personal reasons* for fighting or the larger interests they represented. He discerned their motivation only through their *actions*.

4 Because it looked for clues to character in actions and in external circumstances, the 'discourse of action' tended to foster simple categorizations and to speak of character *types*: Michael thought Shane, at the beginning of the story, was like a priest, 'because he was so clean when he came'. Furthermore, in speaking of the fact that Shane sat at the supper table with his back to the wall, looking out over the entrance to the farm, Michael said that he seemed like an outlaw. And finally, Aaron said that Shane, because he was kind to Bob and showed him how to do things, was like a second father to the boy.

5 It valued *realism* and credibility, and spoke positively of stories that 'could really happen'. For example, Aaron preferred *Shane* to *Tuck Everlasting*, and perceived *Shane* as having more action (something he valued), because *Shane* was more realistic in its treatment of time. His enjoyment of the story was marred, on the hand, when Shane took on five men at once in a bar fight, because he found this 'unrealistic'. Michael, in another example, was disturbed by the fact that the 'Eskimo' people in *Frozen Fire* spoke so much English:

Michael: 'I don't know. It sorta seems weird like when all the Eskimos . . . I hate when they do that they can talk English. Like, not very many of them do. Like especially that wild man? He talked to them in some English and in some Eskimo. You'd kinda think they wouldn't be able to know English.'

He didn't find their English speaking 'believable', and this was a mark against the book because it was 'true' stories that he valued.

The concern, already mentioned, with logic was itself related to these positive feelings toward realism. Those who spoke the 'discourse of action' were seeking a clear explanation of *what* exactly happened and *why* things happened the way they did. They had little patience with ambiguity, and saw it as a weakness in the text (the boys' group for *Tuck Everlasting*, speaking and thinking predominantly in line with the 'discourse of action', and dealing with a story which left them with many unanswered questions, did not like the novel for this reason).

The concern with logic was also related to concerns about possible *contradictions* occurring in the text. The speakers were testing the logic of the text — trying to uncover or explain away seeming contradictions — as their way of testing the worth of the story. In the following discussion, the boys try to apply logic to *Tuck Everlasting*, and in particular to the matter of living forever:

Aaron: 'It wasn't realistic. Like, they didn't have jobs.'

Michael: 'Well, Miles was a carpenter, but that's about it. I don't think he'd earn that much.'

Aaron: 'Tuck, the father, he kept carving and carving.'

Michael: 'Yeah, when Winnie first went to the Tucks it was all the wood shavings on the floor and she said there was sawdust all over the curtains and everything . . . so they might have made a little money off of . . . those Tucks . . . it talks about how they lived forever, but that would be kind of torture, because if they didn't make much money they'd be starving to death, but they wouldn't be able to die . . . so it wouldn't really matter . . . so they could just not eat.'

Aaron: 'Well . . . they'd have to have a birth certificate to get a job.'

When the contradictions arising could not be logically explained, the story seemed weaker as a result. 'Realistic' and 'believable' were the characteristics of good stories.

6 'Action' (i.e. the sequence of events involved in the plot) that was *interesting* and *exciting* was highly valued, and was a source of satisfaction in story-reading, for those who used the 'discourse of action' most frequently. A person's character, as already mentioned, was interpreted and understood through his or her *actions*, as well as through the *events* of the plot. Christopher's description of *The Legend of Huma* is an example of this aspect of the 'discourse of action'. So are the excerpts that I have quoted from Michael and Aaron's discussions of *Shane*. So, also, is this excerpt, in which the boys try to get at the meaning of *Frozen Fire*:

Michael: 'It's good Kayak went out searching with Matthew, or else . . .'

Aaron: 'He wouldn't have been saved at all.'

Michael: 'Yeah. Cuz Kayak got most of the food for them and everything.'

Aaron: 'It was good that Matthew took that mirror off the skidoo, though. Cuz that's what really saved them.'

Michael: 'They sort of both saved each other, cuz when he put the seal blood around the hole, and then Matthew flashed the mirror and then he saw the red blood. And that's what got him (the pilot) to land. It tried to show us how they work together.'

Aaron: 'It wants to show us how an Inuit and a White — or, as he calls him, a Kaluna — can communicate.'

Here the boys use the satisfying 'action' at the end of the novel to illuminate a particular theme.

I will conclude this consideration of the two different styles of discourse found in the transcriptions of the literature-response groups conducted for this study by making this point: both the boys and the girls used the discourse of feeling *and* the discourse of action. But the girls were *more* inclined to use the discourse of feeling, while the boys were *more* inclined to use the discourse of action. A study of the 14 transcripts made showed that *the discourse of feeling* occurred much more frequently in 10 of the groups. All of the seven girls-only groups used the discourse of feeling predominantly. Three of the five *mixed-gender* groups used the discourse of feeling predominantly. And finally, the *discourse of action*, on the other hand, predominated both in the two all-boy groups, and in *two* of the five *mixed-gender* groups.

When a girls' group and a boys' group discussed one and the same novel, a contrast could be seen. In the girls' discussion of *Tuck Everlasting*, there were 15 instances of the discourse of feeling and only 1 instance of the discourse of action. In the boys' discussion of *Tuck Everlasting*, there were 26 instances of the discourse of action (many of them, moreover, having to do with the *logic* of the text) and only 2 instances of the discourse of feeling.

The children of Oak Town did not participate either in literature-response or in literature-study groups on a regular basis, and these practices were not modeled for them by their teachers in their reading classes. Because the children did not associate talk about literature with familar school procedures, they brought to the group the kinds of values and ways of being in the world that had always — whether *in* school or *out* of school — typically constrained and shaped their ways of talking. These they had acquired as part of their gender identities. The girls in these sixth-grade classrooms, who 'did gender' by working hard both at understanding other people and at maintaining human relationships, were thus more inclined to read literature in terms of characters and relationships, and to use a discourse of *feeling* when talking about it. The *boys* in these classrooms, who 'did gender' by being active and by fighting for a place in the social hierarchy, were thus more inclined to read literature in terms of both the plot and event, and to use a discourse of *action* when talking about it. Children 'did gender' in their reading of fiction just as they did gender in all the other social practices that made up their lives.

Boys' Books, Girls' Books

Children and Choice

For the people of Oak Town, fiction for middle childhood fell into two categories: 'girls' books' and 'boys' books'. Elizabeth Segel, in writing (1986) about gender and childhood reading, summarized the implications of the fact that, for the most part, contemporary culture has divided books for children according to gender:

> One of the most obvious ways gender influences our experience as readers is when it determines what books are made available to us or are designated as appropriate or inappropriate for our reading. Nowhere is this fact so apparent or its implications so disturbing as in childhood reading . . . Adults decide what books are written, published, offered for sale, and, for the most part, purchased for children . . . The publisher commissioning paperback romances for girls and marketing science fiction for boys, as well as Aunt Lou selecting a fairy tale collection for Susie and a dinosaur book for Sam, are part of a powerful system that operates to channel books to or away from children according to their gender. Furthermore, because the individual's attitudes concerning appropriate gender-role behaviors are formed during the early years, the reader's choice of reading material may be governed by these early experiences long after she or he has theoretically gained direct access to books of all kinds. (p.165)

Book publishers, who have attuned themselves to the gender division in children's books, will market their books for specific audiences that are defined by *age* and *gender*. The sixth-grade girls of Oak Town, when they shopped at the Eastside Mall, came across at least 15 different series books (like *Satin Slippers*) for girls their age, arranged attractively on the bookstore shelves. There were fewer such series books for boys. The market for boys' books was smaller, and this appeared to be because boys *read less*. Each of the three bookstores found at the Eastside Mall near Oak Town did, however, contain a separate shelf or two for boys' books. On these shelves, one found the Walter Farley *Black Stallion* books, the *Hardy Boys* books, and the *Dragon Lance Chronicles*.

The children of Oak Town themselves had learned to think in terms of 'girls' books' and 'boys' books', and they could even explain the differences between them. Girls' books, according to the children, had both female characters and male characters, whereas boys' books had mostly *male* characters. Girls' books were about people, whereas boys' books were about animals and adventures. The children explained that it was easy to tell a girl's book from a boy's book by both the cover and the title. Alisa and Cara took me around the school library one day in an effort to explain:

> Alisa (picking a book off the shelf): 'Look. I wouldn't read this one. It's a boy's book. *Scrub on Skates*. I can just tell from the title.'
>
> Cara: Here's one I read called *Wart, Son of Toad*. I thought it was a boy's book from the title. But I started reading it in silent reading one day, and it turned out to be a sort of a romance. It was still a boy's book, because it was about a boy, but I sort of liked it.'
>
> Cara: Usually, cowboy books are boys' books, and they're boring. *Cowboys Don't Cry* is okay, though, because it has more sad stuff in it, more feelings. It doesn't have just straightforward boyish talk in it. And it doesn't have disgusting stuff in it.'
>
> Alisa: Usually, it's pretty simple. Boys don't read *Sweet Valley Twins*. We don't read those dog books, like *Big Red*, that Jim and Carl always read. Samantha's brother likes them too. But we think they're boring. *Old Yeller*, books like that. *Hardy Boys* are for boys, and *Nancy Drew* is for girls.'

The girls and boys in sixth grade rarely took each other's books from the book table. For example, Jack got really excited when the new Clare McKay *Mini-Bike* books reached the classroom. Both Mr Peterson and I promoted these as books for boys *and* girls, but after three weeks only *boys* had signed them out.

At this point in their lives, the Oak Town children were, for the most part, already cooperating both with adults and with the publishing industry in supporting a system that divided books into two gender specific types. That system contributed a great deal to the reproduction of cultural beliefs about gender from one generation to the next. It was a system that also operated in school.

The School Literature Curriculum

> I was driving out on the highway toward Oak Town, listening to the car radio. The commentator was interviewing a fifth-grade teacher and her students who had been reading *The Doll* by Cora Taylor. This was a children's novel about the settlement of western Canada. It told the story of a little girl who was able to go back into the past.
>
> The children being interviewed were all boys. The commentator asked each one, 'Did the title bother you? Did this seem like a boy's book? Did you like it?' All the boys said they liked it. One boy said the title worried him a little at first, but the book turned out to be all right.
>
> The teacher explained, 'I know a book like this is an unusual choice to read with a whole class, but the subject matter of the book fit in so well with our Social Studies curriculum. So I chose to stress the adventure/settlement theme for the boys' sake. They liked that. It worked well.'

The teacher interviewed on the radio felt it necessary to defend her choice of a novel with both a female main character and a title that referred to a girl's toy. Indeed, the radio commentator had questioned the wisdom of that choice by interviewing the boys in the class specifically about their reactions to the book. The implication was that reading a girl's book might have caused a problem for the boys.

Matt Peterson said that when *he* chose books for class novel studies, he looked for two things: good, exciting stories, and characters that could act as role models for kids growing up. He wanted kids to experience characters that weren't perfect but grew and changed and improved themselves. However, although most of the children did think that Mr Peterson chose good stories for their novel-study classes, the girls in his class did think that he was tending to give preference to *boys'* books over girls' books. Five of them sat in the library one day and discussed the matter:

> Alisa: '*The Black Cauldron* was okay, but we girls would never read that by choice. Or *The Book of Three* either.'
>
> Julie: 'Yeah. There was only one girl in those books!'
>
> Marcia: 'And they're about wars. Girls' books, I like them cuz they don't have war in them. A lot of girls don't really wanna hear about war. Because they aren't included in it anyways. The *boys* mostly read the ones about wars and adventures.

> *The Lord of the Rings* is a boys' book too. They don't have girl characters very much in that one. They've maybe got three, and the rest are all boys and Orcs and stuff like that.'

Cara   (nodding agreement): 'We never read any girls' books in school.'

Alisa: 'Wait a minute. We read *The Secret Garden* in Grade Four. That was a girl *and* a boy. And we read *Mixed Up Files* this year. That was a girl *and* a boy.'

Jerrica: 'Yeah. And Mrs Frisbee was a lady rat.'

(They all giggle.)

Segel points out (1986) that many teacher education texts promote the notion that girls can, and will, read books about boys, but that boys cannot, will not and *should not* be asked to read books about girls. The basic idea, one which was generally accepted by the teachers at Oak Town School, is that no harm is done to girls when they read boys' books, but that some harm *is* done to boys who read girls' books. Joleen Gagnon, for instance, seemed to believe that boys might lose their interest in reading if they were asked to read girls' books, or that the boys' emerging gender identities might be damaged by reading girls' books.

In Oak Town, although little stigma was attached to girls' reading boys' books, those boys who read *girls'* books, on the other hand, had to do so surreptitiously. Amanda and several other girls, all of whom liked horses, said that they read the Walter Farley *Black Stallion* books. But not one boy would admit to ever having read a girls' book. An element of homophobia might have been at work here. Boys knew that homosexuality was severely punished by society, and that it was not permissible for them to do anything feminine at all (Thorne and Luria, 1986). Girls who were tomboys *could* be tolerated, for this was a society that valued *maleness*, but the boys, on the other hand, had, right from the start, to earn their male privileges by denying themselves anything associated with the feminine (Pogrebin, 1980).

Joleen Gagnon expressed her concern over the fact that the boys in her class didn't like to read and didn't take an interest in the class novel studies this year. She said that they didn't like *Mrs Frisbee and the Rats of NIMH* and they didn't like *The House of Sixty Fathers*. The girls didn't seem to like those books, either, but that wasn't a problem because the girls would cooperate and do the work even when they didn't like the book. Many of the boys wouldn't, however.

Joleen thought that she needed to find a book with more action in it. I suggested *Space Trap* by Monica Hughes, a science-fiction novel about a 12-year-old girl who is captured by pirates and taken to another galaxy where she must rescue her older brother and younger sister before they can attempt to find a way back to their parents. Joleen thought that this book might work: 'It sounds like it has lots of action. Even the boys might like that. Too bad the main character is a girl, though.'

Joleen also read *So Far From the Bamboo Grove* and thought that it would make a wonderful novel study, but she didn't think that she could do it with her class at the time of the study: 'The boys are so immature, and the book has a few things in it they would think are hilarious. The boys laugh at anything that has to do with female bodies. Like the rape, and binding the sister's breasts so the soldiers wouldn't know she was female.'

There was cultural misogyny at work here. Joleen could not choose a book about female people for class-study purposes because it contained references to female bodies, and female bodies, defined sexually by the culture, were considered unclean and inappropriate for children in school. The boys knew this and Joleen was right to predict giggles.

You Can Choose a Book By its Cover

The covers of children's books are worthy subjects in themselves for a semiotic analysis. Various cultural signs that signal certain beliefs about gender are prominently featured in the 'cover art' for children's books.

One such cultural sign found on covers for girls' books is that of the ballet dancer. A typical example (already described in the vignette that begins the introduction to this book) is to be found in the cover photo for the *Satin Slippers* books. Here we see idealized femininity: slim, graceful, pale, soft. The young woman in the *Satin Slippers* photo was not ready to actually dance or move. Her long hair would have gotten in her way if she had. She would have become entangled in the sheer drapes that were blowing around her if she had moved. But the effect matched the culture's definition of 'charming' and 'feminine'. And Sarah and Leah's mother were mesmerized by it. Why?

Perhaps because of its culturally defined perfection. The figure in the picture was perfectly arranged, perfectly clean, perfectly lovely. Her teeth were straight, and her hair had a few stray wisps over the ear, which was accented with a pearl earring. Her skin was white, her hair blonde, and her limbs rounded and well-nourished. This young woman was privileged by her race, her economic affluence, and her own beauty. As we can see from the desire spoken of and enacted in that opening vignette, Leah's mother, who weighed well over 200 pounds, would have liked to somehow secure this young woman's ideal experience of the world for her daughter instead. And Sarah, similarly, would have liked to secure it *for herself*.

The *Satin Slippers* books are not the only books to picture a ballet dancer on the cover. Julie chose to read *The Sisters Impossible* because of the two girls in ballet clothes on the cover. The ballet dancers in question signified some of femininity's most valued qualities: grace under pressure, controlled sexuality, and self-conscious, achieved beauty. Of course, there are other semiotic devices in evidence on the cover of other children's books. One signifier that appears frequently on books intended for boys is that of a *horse*. Often, the horse supports a rider, and on certain occasions the rider wears or holds a sword. The horse and its rider may be a visual metaphor for the power and beauty of nature controlled, wherein the rider symbolizes the physical nature of that control, and the sword he carries represents the potential for enforcing control with violence. *Taran Wanderer*, the other Lloyd Alexander books and many other books for boys have covers that use similar semiotic devices to construct images of power, strength, and the assertion of the will.

Another signifier used frequently on the covers of girls' books is the image of a *threatening man*. This image, when it occurs, is usually placed in the background, in the form of a suspicious and dangerous-looking male figure, with someone, or something, else appearing in the foregound. Amanda, for example, chose *The Egypt Game* from off the book table because 'It looks good. You can see that guy sneaking in the back there through that window.' Several of the *Nancy Drew Files* books show Nancy Drew in the foreground glancing nervously back at a menacing-looking man. (Cara and Julie pointed this out to me). Other mysteries also use this particular motif, which draws on an association between maleness and violence and is consistent with the female-as-victim messages found elsewhere in popular culture.

Book covers thus transmitted gender messages from the larger cultural context to young readers. So did the texts within the covers. The adults had created a world of 'girls' books' and 'boys' books' for the children in sixth grade at Oak Town, and the latter had learned to live in and accept that world. They, their parents and their teachers believed that girls' books, on the one hand, had *female* characters and most often dealt with interpersonal relations, and that boys' books, on the other hand, had *male* characters and dealt primarily with animals and with adventure. They also believed that the school-literature curriculum had to be designed with the interests and needs of *boys* in mind; that boys could be harmed by reading *girls'* books; that they *could* judge a book by its cover (a good cover meant a good book); and that the gender messages conveyed by a cover could go unchallenged.

Children's books, divided according to gender, conveyed powerful cultural beliefs about gender to children, and made a significant contribution to the reproduction of those beliefs in each generation. But those beliefs, as already pointed out, did not go entirely unchallenged in Oak Town when they were encountered in books. Children *were* individuals, after all, and, like all readers, they brought their own needs and interests, and their own backgrounds and experiences, to the texts they read. There was in the data for this study much to show that the girls resisted the notions of female passivity that the 'girls' books' and other books often contained, and that they reworked what they read so as to make it more palatable and less demeaning. (This resistance on their part will be analyzed in the next chapter.) But there was also, in the data, a remarkable instance concerning one boy's resistance to the cultural norms inherent in the children's gendered reading practices.

Anthony's Resistance

The Oak Town girls were quite capable of articulating their beliefs about gender and reading. Samantha said that girls got more emotionally involved with reading than boys did. Karen said that only girls liked to read. Julie said that boys weren't serious about reading. Marcia said that when boys read, they read about things that weren't very important. And Jerrica said that boys never read. The girls said these things in spite of a good deal of evidence to the contrary. Anthony, who read continuously in school and who remained lost in novels for hours on end under their very noses, was all but invisible to most of the girls. Samantha saw him and was puzzled. Cara saw him, and understood. But the others didn't seem to see him at all.

Mrs Gagnon saw Anthony reading in class when he should have been doing his schoolwork, and she was upset by it. She felt he was being 'lazy' by not completing his schoolwork first. She had several confrontations with Anthony over his reading and asked him repeatedly to stop 'sneaking' reading when he ought to be 'working'.

It is interesting that all of the seven focal girls for this study admitted to 'sneaking' reading in class when they should have been doing schoolwork. Of course, they did this only some of the time (while Anthony did it most of the time), but when they did, it was invisible to Mrs Gagnon and Mr Peterson. They never mentioned it.

The other boys, when they saw Anthony reading, interpreted his reading as an act of defiance. They joked about it, patted Anthony on the back as they laughed about it, and referred to the incidents where he 'got caught' with admiration in their voices. They seemed to believe that Anthony's 'sneaking' of reading was a way of bugging the teacher. I, however, see Anthony's reading, in part, as a form of resistance to the norms of the prevailing culture as reflected in the children's gender-associated reading practices.

Anthony read fiction in school for as much of the school day as he possibly could. He read Madeleine L'Engle, Katherine Paterson and Natalie

Babbitt. Anthony read in spite of the fact that the reading of fiction was believed to be a girl's activity. But Anthony's attitude was not defiance. When Mrs Gagnon scolded him for reading in class, his attitude was simply one of endurance: he waited calmly until he could return to his book.

Anthony did not read for the reasons that a girl would read. He did not read, in other words, to emulate his mother, to learn how to 'do gender', or to be part of a community of readers. He was, rather, a solitary reader at school, one who was not able to discuss what he had read with the other boys or girls, or with his teachers. But he continued to read, and in doing so, he resisted both the school's curriculum and the teachers' control of his time. He also resisted the idea that reading was a female activity and that fiction was a female province.

None of the Oak Town girls resisted the school curriculum in this way. None of the girls went as far in resisting teachers' control of their time. Anthony, on the other hand, was empowered to resist by his gender[3]. Because he was male, that is, he saw himself as able to assert his will. When Marcia asserted her will, it was seen as inappropriate for one of her gender, and she was severely punished by her peers for doing so. But when Anthony asserted his will, it was seen as gender appropriate, and his behavior was thus tolerated by his peers. This was the case in spite of the fact that his act of resistance involved the reading of fiction, which was regarded as a girl's activity.

Improper Literacy

Literacy, which is always enacted in literacy events, is never politically neutral. Lankshear and Lawler (1987) suggest that it is perfectly possible that a form of literacy taught in school could actually work *against* the interests of a social group. They call this phenomenon 'improper literacy'. I would like to connect this idea with what was going on in Oak Town, and in particular with the picture that emerged during my interviews with the *parents* of Oak Town. The mothers interviewed had, at one time, been bright little girls who read fiction, just as their daughters were now; and yet none of them had gone on to acquire a postsecondary education. I found myself surprised. The culture seemed to value reading and education, and to connect the two things and yet, despite this, the little girls who read were *not* growing up to be highly formally educated women — not, at least, in Oak Town. I began to wonder if the reading of fiction in Oak Town might have involved a form of 'improper literacy' that worked somehow to reproduce both gender inequality and, perhaps, differences in social class.

I eventually decided that the reading of fiction, as it was taught in this particular school, was not working to reproduce gender inequality in any simple or straightforward way, but rather that gendered cultural norms for reading fiction were working against the interests of girls and of boys in several indirect and complicated ways.

How did the reading of fiction work against the interests of the girls involved? Firtly, this activity, importantly, amounted to a form of literacy that marked gender boundaries, and separated the girls in yet one more way from boys of the same age. And secondly, because it provided both entertainment and an escape from loneliness and boredom, the reading of fiction helped the girls to tolerate both the oppressive nature of adult power and the oppressive nature of time in their daily lives. For these reasons, the way in which fiction was read at Oak Town discouraged any challenges to the status quo.

It also worked to serve *other people's* interests as against those of the girls. Lankshear and Lawler's (1987) concept of 'improper literacy' asks us to try to understand the nature and role of existing forms of literacy both within the established patterns of structural power and in the context of the pursuit of different human interests. Were there competing groups struggling to meet their respective interests through girls' reading practices? Certainly, publishers were making money through the sale of paperback books to girls. And certainly, parents (and teachers) benefited from the girls' reading of fiction because it helped to keep the girls quiet, safe, and occupied. But this analysis seems too simple, and it takes no account of the resistance that the girls practiced through their reading activities.

The design of the school's literature curriculum worked against the girls' interests by making it clear that female experience of the world was not valuable enough for inclusion. Female experience was, in fact, largely invisible in the curriculum. Girls confronted various male experiences in *The Book of Three* and *The Black Cauldron* in a context that suggested that those experiences amounted to *universal* human experiences. And at the same time, the reading pedagogy was demonstrating cultural imperatives that promoted ideas about expecting a hierarchy of power, looking to others for authority, and devaluing any knowledge based upon their own (i.e. female) experiences of the world.

The girls (and the boys) were not encouraged to read and write about literature in order to think deeply and critically about the world around them and about what might be done to improve it. Instead, they were being taught to read merely for information and for entertainment. They were being taught to write to meet certain requirements and to display what they knew. They were being taught a curriculum appropriate to an acquiescent lower-middle social class. Work and success were framed in terms of *getting the right answer* (Anyon, 1980).

The norms prevalent in the practice of fiction-reading at Oak Town worked against the interests of the *boys* as well as against those of the girls. The Oak Town boys had received a cultural message that the reading of fiction did not amount to a worthwhile use of their time, a message which affected their attitudes toward both reading and literature study in school. The data for the present study indicate that while boys enjoyed reading novels in school, many did not take novel studies seriously, and showed resistance when called upon to answer questions, or talk about the fiction they had read.

Smith (1986) has observed that children become fluent readers through the sustained practice of reading. It is this kind of constant practice in eliciting meaning from printed text that leads, in his view, to the ability to decode more easily. The Oak Town boys, who had been encouraged to read only for specific information, did not often enjoy such periods of sustained practice in reading. Samantha's mother expressed her concern about this:

> Daniel gets books out of the library about building things. It took him a month and a half to finish this one little novel that I got him from the library. He only read it in bits and pieces. And yet he'll take out hamster books and carpentry books. He's getting to be just like his father. Carpenter books for children. Yet I cannot get that kid to read a story. And I'd like to . . . although I suppose it's good for him to be interested in the other too. But the thing is, he never reads a book from cover to cover. He just picks out little segments.

Research on reading has created a substantial body of knowledge about gender and reading. We know, for example, that girls often score higher than boys on standardized tests of 'reading' subskills (Coltheart, Hull, and Slater, 1975; Thompson, 1975; Wolf and Gow, 1986). And we know that fewer girls than boys are assigned to remedial reading classes (Ansara, Geschwind, Galaburda, Albert and Gartell, 1981; Chall, 1983; Liberman and Mann, 1981; Smith, 1981). Both findings are consistent with the situation at Oak Town School, where boys did less sustained reading, inside and outside of school, and, generally, did not value reading.

Furthermore, there is a need for all children to read literature that validates female experience. And yet both genders were being denied the opportunity to do so in their school. Segal (1986) explains how the practice of reading only stories that involve *male* experiences, during novel-study classes, is harmful not just to girls but also to *boys*: 'Many boys are missing out on one of fiction's greatest gifts, the chance to experience life from a perspective other than the one we were born to — in this case from the female vantage point'

(p. 183). Joleen Gagnon could have countered the 'girls' books–boys' books' ideology by assigning *So Far from the Bamboo Grove* for reading. When she refused, however, to do this, she effectively denied the boys a chance to confront, through literature, the horror of rape and the reality of sisterhood. In this way, therefore, they were being denied vicarious experience of what it feels like to be female.

The Oak Town girls were receiving, through literature, an education in human feeling that the boys were not. Many girls were becoming more fluent readers as a result of constant reading practice. Furthermore, the girls were not only learning the value of belonging to a community of readers; they were also experiencing the joys of a shared literary experience. They came to the classroom prepared to create their own literature-response groups and their own literature-study sessions. The boys, however, did not. As the analysis of the transcripts of the literature-response groups conducted for this study show, the Oak Town girls, on the one hand, and the Oak Town boys on the other approached literature in quite distinct, gendered ways.

The Oak Town children brought their culture's norms, values and beliefs both about gender and about reading to school with them. At school, they encountered teachers, a literature curriculum, and the additional values inherent in the *hidden curriculum*. Social norms surrounding gender placed constraints upon their reading, and as a result certain of their ways of reading became limiting. Those ways of reading, as we shall see, had a role to play in the creation of gendered subjectivity. So, too, did the children's acts of resistance.

Notes

1 See Appendix A for a fuller description of these literature-response groups.
2 After a lengthy search, and in spite of the best efforts of the reference librarians at my local public and university libraries, I have not been able to find any bibliographic information for this book. The title is not listed as part of Random House's Dragon Lance series. It may be that Christopher remembered the title incorrectly, or that I am spelling the hero's name incorrectly.
3 It is also likely that Anthony was empowered to resist by his social class. He was the child of a university professor who was probably the most educated person living in Oak Town; and Anthony, moreover, told me that his parents *liked* to see him reading. The norms for gender appropriate reading which Anthony learned at home were probably not those of the other Oak Town families. They were those of another social class, marked by differences in occupation and education.

Chapter 5

Identity Practices:
Reading Fiction and Constructing a
Gendered Subjectivity

Constructing Subjectivity

Twenty years ago, when I was teaching seventh-grade English in the United States, one of the anthologies of literature I used contained a play called *Inside a Kid's Head*. It was a fantasy-comedy in which a group of adult tourists became miniaturized and then took a tour of the brain of a 12-year-old boy. The adults (and the reader) could hear what the boy was thinking, see what he was seeing, and thoroughly understand his child's view of the world. In this chapter, I hope to convey some glimpses, like those conveyed in that funny play, of a child's subjective state as I imagine it. I would like to think of subjectivity as what goes on 'inside a kid's head'.

I also hope to answer the original research question for the Oak Town study: what did reading mean to these sixth-grade girls? Although this question may seem at first glance, to assume that reading is an individual psychological act, in fact it does not. This is actually a *psychosocial* question, one posed from the perspectives of anthropology and sociology, and in answering it, we will have to consider the cultural discourses that 'produce' what goes on in people's heads. Answering the question will involve describing the dynamics of the construction of the girls' 'subjectivities'. Weedon (1987) explains the term: '"Subjectivity" is used to refer to the conscious and unconscious thoughts and emotions of the individual, her sense of herself and her ways of understanding the world . . . post-structuralism proposes a subjectivity which is precarious, contradictory and in process, constantly being reconstituted in discourse each time we think or speak' (pp. 32 and 33).

I will argue in this chapter that the thoughts and emotions of the individual girls — their sense of themselves, and their ways of understanding their relation to the world are constituted as a dynamic process. Various cultural messages, as delivered through the discourses of the legal system, the media, medicine, the church, the publishing industry, the school, and other social institutions[1], serve both to position the girls in certain ways and to lead them to think, feel and act in certain ways. But each girl, however, also creates and practices individual forms of resistance to those broad cultural forces. The dialectical process then continues as the culture produces *counter*-messages in order to deal with individual acts of resistance; and for the most part, that culture *succeeds*, in the end, in reproducing itself from one generation to the next.

The process of constructing a 'subjectivity' is not a neat and straightforward one. Solsken (1993) argues that self-definition, especially as it occurs through literacy, is a highly individual matter, rooted both in the construction of social relationships within families and in the orientations toward literacy learned there. And certainly, this process by which a person creates his or her own subjectivity is also influenced by that person's gender, race, and social class. We have seen in Chapter 1, for example, how the people of Oak Town are not only positioned as members of two opposite and antagonistic gender groups, but also made to see themselves, and their relation to the world, in gender divided ways; and we also saw, in Chapter 3, how gender appropriate forms of literacy are taught and learned. The process of constructing a 'subjectivity' is also, however, complicated by a range of individual situations, as well as by the various *responses* that can be made to these situations.

In order to illustrate the process by which subjectivity is 'constructed', this chapter will first look closely at the phenomenon of *boredom*, in an attempt to see both the cultural forces and the sense of individual resistance operating in the girls' psychic lives. The following will not be an *exhaustive* discussion, but it will examine both children's language and children's behavior in school in order to identify some of the cultural factors and individual responses that contribute to the 'construction' of subjectivity. This chapter will then use the same type of analysis to examine both cultural influences and individual resistance at work in the construction of the girls' identities as this occurs during reading.

Boredom

Erroll explained as we strode down the carpeted hallway toward the library:

> One of the main reasons for my teaching Literature to every grade for
> two periods a week is to give the teachers their prep time. I like the

contact with the kids, and the teachers get their time off to plan. I mean the kids have to do something during teachers' prep time, and I figure it might as well be studying Literature with me . . . Of course, I'm the principal, and I don't have a lot of extra time for planning lessons, so I really rely on this Tom Penner Structured Tales Curriculum. It's all right here, what to teach for every grade. He doesn't do Tolkien, but I worked that out a few years ago, and now I could teach *The Hobbit* and *The Lord of the Rings* in my sleep . . . Today I'm going to give the sixth graders a pep talk. They haven't been responding very well lately. I'm going to tell them they've been ignoring my existence, just sitting there staring into space, and I would really appreciate it if they'd try to come back to Planet Earth for Literature Class.

I have seen and felt what Mr Boyle's Literature Class was like for the sixth graders of Oak Town. The children were bored, and this feeling of boredom was very unpleasant. Karen described it this way:

That Literature class is boring, you know. We don't learn anything in it. It just takes up time. We don't have any choice about the books we read in there. And we just have to *listen*. We don't even get to read the stupid book ourselves. I think I might like it better if I could read it for myself. This way I just hate it. Mostly I stare at the wall or the clock and just wait for it to be over. It's so boring.

Boredom in Oak Town School was the consequence of both culturally shaped time constraints and of the externally imposed curriculum. Everhart's (1983) analysis of student opposition to 'the imperatives of a managed environment' in school is relevant here. He suggests that students are aware both that they are members of an organization (i.e. the school) in which they have positions of low status, and that they are expected to be the passive recipients of knowledge and activities that have already been planned for them. He sees their opposition as a reaction against passivity, as a form of resistance to activities that they do not approve of or understand.

Karen's words both about taking up time and about the anguish of passivity tell us a good deal about the prevalent culture at work in the school, as well as about her own rebellious feelings. Because Karen's culture saw time as a valuable commodity, the people with power endeavoured to *control* it. Indeed, the control of time, like the control of money, was a cultural marker of power. Teachers controlled the children's time at school, and were responsible for filling it. And because, also, Karen's culture saw time as a void that had meaning and significance only when it was filled with activity, there was, for that reason, no *unassigned* time at school. The school day had been divided into a timetable, both so that time slots could be allotted to separate activities and so that no time would be wasted.

The children of Oak Town School were thus at the mercy of their teachers, who were, in turn, at the mercy of the timetable they had created. Those teachers who had to teach within small periods of time had to choose and plan exactly what they would teach, and they could not allow the children to choose and to pursue ideas that *they* were interested in. Teachers were accountable for 'using time well', for having 'something to show' for the time that they spent with their students. One thing that they could show was a curriculum that had been 'covered'. Any such curriculum could not be planned in partnership with the children, because that would not only take too much time but would also conflict with the cultural assumption that entitles the adults to control the children's time.

Karen knew that Mr Boyle's Literature class was designed to fill up a timetable slot, and to give the sixth-grade teachers their 'preparation time'. She knew also that it was easier for Mr Boyle to read aloud rather than to try to put a copy of Tolkien into the hands of every child. And she knew that her active participation in the curriculum was neither valued nor even expected. But she knew, also, that she had no choice. Karen's words tell us both that she thought that this situation was unjust, and that what she felt in response to this situation, *boredom*, was the result both of other people's having control over her time in school, and of a curriculum that interested someone else and not Karen herself.

The great majority of the sixth graders agreed with Karen that Mr Boyle's Literature class was 'boring'. In fact the sixth-grade children at Oak Town School used the word 'boring' frequently. It had a variety of uses, each of which identified it either as a response to the oppressive influence of cultural rules about time, or as a feeling of being alienated from those topics in which they had no interest. Samantha and Michelle, for example, both used the word 'boring' to refer to those books that they didn't enjoy. Samantha, who loved problem-realism novels, said that she found Jim Kjelgaard's books boring, and wondered what her brother could possibly like about them. Samantha was also bored by the *Sweet Valley High* books. She said that boring books 'go so slow'. They didn't help to make the time go faster. Michelle, on her part, found the Lloyd Alexander books boring. She said, 'They happen such a long time ago.' And Samantha, Julie and Michael found *Last Chance Summer* (a story about an Indian foster child with a criminal record) boring because, 'We don't know anyone like those boys in that book.' Boring books were often those that were far removed from present time and present experience (though not all such books were boring).

Everyone looked for books that were entertaining, and as a result, everyone was disappointed when a book was 'boring'.

Various examples from the transcripts of literature-response groups served to illustrate the different uses of the word. Firstly, the word 'boring' was sometimes used as part of a defense strategy by those who hadn't read a book assigned to them. The idea seemed to be: '*I'm* not at fault here. It's the *book* that's deficient. I haven't read it because it didn't do its job by getting me involved and interested. It was *boring*.' In this case, the children seemed to be constructing themselves as people who expect to be *entertained*, and yet who also did not assume that they should actively create their own interests. This was consistent with the culture's view of children as the passive recipients of the curriculum.

Having to cope with an externally imposed curriculum, the children often found themselves in a state of not understanding, of not being aware of any significance either in a story or in a section of a text. The word 'boring', also, therefore, was sometimes used to refer to a state of not understanding. For example, it was sometimes used to describe the beginning stage in the reading of a novel, where the author was introducing the action and the characters, and the reader had not yet been drawn into the world of the story. Julie and Alisa said that they found the beginning of *Tuck Everlasting* boring, although they enjoyed the rest of the book; Alisa and Marcia said that they found the beginning of *Bridge to Terabithia* boring, until the point when Leslie won the race; and Karen made the more general remark that the beginning of *any* book was usually boring for her. Several children also mentioned their dislike of the long prologue to *The Lord of the Rings*. In contrast, all five girls who read *Mama's Going to Buy You a Mockingbird* (by choice) were immediately engaged by the opening scene. They understood at once that they were reading an account of an argument between a younger sister and an older brother, and they felt that they got to know both characters right away.

Elsewhere, again, the children spoke of boredom as being related to the length of time that something took to accomplish. They wanted time to seem to pass quickly. Lacey said that she fell asleep in Phys Ed when Mrs Gagnon took too long giving the instructions; Jerrica said that *Mrs Frisbee and the Rats of NIMH* was boring because the unit took so long to do; *everyone* complained that the Tolkien book was taking too long; Karen pointed out that the *long* books were usually more boring; and Marcia, finally, said that writing in the Tolkien journals was boring because each entry took so long to do. It may be that whenever something *seemed*, to the children, to take a very long time, it was because the activity in question was a *boring* one.

It was clear from the children's tone of voice and facial expression and body language that boredom was a stressful and unpleasant state. They hated the feeling that being without understanding and engagement and interest brought, that the void of time was empty and that life was meaningless. Boredom meant that time passed slowly and painfully. The teachers at Oak Town School controlled the classroom agenda, expecting children to act as passive recipients of an externally imposed curriculum. Not recognizing the power of the rules about time that shaped their teachers' behavior, the children felt resentful and estranged. And because they did not understand the significance of the curriculum imposed upon them, they also felt bored. Everhart's (1983) conclusion was as apt for the children of Oak Town School as it was for the children that he was studying: opposition, or resistance, grew out of boredom and out of a situation where students were choosing to involve themselves to a *minimal extent only* in activities that were intended to consume much of their time.

The feeling of boredom inspired a search — a *struggle* — for relief, and the children of Oak Town responded to their own feelings of misery by devising various strategies for fighting boredom.

It was January and it was snowing outside Mrs. Gagnon's classroom window. James was bored. Several of his classmates were watching it snow. Mrs Gagnon was standing at the front chalkboard showing the class how to write a diamente poem.

'You see,' she said, 'it has seven lines, and the first and the last lines are opposites. Let's write one together as a group. It'll be about *day* and *night,* so the first line is *day* and the last line will be *night.* Now, give me two adjectives to describe "day".'

Nicole raised her hand and volunteered: 'Bright, sunny.'

'Good!' said Mrs Gagnon. She wrote 'bright' and 'sunny' on the board. 'Now we need three words that end in "ing" to go with "day". James?'

'Sleeping.'

Mrs Gagnon turned toward the chalkboard, saying, 'Well, let's save "sleeping" to go with "night". More people sleep at night.'

James exchanged a small and knowing smile with Jake.

He and Jake continued to volunteer words that were slightly off the mark, and to exchange small smiles as Mrs Gagnon wrote her group poem on the board. Time passed more quickly.

It was easier for the children to fight boredom at *home.* They had a number of ways. They watched television, they got something to eat, or they wandered around, outdoors, with their friends when the weather permitted[2]. Marcia, for example, liked to mess around with her usual schedule: on weekends, she stayed up really late at night, watching the wrestling on television and talking to Michelle on the phone.

However, there were fewer ways to fight boredom during *school* time. Doodling was one way, talking to friends and trying not to get caught at it was another. Not to mention sabotaging the teacher's lesson. For a while, also, the boys all had hockey cards in their desks, and spent their time trying to trade them around without attracting the teacher's attention. Then the girls started braiding friendship bracelets out of narrow strips of plastic. When a girl got one of these started, she could keep it in her desk, and when things got boring, she could just reach in there and continue braiding. One very effective strategy for fighting boredom, however, was *reading*. It was no secret, among the children, that nearly every girl kept a library book open in her desk, and that when a lesson got boring, she would sneak it into her lap and start reading. Some of the boys, moreover, did the same thing.

Anthony, as we saw earlier, didn't even worry about getting caught. He was always reading in school, even during Math, and sometimes Mrs Gagnon did catch him. But what could she say? It wasn't, after all, such a crime to read a book in school, even if you were supposed to be doing something else. Reading was quiet and it didn't bother anyone, and certainly it kept the children from looking at the clock. It gave them something pleasant to do, and it made the time go by much faster.

Anyon's (1984) words about accommodation and resistance come to mind. Here is an instance of children accommodating their culture's demands while at the same time resisting them. They chose *reading* as their means of controling their own time because reading was a quiet activity, and one which allowed them to remain at their desks during the teacher's lessons, and because they could also *appear* to be cooperating with the demands of the existing timetable and the curriculum. Reading, as an act of resistance, did not appear to disturb the status quo.

Reading allowed the children to escape the tyranny of the teacher's curriculum because it replaced that curriculum with something else, something that *they* had chosen, something that *they* found preferable. Reading was also a way both of eliminating boredom, and of affirming one's own ability to take individual action. Reading was thus a way of asserting *some* control over the period of time that the children spent at school.

Girls and Reading

The experience of boredom in school appeared to be similar for both genders. All the children were positioned, through prevalent cultural beliefs about time, to be the passive recipients of an imposed curriculum. However, the experience of passivity in relationship to this curriculum took a different form for the girls of Oak Town because for them it was part of a *larger* picture of female passivity, a picture that the culture itself was painting for them. Various discourses of femininity and masculinity were at work, positioning female people as passive, on the one hand, and male people as active and assertive on the other. Weedon (1987) puts it this way:

> Dominant discourses of female sexuality, which define it as naturally passive, together with dominant social definitions of women's place as first and foremost in the home, can be found in social policy, medicine, education, the media, the church and elsewhere.
>
> (p. 36)

I will argue that although the Oak Town girls were subject to a cultural emphasis on female *passivity*, they did, at the same time, resist this ideology of female passivity in some areas of their lives, while still receiving messages that amounted to the culture's attempt to *counter* their resistance: messages about the threat of violence against women. Throughout this process, the girls were 'constructing' gendered subjectivities as well as arriving at an understanding of themselves in relation to the world.

Agency and Resistance

The sixth graders of Oak Town were struggling to live their lives more independently. They were learning to keep track of their homework, their gym equipment, their lunch money, and their book order forms; and they were learning to stay clean and well-groomed, to contribute labor to the maintenance of their households, and to meet their obligations to the community organizations which they joined. All of these things they were learning and practicing with varying degrees of success, and they moved in and out of states of determination and rebellion. They would say: 'I have so much more to do this year. Life was easier in fifth grade.' They worked toward growing up. They yearned to *be* grown-up.

The attractive thing about being grown-up was that grown-ups had *agency*, the ability to exercise power, the ability to act, and produce an effect, upon the world. Grown-ups seemed to be instrumental in changing the world around them in a way that the children would have liked to emulate. They felt keenly their own lack of such instrumentality.

The word 'agency' can refer either to the power to act in one's own interests, or, as in anthropology, to a culture's *approved* ways both of acting upon the world and of producing an effect within a community. Hoskins, for example, has described (1987) the complementary forms of male and female agency as found in the Kodi culture of Eastern Indonesia. The Kodi people believed that while women, on the one hand, exercised agency in the private sphere of home and family, men, on the other hand, exercised agency in the public sphere of daily life. It can be argued that mainstream North American culture, as manifested in Oak Town, subscribed to ideas of complementary male and female agency that were much like those of the Kodi. The notion of complementary agency suggests that one way in which we distinguish between male and female people is through their modes of acting upon the world. In Oak Town, men believed that they had to act primarily in a public sphere, while women, on their part, believed that they had to act primarily in the private sphere. Men were thought to act directly, while women, in turn, were thought to act indirectly. The two gender roles thus complemented each other because they were opposites. (It may help to remember that I am speaking of what people *believed* and not of what they actually experienced.)

Children of both genders desired *agency*, but the *kind* of agency that a child both desired and expected (eventually) to achieve was determined by the particular *gender* of the child in question. The Oak Town children were learning about the different gender–appropriate forms of agency that were approved by their culture from their parents, from their teachers, from the books they read, and from the activities that they engaged in; and the gender appropriate division of daily activities served to demonstrate and teach these contrasting forms of agency (Thorne, 1986). The boys were encouraged to participate in those organized sports, like hockey, which taught them both the use of physical aggression and the public display of power, while girls, for their part, were encouraged to work indoors, to shop, and to act as consumers. These are generalizations, of course, and there were wide variations in the extent to which these things were taught within individual families, but nevertheless, notions of complementary agency *were* being both learned and reproduced in Oak Town.

As we have seen, one important site for the learning of the culture's gender ideals was the girls' practice of reading fiction. While their brothers were playing hockey and building things, the Oak Town girls were filling the empty hours, on their way to being grown-up, with reading. Through their reading of fiction, they were receiving instructions about the intricacies involved in human relationships, and learning a good deal about 'common sense'. Romances and the girls' series books were promoting those particular notions of female agency that were approved by the culture at large. If we think of common sense as comprising statements of dominant cultural meanings, as communicated through the media, general education, relatives and friends (Weedon, 1987), it becomes clear that common sense represents certain specific values and interests. The girls' reading matter, full, as it was, of common sense, served as an important instrument of cultural reproduction.

Another thing that the girls of Oak Town resisted was the imposition of *limits* upon their lives. Critical educational theorists have frequently used the word 'resistance' to signify the actions of individuals and groups by which they assert their own desires, and contest the ideological and material forces that are imposed upon them by the prevailing culture (Weiler, 1988). McRobbie (1989) has suggested that 'negotiation' may be a better term than 'resistance' for the processes by which individuals come to terms with cultural forces. Similarly, Anyon's (1984) study of school girls' attitudes toward contradictory gender role ideologies in the world around them has suggested that the girls both *resisted* those roles as they accommodated them, on the one hand, and *accommodated* those roles as they resisted them on the other. She writes:

> The dialectic of accommodation and resistance is part of all human beings' response to contradiction and oppression. Most females engage in daily conscious and unconscious attempts to resist the psychological degradation and low self-esteem that would result from the total application of the cultural ideology of femininity: submissiveness, dependency, domesticity and passivity.

In this chapter, I will be using the word 'resistance' to name the processes by which the Oak Town girls negotiated their *own* meanings for the cultural scripts that they encountered in fiction, and in other cultural discourses.

Using Fiction to Explore Agency

The sixth-grade girls of Oak Town used their reading of fiction to explore the various possibilities that existed in connection with their own places as agents in the world, and they often as part of this process of exploration imagined themselves *in conflict* with the roles that their families suggested for them. Alisa, for example, resisted her mother's vision of her attending law school; and other girls, in a similar vein, generally resisted their parents' vision of them as grown-up 'good' girls who behaved decorously, pleased others, and served their husbands. Even when the very fictional texts they were reading suggested one particular kind of female agency, the girls would still sometimes read those texts as a means of exploring other, *different* kinds of agency.

Consider this example: the *Babysitters Club* books by Ann Martin did not seek to promote social revolution. They were stories about middle-class, preadolescent girls who lived in the same neighborhood, and who supported each other cheerfully in their dealings both with parents and teachers, and with the families that they babysat for. The girls in those stories were 'good' girls whose struggles with their respective parents took place in a rather low key. The girls who belonged to the Babysitters Club beautified themselves diligently, did their chores conscientiously, loved their families well, and served the children of their community faithfully. Clearly, this was one model of 11-year-old female agency that promoted a comparable model of adult female agency.

But the girls would *renegotiate* the cultural messages of these texts: they saw the Babysitters as making money that they would then use to achieve their *own* ends; they saw the Babysitters shaping the action around them so that things worked out the way they wanted them to; and they saw girls of their age acting as agents in their own right. Ellsworth explains (1984) how, in a similar fashion, a group of feminist women interpreted a particular film in a way that not only served their *own* purposes but also created an interpretative stance that was in direct opposition to the stance intended by the film's own makers. She found that these women, sharing a common political orientation and beliefs about women's oppression, formed an interpretive community when considering *Personal Best* (the name of the film in question). The Oak Town girls engaged in a similar sort of renegotiation process, forming their own 'interpretive community', and developing their own oppositional readings of mass-marketed fiction.

In *Mary Anne Saves the Day*, for example, the babysitter Mary Anne was sweet and timid and largely controlled by her father at the beginning of the story. She was allowed, by her father, to meet her girlfriends, or to go out babysitting, until 9.00 p. m., but she was not allowed either to wear make-up or to assert herself in any way. When one of her babysitting charges became ill, Mary Anne demonstrated that she was a capable person by caring for the sick child and getting help. Her father's attitude toward her then changed. Mary Anne was both the compliant female child and the effective agent. She did not rebel, and yet she successfully demonstrated her capabilities, and in so doing, convinced her father to remove his restrictions. The girls of Oak Town who read the book saw a worthy individual triumph over the gender restrictions of the culture at large; and more importantly they were learning that such individual triumphs were something that *they too* could achieve.

'I loved that book,' said Alisa. 'She was so smart, and then he couldn't treat her like a little girl any more. I felt proud for Mary Anne.'

In a similar way, the *Sweet Valley High* books served to encourage Jerrica and Marcia, and the other girls who read them, to take risks. Jessica, the 'bad' twin who did as she pleased and got into trouble, was the twin they applauded and would have liked to emulate. Elizabeth, the 'good' twin who was beloved by all because she made everything turn out all right in the end, was much less interesting to them.

It seems probable to me that the girls used fiction to explore agency because the desire for agency was so strong in their daily lives.

Karen's face was grim. She pulled her chair up to the table where the literature-response group was about to meet. She spoke across the table to Jerrica. 'Did you hear what happened to Lacey in Social yesterday? Mrs Johns was absent and we had a sub. We were working on our reports and the sub came around to see what we were doing. Lacey showed her her report — and the sub wrote all over it! She drew arrows on it and crossed out things and she changed it all around. Lacey was so mad! If it had been my report, I would have killed her.'

Later, Jerrica and Karen and Alisa munched their sandwiches in the lunch room. Jerrica said, 'I had an awful weekend. Sunday School was the worst. I hate it so much.' Alisa nodded and said: 'I hate it too. My whole family does. We don't go as much as we used to.' Karen sighed, and said: 'I wish *we* could stay home as much as you do. Sunday School is so worthless. We fill out these lessons, and nobody understands them, and I'm so far behind. I hate it.'

For the sixth-grade girls of Oak Town, life was full of situations over which they had no control and in which they had no choice. They could negotiate with teachers, but when a substitute arrived they had to put up with whatever she chose to do. Certain features of their lives, furthermore, were imposed on them by their parents: for example, Sunday School and church attendance, both of which meant little to the children, were imposed on them by their parents. Frequently, music lessons were too, and as a result the children often practiced music not because they wanted to, but because they had to.

Although the children actively resented these things, they realized that they had no real choice in the matter. They had to cooperate because they were dependent people. Cara described the situation thus: 'My Mom and Dad are really the most important people in my life. I like my brother, but he's really not important to me at all. We both depend on Mom and Dad. There isn't much that we could do to help each other.'

The girls, as already mentioned, would have loved to have had more control over their own lives, and they looked forward to the day when they *would* have it. Jerrica related an anecdote: 'I was helping my mother get supper the other night, and she said to me, "Jerrica, some day you'll be able to fix your husband a nice supper." I got so mad, so I said to her, "Oh no you don't. *He's* gonna fix my supper!"' Julie, similarly, explained that when she grew up she wouldn't be doing all the housework: it wasn't fair that girls had to do it all, and she wasn't going to stand for it. At the age of 11 these girls were already 'resisters' — especially prone to questioning the ways in which women submitted to male authority (Gilligan, 1989) — and they enjoyed imagining themselves as adults who would not only make choices but also be able to assert themselves.

This desire for agency was clearly visible in the girls' various interpretations of the different library books that they read. Lacey read *The Secret Garden* and said that she didn't like the way (in the book) that Colin bossed Mary around: 'If I was Mary, I'd just tell him to stop it.' Several of the girls read *The Haunting at Cliff House* by Karleen Bradford, in which a young girl solves a mystery and rights an ancient wrong. Rene, Cara, Nicole and Alisa all agreed that it was a great book. 'She didn't let anybody stop her,' said Alisa with admiration in her voice. 'She just went ahead and did it.'

When Mr Peterson asked the children to follow their reading of *The Book of Three* with an activity in which they 'gave gifts' to the different characters in the book, the girls, who enjoyed this idea, thought long and hard about what to give the character called Eilonwy. Finally, Karen hit upon the perfect present: 'Let's give Eilonwy a sword! Like she always wanted to fight and everything. She didn't want to be considered just a little girl.' A weapon seemed to Karen to be all that was needed to equip Eilonwy to fulfil her desire for agency.

Furthermore, when the girls recommended various books to each other, they often identified those particular stories that involved *female agency* as the 'good books'. For example, Samantha suggested *Kid Power* to Alisa, saying, 'It's about a girl who needs to earn some money, so she starts her own business;' Karen told the others about *Julie of the Wolves*, saying that Julie was very smart and independent, and 'believed in herself'; and Jerrica recommended a book about the aftermath of nuclear war because the ending showed the children managing both to survive and to secure help for their injured mother.

The girls exercised agency wherever they possibly could in their daily lives. Amanda, for example, who had been strictly forbidden by her mother to see the movie *Flowers in the Attic*, arrived at Nicole's birthday party to find that Nicole's parents had rented *Flowers in the Attic* for the evening's entertainment. Nicole chose to say nothing, and watched the movie. Marcia and Julie, for their part, often chose to 'hide' and read when they were supposed to be doing household chores; and they willingly paid the consequences for this act of defiance later. And *all* of the girls 'sneaked' reading in school at certain times when they were supposed to be 'doing schoolwork'. In resisting the teacher's assignment of their time, and exercising some choice in what they would and would not do, the girls were incorporating agency into their daily lives.

It seemed to me that the girls felt freer to explore agency in those matters that related to money, entertainment, and material possessions. The affluence in which they were growing up allowed them to make choices about what they would wear, what they would eat, which movies they would see, and which books they would read. Parents took them shopping and encouraged them to make choices — encouraged them to buy what they *wanted* to buy. Parents took them to the video rental store or to the public library and allowed them to choose whatever they liked (although most of the time, however, they were *not* allowed to choose anything with an explicitly sexual content). After they had met their obligations to do household chores and practice for music lessons, the girls were encouraged to organize their own time at home. The girls took these opportunities to exercise agency, and they *enjoyed* them.

In many other areas of their lives, however, the girls were not encouraged or allowed to exercise agency. They had (as already mentioned) no say in the school's curriculum, or in the ways in which they were expected to use their time at school; they were not allowed to choose boys as companions or friends; they were not allowed to travel where they wished to at will (but instead were obligated to keep their parents informed of their whereabouts at all times); they were certainly not allowed to exercise agency in matters of sexual expression. Each girl *did* resist the constraints that were imposed upon her exercise of agency — at school, within the family, and in cross-gender relationships — but at the young age of 11 or 12, they were not in a position to risk open rebellion.

Instead, I believe, the girls explored the various models of agency through their reading of series books. Those who read series books seemed to find in them a complete and real world that was 'continuous' with their own world (Radway, 1984); and the fact that this parallel world of the series could be treated as a real world made it easy for the girls to think of the characters in the series books as real girls, girls with problems similar to their own. The sixth-grade girls of Oak Town read series books for the same reason that they would watch each other: to look both for cues as to acceptable ways to behave, and for examples of ways to be in the world. Desiring agency for themselves, the girls, at the same time, desired agency for the girl characters in their series books. They admired them for exercising agency when and where they could, and they imagined *themselves* exercising agency in a similar fashion. They thus fantasized about the texts they read in order to fulfill their own desires.

> Tanya sat at her desk, her math homework finished, reading her *Sweet Valley High* book. The cover said that it was *Book #5, Out of Reach.* The picture on the cover showed an attractive Oriental girl with an athletic towel around her neck, looking pensively off to one side. Blonde and beautiful Elizabeth Wakefield stood beside her, looking at her supportively. The sentence on the cover below the picture read, 'Will Jade Wu have to defy her father to get what she wants?'
>
> Tanya read intently, turning the last few pages slowly. She finished, sighed, and closed the book. 'That was an excellent book,' she said to the girl across from her. 'She got it.'

Daly (1989) has pointed out that the *Sweet Valley High* series does nothing at all to question either consumer values or class consciousness. The twin heroines, Jessica and Elizabeth Wakefield, live in a Californian world of shopping malls, television programs and junk food that was perfectly familiar to the residents of Oak Town. The Wakefield twins glory in their affluent lifestyle, and enjoy their privileges without questioning them. One of them, however, *does* question cultural gender constraints. Jessica is not the 'good girl' that ideal girls are supposed to be. Daly suggests that Francine Pascal, the author of the *Sweet Valley High* series, has split the mixed emotions that girls feel in response to their gender–constrained social development between her twin heroines (p. 53): where Jessica feels rebellious and assertive, competitive and selfish, even angry, Elizabeth feels saintly and sweet, concerned for others, and helpful, calm and loving; where Jessica indulges in openly sexual behavior, Elizabeth refrains from any such behavior; and where Jessica pursues her own self-interest relentlessly, Elizabeth is entirely selfless.

Jessica allowed the Oak Town girls to fantasize about exercising agency in one of the very social domains where such agency was forbidden to them: the domain of sexual behavior. Jerrica, Marcia and the other Oak Town girls who read *Sweet Valley High* books all faithfully admired Jessica, and identified with her independent behavior, even when she was severely punished for it. Marcia explained in her dialogue journal:

May 1

Dear Mrs Cherland,

Characters can be boring at times, but Jessica never is. My favorite character is Jessica because she always does these neat things and always takes risks.

In *All Night Long* Jessica took so many risks and it had a lot of adventure, too. It was about Jessica going out with a college guy who had a Ferrari (some sort of car). He invited her to a beach party with all these other college students. When she gets there, she starts drinking beer and they are smoking pot. Then he takes her to an abandoned shack and tries to abuse her. She started screaming so he took off to his cottage and left her there in the dark. She made her way back to the cottage, and all his friends are still there, but she can't get home, and a telephone isn't within ten miles. So she is forced to stay overnight there. When Elizabeth finds out that her sister hasn't been home, she has to be Jessica and Elizabeth at the same time.

Truly yours,

Marcia

Marcia enjoyed reading about Jessica's risk-taking, even when her risk-taking nearly ended in disaster, and she loved it when Elizabeth rescued Jessica from one awful situation or another. And Jessica, whose life was not all trouble, did, indeed, seem to enjoy herself when she was exercising her own agency. In *Slam Book Fever*, for example, Jessica chose to pretend to be meek and mild in order to attract a certain boy, and she succeeded, choosing short-term happiness and instant gratification over long-term well-being — and relying on Elizabeth, again, to save the situation in the end. It appeared to the Oak Town girls that Jessica made wise choices.

Because the two characters of Jessica and Elizabeth were framed in terms of binary oppositions, it seemed clear to the girls that one could not be *both* Jessica and Elizabeth, and the discourses exemplified in *Sweet Valley High* books certainly worked to position the girls to see sexual choices very much in an either–or light.

Not all the sixth-grade girls enjoyed *Sweet Valley High,* however. Those who did may have enjoyed the fact that Jessica and Elizabeth were older than they were, and therefore seemed so much more powerful. But most of the sixth-grade girls preferred the *Sweet Valley Twins* series in which Jessica and Elizabeth (the same characters) are 12 years old. Their characters are the same: Jessica is selfish, Elizabeth is saintly. And again, it is Elizabeth who repeatedly rescues Jessica from the awful situations that she gets herself into. Alisa responded to the *Sweet Valley Twins* books in the same way that

Marcia did to the *Sweet Valley High* books: 'I love it when she gets into trouble. Those are the books I like.' Getting into trouble required the exercise of agency.

The *Babysitters Club* series, although it offered less such 'excitement', did, on the other hand, seem to meet the girls' need to feel more confident and capable. In this particular series, a familiar group of characters faces challenges to their babysitting success that are not too dangerous but that are rather realistic, and are *always* overcome. The featured babysitter is always shown to be clever and competent and well-liked by all. The *Babysitters Club* reader, who can say, with Lacey, 'I feel like I *know* those girls,' is reassured that she too can be useful, and can contribute something to the world of material production. The *Babysitters Club* characters are not 'used' as babysitters. Instead, they do something praiseworthy and challenging and worthwhile that gives them agency within those social domains where such agency is acceptable: the home, the peer network, and the local community. (The *Nancy Drew* books also show a young girl acting effectively and capably upon the world, solving mysteries that have the grown-ups baffled, and keeping both herself and her family and friends safe.)

The girls' use of reading in order to exercise agency within approved social domains seemed to me to represent a way of coping with two kinds of tension in their lives. Firstly, just as romance reading for women may be 'combative' because by reading such romances the woman temporarily ignores the otherwise constant demands of her family (Radway, 1984, p. 211), so the activity of reading series books may also have been 'combative' for the Oak Town girls, since by engaging in such reading, the girls could temporarily escape the constant demands being made upon them to be 'good'. When they read, they *were* being 'good'. Anyone (parent, teacher, girl, or boy) who saw them reading would see them sitting quietly and engaging in an activity that was approved for girls of their age. No one could know what they were imagining, what they were 'constructing' via their interaction with the text before them. No one could know what kind of renegotiation of their lives, what kind of resistance, what private practices were hidden behind their publicly conformist stance.

The activity of reading may also, however, have released a *second* kind of tension. Just as romance reading for women can be a 'compensatory' (Radway, 1984) activity, insofar as, by reading, women are making up for the emotional deprivations of their daily lives, so it is possible that series-book reading, for the Oak Town girls, was likewise a 'compensatory' activity, insofar as, by identifying with the characters they were reading about, and by fantasizing and dreaming, the girls could feel more powerful than they were allowed to feel in the real world. The practice of reading thus released two different kinds of tension, by granting the girls both some 'psychic distance' from the demands being made upon them to be 'good' and a sense, denied to them by the culture in which they had grown up, of their own *power*. Moreover, another reason why reading served the girls as an ideal compensatory and combative strategy was that it did not attract the kind of attention and disapproval that would, in turn, have created *new* tensions in their lives. Reading was accessible, and it was not punished — as other combative and compensatory forms of behavior might have been.

I have been discussing the girls' reading of popular series books, but the Oak Town girls also explored their desire for agency in the literature-response groups. An analysis of the literature-response-group transcripts provided more relevant information about the girls' ideas, and feelings, about agency. Their talk about literature showed the girls to be both attributing agency to fictional characters, and *admiring* the exercise of agency. Their talk also showed the girls' desiring agency for themselves, as well as lamenting their present lack of such agency. In their discussion of *Tuck Everlasting*, for example, the girls empathized with the main character, Winnie Foster, who was strictly controlled by her family, and who lived in a 'touch-me-not' house, but who also made decisions about the course of her future life. It became clear that Alisa, Julie and Cara all believed both that Winnie *freely chose* to pour the precious water of immortality onto the frog (and not save any for herself), and that Mae Tuck, similarly, *freely chose* to kill the man in the yellow suit — the man who would have betrayed the Tucks' secret. And finally, they also believed that Winnie again *freely chose* to run away from home in order to escape the demands both of her parents and of propriety. Alisa explained:

> I think she ran away because her parents, like they wouldn't let her out of the yard and like she had to eat with . . . like she couldn't lick her fingers at the dinner table. She had to follow all these rules and she had to be polite and stuff that way.

The other girls agreed with Alisa that Winnie wasn't really kidnapped by the Tucks. They believed that she *chose* to accompany them to their home, and they minimized the importance of circumstance in causing this to happen. In believing this, the girls were crediting Winnie with agency in those domains in which they themselves were allowed very little, or none at all: Winnie did not keep her parents informed of her whereabouts, she left home secretly at midnight, and she nearly entered into a relationship with Jesse Tuck. Her actions, in their view, portrayed Winnie as *choosing* to exercise the agency that her family had denied her.

Because they attributed agency to such characters, the girls also held those characters responsible when their 'choices' didn't work out well. For example, Alisa and Julie expressed their annoyance at Winnie for pouring the water on the frog; Julie said that Mae's choice to kill the man in the yellow suit was stupid; and *all* the girls expressed their disappointment at the fact that Winnie had not swallowed the water of immortality at the age of 17 and married Jesse Tuck.

In the literature-response groups, as in the activity of reading the series books, it became clear, as already mentioned, that the Oak Town girls admired the exercise of agency, especially in those areas of life where they themselves enjoyed little or no agency. Alisa and Marcia both said that the first event in *Bridge to Terabithia* to capture their interest was Leslie's winning of the foot race against the boys (the Oak Town girls *never* met with success when competing against the boys in sports). In another discussion, Karen recalled from memory the sentence, in *Julie of the Wolves*, that said that the pink room in San Francisco was filled with Amaroq's blood. In doing so, Karen was demonstrating her approval of Miyax's decision not to abandon her Eskimo way of life. Karen admired this decision, because in contrast, she and the other Oak Town girls had no authority at all for making decisions about where and how they would live. In another group, furthermore, Marcia applauded Wanda's decision, in *Summer of the Swans*, to defy her Aunt Willie and to ride off on the motorcycle with Frank. 'Because when she wanted that ride from that guy, she went, "I don't have to listen to you" to her aunt, because she was nineteen, like, "I don't even have to live here" and stuff. She didn't have to follow the rules that much.' The Oak Town girls, however, did have to live at home and follow the rules.

During the literature-response group meetings it became clearer to me how much the girls wanted agency for themselves in these other domains. Although they were at the mercy both of the school's timetables and of their teachers' decisions, they were always anxious, for example, to know on which days I intended to be there, so that they could plan for my visit ahead of time. They wanted to feel as much in control of their time at school (i.e. in their public world) as they were at home (i.e. in their private world).

In experiencing this desire for agency, the girls often connected the circumstances of their own lives with those occurring in the books that they were reading. In a discussion of *Bridge to Terabithia*, at a point in the story when Jess is anxious not to be caught near the girls' bathroom, Jerrica recalled with admiration an act of defiance that occurred in school when three girls from her class actually entered the boys' bathroom. Alisa, too, admired this action.

> Alisa: 'Jess was gonna go in, but he decided not to because it was a girls' bathroom.'

Karen: 'That was a mean principal at their school . . .He wouldn't even let a boy be seen *near* the girls' bathroom . . .Big hairy deal . . .'

Jerrica (laughs): 'Once, at recess, some of the girls went in the boys' bathroom. Right into the boys' bathroom.'

Alisa: 'Yeah. It was at that babysitters' course last year. That was so funny.'

Jerrica: 'Yeah, there were some boys in there teasing, "Come on, girls, come on in . . ." So they went in! It was great.'

The girls also claimed, and celebrated, agency during a discussion of *Summer of the Swans*, which began as they talked about why everyone referred to Sara's guardian as 'Aunt Willie'. They spoke of calling their own friends' parents by their first names.

Jerrica: 'So that's probably why Frank and Mary called her "Aunt Willie". Because they're good friends and they don't wanna call her "Miss Godfrey" or something.'

Karen: 'When I go to Jerrica's house, I don't like calling her mom "Mrs Scott". My mom told me to, but it sounds so dumb. It sounds like I'm on a business trip or something.'

Alisa: 'My mom says it's disrespectful to call a friend's mom by her first name.'

Jerrica: 'So does mine.'

Cara: 'So does mine.'

Alisa: 'But I think that's too formal. The mom is really my friend too, and I can call her what I want to.'

Jerrica: 'Yeah.'

The girls felt comfortable with this practice, and they *wanted* to do it, even though their own parents had asked them to use titles and last names when addressing these adults. The parents wanted their children to respect this marker of deference to age, but the children, on the other hand, wanted to see themselves as the *equals* of the adults in question, equals with agency that enabled them to act on that equality.

This was not, however, the case in their relationships with people *younger* than themselves. For example, Karen thought that the fact that Sara in *Summer of the Swans* had feet as big as Jackie Onassis must have been disheartening for Jackie Onassis; and she told of her own feelings of embarrassment when meeting a very little girl at the mall who had a jacket exactly like her own. When Karen was the older person, age markers like dress were very important in establishing status, and in indicating relative power.

Where the girls did not feel in control, or where they read about a character whom they felt *ought* to take control, they expressed their dissatisfaction. Samantha lamented the fact that she kept choosing books that ended with death, even though she didn't intend to. Marcia, on her part, felt dissatisfied that Sara in *Summer of the Swans* didn't take charge of her life; she felt that Sara ought to be phoning people and making more of an effort to see her friends. Later, she also expressed her dissatisfaction at the way that the book ended just where Sara ought to have been *starting* to exercise agency in her relationship with her friends. Marcia saw such a lack of agency in the field of interpersonal relationships as a cause for unhappiness.

The Oak Town girls used their reading to envision themselves as agents both within approved domains (through The *Babysitters Club* series, for example), and within *forbidden* domains (through the *Sweet Valley High* series, for example). But it is important to point out, again, that the girls were not engaging in any form of open rebellion. Instead, they chose an *approved* behavior, namely reading, as an arena for their dissenting visions of what they ought to be. While they behaved with discretion, while they continued to be 'good' girls who took care of their appearances, worked at their relationships with friends, and did as others expected them to do, they filled their time with quiet reading. But they were using that reading to *escape* those constraints on their time, and to explore alternative ideas both about agency and about gender.

Horror and the Denial of Agency

In her study of high-school sex education, Fine has suggested (1988) that while adolescent boys are treated in our culture as sexual agents, girls, on the other hand, are treated as sexual *victims*, and this ideology of aggressor and victim is reflected in the language of various sex-education-curriculum materials. The motif of aggressor and victim can also be found in fiction for children; indeed, the Young Adult rack in the school library and the public library frequently displayed books that contained aggressor–victim stories that were overtly sexual in content. When the Oak Town girls, seeking stories of female agency, encountered these, they sometimes became profoundly upset.

> 'This is that book I was telling you about.' Samantha pushed it across the library table toward me. It was a paperback with a picture on the cover of a schoolgirl who might have been 12 sitting nervously in a dentist's waiting room. The title was *The Trouble With Wednesdays*. The spine was labelled *YA*. It must have been

from the city's public library. I turned it over. The back cover said, 'This book is about learning not to let grown-ups abuse you.'

'It's good,' said Samantha quietly. 'But at first I didn't like it. I got to Chapter Eight and I really felt bad about it. I cried. I gave it back to my mother and said, "Take this back to the library!" So then she read it, and she said I really should finish it. So I did.'

'What's wrong with Chapter Eight, Samantha?' 'It was gross. I really didn't like it. I felt too sorry for the girl . . . You can look at the book, if you want to.'

Samantha returned to class and I turned to Chapter Eight. The girl in this story had been going to the orthodontist every Wednesday afternoon and he had been molesting her, feeling her and rubbing up against her. She hadn't been able to get her parents to listen and believe her explanations of what was wrong. She felt sick and powerless.

I flipped to the final pages. She did get her parents to listen. They helped her. She felt better as the story ended.

Samantha thought Chapter Eight was 'gross'. Alisa and Lacey thought *Flowers in the Attic* was 'gross'. Cara thought it was 'gross' when Daniel forced his kisses on Miyax in *Julie of the Wolves*. The girls seemed to use the word 'gross' to mean 'nauseating and extremely unpleasant', and they used it, in particular, to refer to any violent or sexual (or both) events occurring in the stories that they were reading.

This is not to say that violence and sex, as found in such stories, *always* triggered this reaction, since, after all, the girls were *interested* in sex, and they didn't seem, moreover, to fear it. For example, they seemed to take positive delight in the developing relationship between Winnie and Jesse in *Tuck Everlasting*, as well as in the occasional kisses that the *Babysitters Club* members exchanged with the boys in their lives; and they talked openly about the incestuous relationships in *Flowers in the Attic* without disgust — and Jerrica even made a chart on a piece of scrap paper outlining incestuous liaisons across several generations as she went on to read the whole *Flowers in the Attic* series. Violence did not necessarily offend them either: Mae Tuck's murder of the man in the yellow suit did not upset them; and when the white hunters shot the wolves from airplanes in *Julie of the Wolves*, the girls felt anger, but not disgust. Clearly, something other than sex and violence called for the use of the word 'gross'. Something else upset Samantha when she read *The Trouble With Wednesdays*. I would suggest that the word 'gross' was called for in those cases when someone was powerless to resist violent treatment or abuse. And when that powerlessness and that abuse was associated with sexuality, the girls perceived it for what it was: a gender-specific threat.

Girls who were reading in order to explore the possibilities for female agency in the world around them valued any stories that demonstrated those possibilities. They resisted the cultural messages that conveyed images of female passivity and submissiveness, but despite this resistance, the culture continued to reproduce itself. The great majority of girls, it seems, were growing up with a view to keeping their places in the gender hierarchy, and were not attempting to subvert the social order. Brownmiller (1975) has suggested that the existence of the act of rape produces in women an attitude that makes them fearful of men as a group, and that that same attitude of fear helps to maintain patriarchal control of society. I would suggest that the presence of the aggressor–victim motif in stories for children works in the same way. The message is clear: female agents had better watch out because the threat of male sexual violence is always there in the world; and this threat holds for *all* women. The girl in *The Trouble With Wednesdays* did nothing to bring on her victimization; it was just waiting for her there in the orthodontist's office. She found out that it isn't really possible to take care of yourself.

I believe that in Oak Town the gender-specific threats of violence found in children's fiction amounted to the prevailing culture's *counter*-move to the girls' resistant desires for agency. At first, it surprised me that references to horror as entertainment would appear so frequently in the field notes for this study. After all, these field notes centered only on classroom life. But classroom life is social life, this situation, like any other, acted as a forum for the beliefs and values of the culture within which it existed. Cultural discourses concerning gender (as well as race and class) entered the classroom with the people who spent their days there. Curriculum materials and activities were chosen according to guidelines shaped by cultural constraints, and people wore and ate and carried with them cultural items (like paperback novels) which were the products and the carriers of many discourses. It is not surprising, therefore, that horror stories made a real impact in the school.

Early in the school year, before the snow came and the roads got icy, Lacey and her family drove for seven hours to a huge and elaborate mall in order to shop. While there, her family paid the $10 'family fee' to see the Medieval torture devices on display. Lacey told a group of girls about it during recess: 'It was so interesting! At first my Dad thought that $10 was an awful lot to pay, but afterwards even he thought it was worth it.'

Later that month, at Halloween, Matt Peterson casually brought the video of 'Thriller' to school, thinking that the kids might enjoy watching it with their Grade Three reading buddies. But the kids had all seen it too many times to find it interesting.

Then, in November, Marcia showed me the horror novels that she kept in her desk. She said that they belonged to her mother, but that her mother didn't mind if she read them. One was called *The Unloved* by John Saul. It had a picture on the cover of a woman with a young body (wearing a blue nightgown), on the one hand, but with a horrible skull for a face on the other. Marcia said that she had stayed up past midnight on Saturday reading it.

In December, *Flowers in the Attic* came to school. For two full weeks, the girls could talk of nothing else. Many had with them at school the copies that their mothers had bought at the drugstore, and all the girls were either reading it or at least trying to read it. At lunch and during recess, the girls would review the plot, make comparisons with the movie, and examine copies of the other books in the series. Several told me: 'V.C. Andrews is my favorite author.'

It was clear that horror stories were making an impact in the school, and that this was a direct reflection of a similar impact being made by horror stories in cultural discourses *beyond* the classroom. I wondered why horror might be so popular. If the huge shopping mall, a Canadian cultural Mecca, was displaying torture devices, it must be because someone expected that such devices would have a strong enough appeal to attract large numbers of people, and so make money. *Flowers in the Attic* was a raging best-seller. Stephen King had a popular novel coming out every few months. What was it about horror in general, and horror stories in particular, that the people of Oak Town and others like them found so appealing? I began to seek an explanation.

Horror has been a part of popular culture for a long time. Twitchell (1985) traces horror back to the cave paintings of the Magdalenian people, paintings made circa 10,000 BC. He goes on to state his belief that certain of horror's images have been a part of popular culture since the turn of the nineteenth century. He examines three such images, those of the vampire, the Frankenstein monster and the werewolf, pinpoints their origins in the Gothic novel, and follows their development both in the novels of the 1890s and in the films of the 1930s. Twitchell suggests that we are currently in the midst of a revival of horror in popular culture. Horror is everywhere: in music (the monstrous makeup of the kind worn by the rock group Kiss is now a commonplace affair), in music videos, in books, in painting, on television (almost half the made-for-television movies are 'terror-jerkers'), and even in the names of breakfast cereals (for example 'Count Chocula' and 'Frankenberry').

What does it mean? Twitchell, in a chapter entitled 'The Psychological Attraction of Horror', explains that horror monsters may frighten us because they are acting out those desires that we fear, and he creates a Freudian analysis to suggest that horror stories make visible the repressed desire for incestuous relationships. In a similar vein, Reed argues (1989) that the reason why the demon-lover motif of horror stories has survived for so many centuries is that it represents a powerful projection of evil arising from repressed personal and social conflicts. Count Dracula's sucking blood from a comatose virgin's neck, Frankenstein's carrying off his screaming bride, and the well-behaved gentleman's turning, against his will, into a ravenous monster (i.e. the werewolf) on the eve of his wedding, are all images of evil that reverberate with meaning, both within the individual and within the culture. And all, moreover, present images of male aggressors and female victims.

It is clear that the classic horror stories involving Count Dracula, Frankenstein, the 'Phantom of the Opera', and the Werewolf are all stories of male aggressors who seek female victims, and that the pleasureable emotion which horror excites is in fact a form of fear. Psychological responses to horror are socially shaped. Twitchell writes (1985) that, in preparation for his book on horror, he watched hundreds of hours of film and video material that was much like pornography. It was rife with misogyny, incest, rape, and aggressive antisocial behavior directed against women. He notes that although, in the horror movies of the 1930s, sexual violence was never actually shown on the screen, 'it was always there; we're just now getting a good look at it' (p. 70). Modern horror films include such genres as 'slice and dice' and 'stalk and slash' films, in which women are pursued, stabbed, and dismembered. Gene Siskel, film critic for *The Chicago Tribune*, has suggested that it is not a mere coincidence that these films should happen to have proliferated in the years in which the Women's Movement was flourishing. These films have a clear message: women should get back in line (p. 69).

Whatever the psychological attractions of horror, horror nonetheless represented a form of entertainment that was accessible to the children of Oak Town: they could read the horror novels their parents bought; they could (often) watch the horror movies their parents rented; and they could find 'scary' and 'spooky' books in the school library. However, although the girls did seem to enjoy 'scary' books as much as they enjoyed 'sad' books, the 'scary' library books were in many ways quite different from 'scary' horror movies, and the girls did sometimes encounter horror stories that upset them profoundly. What was the difference?

There was what might be called a 'horror-in-literature continuum' in the fiction that the Oak Town girls read. Some of what they read, on the one hand, was mild enough for them to enjoy, while some of what they read, on the other hand, was extreme enough to frighten them. The girls were anxious to help me understand what *was* and what *was not* acceptable to them. Jerrica explained: 'I love to read scary things that give me the shivers in bed. Have you ever read *Blind Date*? I don't know who the author is, but it was pretty scary.' Alisa offered this: 'I love mysteries and scary books. But not too scary, because then they give me bad dreams. *Deadly Rhymes*, that book about the mystery in the boarding school that I gave you to read, that one was just right.' Samantha added: '*Holding Me Here* was a really good book. It was scary all the way through. This lady had a husband who drinks and he forced her to stay in the house, and he *almost* beat her up. It was scary like *The Haunting at Cliff House*. Same kinda book, you know? At the end he comes in the house looking for her! It was scary!' And Cara, finally, made this comment: 'The best books I read all year were *Weekend* and *Slumber Party* and *Locked in Time*. They were all mysteries that Jerrica found on the Young Adult rack. They were all scary and they were all *excellent*.'

The kinds of mysteries and the scary books that the girls enjoyed so much were, I believe, distant relatives of the 'stalk and slash' horror movies. In claiming this, I am making an intertextual connection that the girls themselves did *not* consciously make. Like the horror movies, the 'scary books' in question often featured some sort of threat, directed at a girl or woman, and in the girls' novels in particular, the female protagonist often found herself in a graveyard at night, or in a murky fog, or in a dark old house, faced with the ever-present possibility that something unnamed and unknown might jump out at her. In these books, however, such a possibility only very rarely materialized; and when something *did* jump out at her, it usually turned out to be harmless: a friend who followed her there, or a bat on the wing.

The *Nancy Drew Files* were instances of this kind of 'scary book'. Cara described the *Nancy Drew* plots to me: 'There's always some boy in the story who's trying to kill her or one of her girlfriends. He's always hanging around in the background somewhere. Sometimes they even put him on the cover.' Alisa also noticed this. The *Nancy Drew* covers always looked the same. And it is Nancy Drew, of course, who always solved the mystery — that was always the same too. Hardly surprising therefore, that, although the sixth-grade girls did still occasionally read a *Nancy Drew*, they all felt that they'd outgrown them. The focal girls for the study, all of whom could read easily, had now turned to the Young Adult racks for their mysteries. Many of these 'scary books' were highly satisfactory. Some however, they found very upsetting.

The Trouble With Wednesdays, found by Samantha on the Young Adult rack, moved one step further along the horror-in-literature continuum towards a more explicit form of gender threat. In this book, the female protagonist did not solve her problem through her own agency. Her parents, instead, solved it for her. In this way, the book resembled the two *Sweet Valley High* books, *Hostage* and *All Night Long*, in which Jessica was faced with the possibility of rape, but was rescued both by luck and by her sister Elizabeth.

Marcia enjoyed the Young Adult mysteries, but she had also taken an interest in those kinds of books that seemed to take the next step in the horror-in-literature continuum: adult horror novels. Marcia, for example, read her mother's John Saul and Stephen King novels and enjoyed them very much. She said she preferred John Saul's books because they were more like mysteries, and because things always turned out all right at the ending. Evidently, it disturbed Marcia that Stephen King sometimes left things unresolved at the end of a story. In Stephen King novels, the horror was not always eliminated, nor was it always fully understood.

The girls seemed to have different levels of tolerance for horror. Alisa and Samantha were perhaps the two girls who were most sensitive to frightening things. Julie, for her part, enjoyed mysteries, but said that after reading the beginning of one particular Stephen King novel at home, she had a nightmare, and her mother warned her not to look at Stephen King again for a good long while. Many of the sixth-grade children saw a movie called *New Kids*, and it passed unremarked. But Jennifer told Alisa not to watch it. She explained: 'There's this one part where the girl is taking a shower. The bad kids take her pet rabbit and cut its throat and throw it in the shower with her! You don't want to see that.'

Sometimes, as mentioned, the horror was *too* horrifying — even for Marcia, who had the highest tolerance for horror among all the girls. When Marcia's parents rented three Freddy Krueger movies over the Christmas vacation, Marcia watched them all. She was sorry she did. She told me about it. 'Freddy Krueger, like people burnt him and then he comes back and he's like a ghost, and he's got razor blades for fingers and he chops people up and when he was alive he used to take girls and he used to kill them in a broiler! He lurks in this factory, it's where he lives, and he can do anything. And he grows into your dreams? And when you dream he always, well, you can't really sleep, cuz when you do if you get killed in your dream, then you're really killed in life? And they usually wake up screaming. After I saw that, I couldn't eat. It was disgusting and it didn't make sense, either. And I couldn't sleep for two weeks. Sometimes he comes back with you in your dream, and when you wake up he's still there. And he's in your house and stuff . . . You're helpless.'

It is interesting to note that Marcia's parents seemed to be *unaware* of her response to the Freddy Krueger movies. They allowed Marcia to read and watch horror stories, and they themselves saw no harm in it. Like most people who lived in Oak Town, they thought that horror stories were harmless. They had read horror when they were children, and they didn't believe that they had suffered any adverse effects from it.

If *Nancy Drew* was at one end of the horror continuum for children, Freddy Krueger was at the other. Different children, as mentioned, could tolerate different levels of horror, and it seemed that, like adults, they learned to tolerate *more and more* violence and gender threat as they moved along the continuum in their reading and viewing choices. One explanation may be that horror had a numbing effect. What might have been frightening at first grew less frightening on repeated viewing. While Frankenstein and Count Dracula were frightening 50 years ago, nowadays they no longer made people feel anything more than amused. Perhaps contemporary audiences now required real blood, dismemberment and death before they could feel anything.

What, then, do people actually experience when moving along this horror continuum? I believe that it is likely that women and men feel different things in response to horror. Twitchell reports (1985) that among the large proportion of teenagers found in the audiences at horror movies, it is predominantly the teenage *women*, and only a few of the teenage men, who call out warnings to the female victims on the screen. The other teenage men, and nearly all the older men, in these audiences call out encouragement to the *stalker* instead. And the movie itself, what's more, is nearly always filmed from the stalker's point of view (p. 69).

If the horror audience is invited to identify with the monstrous aggressor, so may be all those men who grow up in a patriarchal culture. Such men would be encouraged to take pleasure in the feelings of power, dominance and gratification that the horror protagonist himself experiences. But it is not likely, however, that those *women* who grow up in the same kind of patriarchal culture would feel immune from the threat to the female that is also central to these horror stories. On the contrary, for women, it would be much easier to identify with her *helplessness*.

Although the Oak Town girls, as already mentioned, enjoyed the 'scariness' of most mystery books, the ones which they were best able to tolerate were mystery stories in which the heroine could eventually both *understand* and *control* whatever was threatening her. On the other hand, they were disturbed by any tales in which the heroine had to rely on others for protection from threat; and they were truly horrified by any tales involving senseless violence directed at helpless people.

Variations on the Theme

There were eight girls around the table in the school lunch room, leaning on their elbows, looking at each other over the debris of sandwich crusts and saran wrap and apple cores. Jerrica tossed her mane of hair and said, 'It's really good. It's about a brother and a sister who get married and have children.'

Karen interrupted. 'No, it was her *uncle*.'

Alisa leaned forward. 'No, that was in the second book. My mother said!'

Lacey made a face. 'Oh, yuck! Tell us the story.'

Jerrica took a breath. 'Well, the grandmother and the mother lock the four kids in the attic. The grandmother puts hot tar on the girl's head, and they starve them so they have to drink each other's blood!'

Lacey gasped. 'Why did they give it that title?'

Jerrica explained. 'The kids made flowers in the attic because they could never go outside. They made flowers and a garden up there, and a swing. The grandmother said she'd give them food and shelter, but never love and kindness. Because they should never have been born.'

There was silence. Amanda straightened her back. 'My mom would never let me read a book like that. I mean, I'm just guessing, but I don't think she would.'

Jerrica said, 'Well, my mom said she didn't think it was right for me, but she let me read it. It took me two weeks to finish it.'

Alisa spoke. 'My mom said it was really, really good. She read it in two nights. But I just read the first chapter, because it made me sick. It's a true story, isn't it?'

Lacey was disdainful. 'No it isn't! You don't think people would really *do* that, do you?'

Jerrica announced, 'I have *Petals on the Wind*, the sequel to this book. There are five in the series.'

'My mom has the whole set,' said Leah. 'She won't let me read them, though, and she won't let me see the movie. She says I can watch it when I'm older. But I'd rather read the book. Can I borrow yours, Jerrica? Books are better than movies anyway, because they tell more detail.'

The bell rang. The girls rose, cleared away their lunches, and walked back to the classroom.

Flowers in The Attic was not a classic horror story: no weird monster threatened and stalked a female victim. Instead, an ordinary mother was transformed into an emotionless, greedy madwoman who imprisoned her four children in the attic. There she and her mother starved and mistreated them for a period of two years. *Flowers in the Attic* was a story of child abuse.

The Oak Town girls didn't think that *Flowers in the Attic* should be classified as a 'scary' book: Marcia said that the book wasn't scary but *exciting*; Cara said that it wasn't scary but *sad*; and Nicole said that it wasn't scary but just *interesting*.

The girls were clearly fascinated with the details of the plot. For two weeks they sat at lunch every day reviewing it for the benefit of those girls who hadn't yet read the book. Nicole said: 'The most terrible thing was when the mother put arsenic on Cory's donut and he died. He choked to death.' Alisa added: 'You know what the grandmother did to her? She poured tar all over her hair!' Jerrica offered: 'It was so awful when they were starving to death because they couldn't eat the poisoned food, and they had to drink blood to stay alive.' Lacey was able to hum the suspenseful music from the movie version, and said that she liked the way in which they filmed the mother being strangled by her own scarf.

All the girls were interested, but some were more frightened or repulsed than others. Several of the girls found themselves unable to read more than the first chapter. Alisa wanted to read *Flowers in the Attic* because she'd watched the movie and heard the other girls talking about it, but she read the first chapter and then stopped. She explained. 'It wasn't scary, but it had a lot of sick things in it. My sister saw the movie, and she never slept for a week. She was petrified. Do you think it's a true story?' Lacey's reaction was similar: 'At first I liked *Flowers in the Attic* because everyone else did. But it turned out to be so slow to read, and really disgusting. I quit reading it.'

Neither Alisa nor Lacey understood the incest theme that was central to the plot of *Flowers in the Attic* until Jerrica explained it to them. Lacey was shocked. 'Oh, no!' she responded. 'You're kidding!' Alisa was silent for a minute, and then said again that she didn't intend to read the rest of the book. 'It's boring, stupid, and gross.' And yet Jerrica and Marcia were fascinated by the incest theme, as well as by everything else about *Flowers in the Attic*, and they pored over each of the books in the series. Jerrica was especially interested in the implied connection between the incest that went on in the current generation and Bart's mental illness a generation later.

While the sixth-grade girls at Oak Town School devoted themselves to discussing *Flowers in the Attic*, Meryl Streep's new movie, *Cry in the Dark*, was being released. This movie told the story of an Australian woman who was accused of murdering her baby. In that week also, a child-abuse case was concluded when a lawyer was convicted of beating his five-year-old daughter to death; *People* magazine had covered the trial. And what's more, John Saul's novel *The Cradle Will Fall* appeared in Marcia's desk at school. People were fascinated with stories of child abuse. It seems to me now, several years after that time, that *Flowers in the Attic* was one of several 'texts' that proved popular at that historical moment, each related in theme and each existing *in intertextual relationship* with the others. The Oak Town girls had access to all the texts I have named, texts which shared a *dialogic* quality. By this I mean that each text assumed that the reader had some prior knowledge of other texts of its kind, and interpreted its readers as people who shared certain attitudes toward child abuse. The Oak Town girls were learning to be interested, through their interactions with cultural discourses characterized by intertextuality (Fairclough, 1989).

I began to wonder if stories of child abuse amounted to a new form of horror. If so, they were certainly not gender-specific in the same way that classic horror stories were. They did not confine themselves to male aggressors and female victims, and yet they were still stories of aggressors and victims, stories of the powerful preying upon the powerless. The sixth-grade girls, who routinely read fiction, and helped themselves to their mother's books, tried hard not to see themselves as powerless people, but they knew that as children they *were* virtually powerless in relation to the adults in their lives. The Oak Town boys, being children as well, also felt powerless in this way, but they were *not* reading and discussing and dwelling on stories of child abuse — and thus being defined by a whole range of cultural texts as passive victims — in the same way that the girls were. The reading of fictional stories of child abuse may have served to reinforce the girls' feelings of powerlessness in much the same way as did the other kinds of horror stories.

Flowers in the Attic similarly derived much of its shock value by perverting a traditional, and gender-specific, cultural message: a mother's love is selfless and unchanging. Perhaps the horror story was more horrifying when the perpetrator of violence involved was female, because patriarchal culture has always promoted the view that it is the *female* members of society who are responsible for providing love, and sustaining human relationships. Horror stories with female monster-protagonists flourished in the 1980s. The highly successful movie *Carrie* is but one example.

Why, therefore, was it *fun* for Jerrica and Marcia and so many of the other girls to read *Flowers in the Attic*? One reason, which it would not be wise to overlook, may be the fact that the novel also contained sexual scenes between the two older children that were designed to be both sentimental and titillating. Episodes of abuse alternated with episodes of self-conscious nudity, declarations of devotion, and lengthy expressions of physical affection that were meant to be erotic. The association of the *sexual,* on the one hand, with the *violent* on the other may have led the young reader to associate the two. Adrienne Rich has said (1970): 'When you strike the chord of sexuality in the patriarchal psyche, the chord of violence is likely to vibrate in response, and vice versa.'

While horror mixes sex and violence and is intended to provoke fear, it is pornography, on the other hand, that mixes sex and violence with a view to provoking *sexual arousal*. It is hard to distinguish between the 'stalk and slash' subgenre of horror, on the one hand, and hard core pornographic films where women are chained and slashed and put through meat grinders on the other. And what is also interesting to note is that in recent years, with the proliferation of cultural texts centered on child abuse, more pornography has been produced that involves children. The intertextual connections are there: when popular entertainment media, such as films, pulp novels, and magazines, provide texts centered on a 'child-as-victim' theme, the field of pornography then begins to take advantage of, and contribute to, those kinds of cultural discourses which create a popular interest in child victims.

The Oak Town girls did not seem to have access to any hard core pornography. They did, however, have access to horror stories in which the powerless people were exploited, and this meant that they were engaging in 'private lessons', during the course of which they were learning how to enjoy horror. They were encouraging their girlfriends — and, in turn, being encouraged themselves — to move further along on a continuum of horror stories that began with female characters who could understand and control what threatened them, and ended, with victims who were horribly abused and then finally obliterated.

Gendered Subjectivity

A substantial part of the answer to the question 'What does the practice of reading mean to the Oak Town girls?' has to do with the ways in which the girls constructed their individual and yet gendered identities through reading. If a girl's 'subjectivity' does indeed consist of her conscious and unconscious thoughts and emotions, her sense of herself, and her ways of understanding the world (Weedon, 1987), then we can begin to see how certain aspects of a girl's identity came into being in Oak Town as a result of her reading of fictional texts. This is not to psychologize reading, or to make it seem that a girl's responses to fiction are ever only private and personal in character. The creation of the girls' identity is largely framed by discursive practices aimed at regulating conflict and rebellion (Foucault, 1979). In the present case, these practices are aimed at regulating the human desire for agency, as well as the degree of autonomy of those people who must be controlled. Cultural discourses involving images of aggressors and victims were working in Oak Town to produce female citizens who accepted the moral order by 'choice' and by 'free will'. There was a concrete and physical connection between discourse and subjectivity: cultural discourses were working to construct the identities of people who, in turn, would regulate their own behavior.

I believe it happened in this way. The desire for agency inevitably developed, in Oak Town, among the older children, who were beginning to understand their own powerlessness at the hands of adults, and becoming less able to take it for granted. Cultural discourses promised such children that they would have agency, when they reached adulthood, in the more public domains denied to them as children. But it promised them only gender appropriate forms of agency. As a result, boys now expected to grow up to become men who would act as agents in the world at large, and who would wield economic and political power, while girls, on the other hand, now expected to grow up and become women who would act as agents within the family, and who would wield power in the domain of personal relationships. Such were the gender-specific forms of adult agency found in Oak Town. It is not surprising that female children were dissatisfied with these arrangements. They too would have liked to enjoy a wider sphere of influence in the world when grown-up. This female desire was personally 'constructed' by every Oak Town girl I came to know. It was pervasive.

But it was also profoundly threatening to the social order. If the majority of female people were actually to insist upon exercising agency in the public world, if they were to ignore their culturally assigned responsibility for maintaining and nourishing the private world of human relationships, the whole gender hierarchy would crumble, and the world might crumble with it. The Oak Town girls used their reading of fiction as a means of exploring new possibilities for female agency. They took the books that the culture produced for them and used them to try on, and analyze, forms of behavior that went *beyond* what was culturally approved for them. In short, they *resisted*. But the prevailing culture then *countered* that resistance by providing horror stories. Horror may mean different things to women and to men, or to people of different ages. To the sixth-grade girls of Oak Town, it seemed to convey the message of female helplessness in the face of a pervasive and gender-specific threat of violence.

The Oak Town girls were not simply considering these matters analytically. They were actually fantasizing about exercising agency, and engaging psychically with aggressor-victim motifs that inspired feelings of horror and revulsion in response to images of violence and powerlessness. As a result, they became, in all likelihood, less able to act upon their desires for agency. Walkerdine throws light upon this psychic conflict which arises in response to the cultural messages implicit in the fiction that girls read. She suggests (1984) that when girls read fiction, 'the positions and relations created in the text both relate to existing social and psychic struggle and provide a fantasy vehicle which inserts the reader into the text' (p. 165). Girls could thus imagine themselves quite easily as powerless, as victims.

The threat that the Oak Town girls felt was a gender specific one, because the violence that gave rise to it was associated with *sexuality* in the particular discourses of that culture. The girls learned to associate violence with sexuality whenever instances of sexual titillation were included in the mystery and horror novels that they read. Pleasant sexual feelings arose, but these were paired with apprehensive ones, and as a result, the girls learned to associate the *pleasantly erotic*, on the one hand, with the *threatening* on the other. The more horror stories they read, the greater the threats that they learned to tolerate.

Here, then, we have a portrait of 'subjectivity' that is indeed 'precarious, contradictory and in process, constantly being reconstituted in discourse' (Weedon, 1987). Although mysteries and horror stories (at least *some* of them anyway) were fun for the girls to read, Freddy Krueger films, on the other hand, were still disgusting. The desire for agency persisted, but the counter-messages of powerlessness and helplessness that the extremes of horror conveyed were too painful for the girls to tolerate. Accordingly, at the age of 11 or 12, they were taking in the same message but in a gentler form: 'Moving freely in the world was dangerous. There were forces out there that could get you if you didn't watch out. Taking risks could get you into real trouble.' Being a 'good' girl was the wisest choice.

Notes

1 Weedon provides (1987) an excellent description of 'language as discourse', if the reader would like a fuller explanation of how cultural forces work in such a way as to 'construct' an individual's subjectivity.
2 I have wondered about the extent to which the *Canadian weather* is a factor contributing to children's feelings of boredom during the winter months. There are times when the weather is so cold that children cannot safely spend time outdoors, either 'playing' in the company of their friends or hanging out at the local convenience store, in the way that their contemporaries in warmer climates might. The Oak Town children stayed in touch by telephone during these cold periods, and used Nintendo games, videos and all the other amusements that their affluence brought to them to fight boredom when they could not leave their homes. Certainly, the severe Canadian weather played *some* part in the children's feelings of boredom. Marcia's mother, for example, told me that the very cold, 18-day-long Christmas holiday that took place during the year of the study kept the whole family confined to the house, 'and nearly did us all in'.

Chapter 6

Private Lessons

Revisiting a Vignette

The introduction to this book promised an explanation of this moment of classroom life:

> I stood at the book table at morning recess time. Kids were milling around this sixth-grade classroom, eating and visiting, strolling out to their lockers in the hallway and back again. I watched Leah and Sarah talking at the desks. Both had permed, chin-length hair, parted on the side and clipped with a pretty barrette. They wore pastel sweaters and knee-length black pants, spotless white socks and white runners. Leah had an apple, Sarah a muffin.
>
> I straightened out the books on the table and tried to make the covers visible. Matt Peterson, the teacher, had pushed the table right up against the wall under a bulletin board displaying three large laminated illustrations of Lloyd Alexander's *The Book of Three*. Matt had drawn the pictures himself, using pastels. Done in shades of rust and green and gold and brown, these all showed the character of Taran on horseback, fierce and heroic, drawn sword in hand, battling several ugly creatures at a time.
>
> Leah wandered over to the table and picked up a paperback with a photo on the front. The title said *Satin Slippers #1: To Be a Dancer*. She told me 'I've read this one. You can get all these *Satin Slippers* books at Coles bookstore. I have the first six, and I'm going to be getting #7. My mother thought they looked good, so she started buying them for me.'

Sarah joined us. 'She did? She just bought them for you'

'Yuh,' said Leah. 'We were in the store, and she just said to me, "Oh, Leah, this looks like a great set!" And when I got to reading them, I liked them too, but first my mother just fell in love with the cover of them. She bought me the first three because she liked the cover so much.'

I looked at the cover. It was made from a photograph of a tall, slim young woman in pink tights and leotard with a gauzy skirt and toe shoes. She stood by a tall window in a graceful pose, long blonde hair flowing, arms extended. It was a hazy photo, in soft focus.

Sarah said, 'I read this one, the first one, and it was okay. But I just love the cover too. I stare and stare.'

The end-of-recess bell rang and the two girls moved to their desks with everyone else. It was silent reading time. Sarah took *Satin Slippers #1* with her and placed it flat on her desk. She sat, hands in her lap, gazing at the cover.

Detailed theoretical explanations of the cultural discourses and processes which appear in this vignette have been presented in the first five chapters. But, as a first step toward bringing this book to a conclusion, I would like to provide three more general comments. Firstly, this vignette is a portrait of *privilege*. Secondly, this vignette shows us adults working, as representatives of a dominant patriarchal culture, to shape children's lives in culturally appropriate ways. And thirdly, it shows children engaging with cultural discourses through the specific interactions of their daily lives.

As we have seen repeatedly, and again in revisiting this vignette, the Oak Town children lived comfortable lives of affluence and economic privilege: they dressed well, and ate well; they received their education in comfortable surroundings; their classrooms were carpeted; there were plants in the school's main entryway, paintings on the walls, and plenty of books for them to borrow, both in the library and on the classroom shelves; and they spent lots of time in well-equipped music, drama, home-arts and science rooms.

Certainly, their privilege was both economic and racial in character. The influences of race and class are harder to see at work in homogeneous groups such as that group found at Oak Town, but they surely are there. I have been free to leave race and class unmarked for the most part in this account of life in Oak Town. This is because I can assume that many readers will recognize, and to some extent identify with, this community. They were, in a sense, members of the dominant North American culture, familiar to so many. But consider the contrast between Oak Town School and the inner-city American schools described by Taylor and Dorsey-Gaines (1988). Their ethnography of home and school life portrayed grim, cold, concrete school buildings with bars at the windows, and very few resources. Indeed, only 20 minutes away from Oak Town School, in another such inner-city neighborhood, Canadian Indian children were attending school without many of those material comforts that the Oak Town children took for granted. Privileges of class and race were factors in their daily lives, even though the people of Oak Town were not aware of it.

The people of Oak Town took their places as members of the Canadian middle class by virtue of both their race and their relative affluence, rather than by virtue of their level of education. Of the 14 parents (of the 7 focal girls for this study), 5 did not finish high school; and only a few had attended university. And yet *all* seven of their girls now lived in homes marked by the kinds of material resources and privileges that conditions of affluence serve to provide[1]. Their parents had money to register them for swimming lessons and gymnastics, and other activities, to provide them with transportation there and back again, and to buy them any special equipment that the activities required. They also had enough money to indulge in both fashionable clothes and fashionable hair-care. The Oak Town children and their parents expected a certain kind of lifestyle. In particular, the parents expected to have time to do coaching and other forms of volunteer work; and their relative economic security left them free enough from worry to be able to do these things. In other, quite different communities, parents worried about providing enough food and heat, and about how safe their children were both during and after school time. Not in Oak Town, however.

The children's expectations both for economic security and for their level of success in school were shaped in part by their race. Ogbu (1985, 1990) has written of the ways in which larger cultural forces shape the expectations that Black children have about their experiences in school. The children that he studied eventually came into conflict with the school's explicit demands for conformity to the language, and with the other various requirements imposed by the predominantly White culture. And they rejected school education as a result. The Oak Town children, on the other hand, because they were White, accepted the demands of the school more easily and complied with them, at least superficially. Later, I will explore some of the ways in which race and class shaped the children's experiences of gender in Oak Town. The point I want to make here is simply that the subjectivities portrayed by the vignette above were 'constructed' by discourses of *class* and *race*, as well as by discourses of gender.

The opening vignette also shows us adults at work in children's lives, teaching the culture's values, and encouraging children to behave in cultur- ally appropriate ways. The children's teacher's cultural influence is represented, in this vignette, by the portraits of Taran that he created and then used to decorate the classroom. Matt Peterson cared enough about the children to try to stimulate their interest in the novels that they were to study, and to work at maintaining an attractive classroom space for them. But at the same time, he was blind to the influence of gender as a factor in literary experience, and he was not aware either that girls saw Lloyd Alexander's books as 'boys' books' or that pictures of warriors on horseback proved not reassuring but *alienating* for the girls in question. Nor was he aware of how, through his paintings, he was positioning boys, on the one hand, as people of action and violence, and girls, on the other hand, as *invisible people*.

The parents are represented in this vignette by Leah's mother, who was demonstrating her own attachment to cultural ideals of femininity, as well as her acceptance of the reading of fiction as an appropriate activity for her daughter: she gave financial as well as moral support to the publishing industry's marketing devices; she unconsciously and uncritically accepted the imposition of certain cultural values both on her daughter and, indirectly, on her daughter's friend; she encouraged their participation, in gender-appro-priate ways, in the consumer economy.

Publishers and bookstore owners, and indeed all adults who make money from the production and sale of children's books, are also represented in this vignette. Because they are engaged in the struggle to make a profit, they are *not* blind to gender as a factor in children's reading. But at the same time, they are not interested in what the effects of gender might be in the lives of the children themselves. They see gender as a mere marketing factor, and concentrate on using what they know of people's beliefs about gender to manipulate children in such a way as to increase their own profits. This strategy has met with tremendous success. Consider the phenomenon of the *series book*, of which millions of copies have been produced and sold. It is successful because it appeals to cultural gender ideals, because it takes advantage of the cultural obsession with time, and because it provides yet another material possession for the girls to acquire.

Finally, the vignette provides us with a convincing portrait of a particular child's engagement with a particular cultural message that has been delivered through a photograph and via a piece of text: Sarah is mesmerized by *Satin Slippers #1*. Although the message represents the *culture's* view, and although it has been put into her hands by adults, there is no denying that Sarah herself is also busily at work responding to and internalizing some version of that message. She is not merely acted upon — she is herself *active*.

The opening vignete thus makes it clearer as to how both children's lives and the work of teachers are created and shaped by cultural forces. Turning away from those traditions of research which *psychologize* reading, I hope instead to conclude this book by looking at the girls' reading of fiction through three very different 'lenses' — to focus on this cultural phenomenon from three different perspectives, if you will. Firstly, I will reconsider what we've learned about the Oak Town girls' reading from the perspective of one who views reading as a *social practice*. Next, I will look again at what I've learned about the girls' reading activities, but this time from the perspective of one who views gender as a *cultural construction*. Finally, I will look once more at the educational context in which the Oak Town girls were growing up.

Focus on Reading

So much is missed when we think of reading merely as an internal, psychological process; or when we assume that it takes place only within the minds of individuals; or when we assume that it goes on without regard either to time and place, or to human relationships. The previous chapters offer a wealth of ethnographic evidence in support of the premise that the activity of reading is in fact an external, social one. They make the point that reading always occurs in a particular cultural context, and that what might be seen as the individual psychology of reading is 'constructed' and then enacted in response to forces operating as part of that particular culture.

So much becomes visible when we realize that large groups of people *share* certain kinds of norms and practices that govern how we act as readers, how we go about teaching reading, and how we go about learning to read — and the norms in question differ from group to group. The people of Oak Town formed one such group. Reading is not idiosyncratic, but is always constrained by certain social norms. At Oak Town, these cultural norms served both to shape the various forms and uses that reading, as an activity, acquired at home and at school, and to determine, to a large extent, *what* exactly was read by the children involved.

Reading at Home

Jerrica sprawled on the bed, teddy beside her, a *Sweet Valley High* paperback in her right hand, a can of Pepsi in her left. She wasn't reading. She was listening to the radio, and looking at the digital clock on the night table next to her. It was 7.00 p.m.

She sat up. The CKCK Radio disk jockey was announcing the winner of 'Monday Night Favorites'. Jerrica and her friend Rene had both sent letters to CKCK for the Monday-night draw. Jerrica listened for both of them every Monday becaue Rene had her dance lesson and couldn't be at home.

Then the announcer read Rene's name! 'Just give us a call, Rene, and you'll be a winner! Call us now at 987–6543. Call within five minutes . . . and the records are *yours!*' Jerrica ran to her desk, pushed things out of the way, and grabbed the pink telephone to dial the CKCK number. She gave Rene's name, and the voice at the other end told her that the five records would be sent to her home. 'Congratulations, and thanks for listening!'

Jerrica ran downstairs to tell her parents. They shared her excitement for a little while, and then Jerrica returned to her room to wait for Rene to get home. Jerrica was excited and restless. She pushed her stuffed animals into a neater pile, picked up a few clothes, reshuffled the piles on her desk, straightened the 20 or so *Sweet Valley High* books on her bookshelf. She tried to settle down to read.

At 10.00 p.m. she was finally getting into her story. She'd talked to Rene on the phone, discussing the possibilities for splitting the five-record prize. She'd called Cara and Nicole to tell them about Rene's winning. She'd written a letter to her pen pal and she'd written in her diary. Now she was sitting in her pink and white pajamas, immersed in *White Lies*, feeling John's distress over the fact that the girl he loved loved someone else. She hadn't looked at the clock for half an hour.

The door opened. Mom. 'Jerrica, for heaven's sake, it's after 10 and you have to go to school tomorrow! Get this light out and let's get to sleep!' Jerrica didn't take her eyes from the page. 'Jerrica!'

Her mother marched in and took the book out of her hands. Jerrica was annoyed. 'Mom, I'm really not tired.'

'You won't be saying that in the morning. Now that's enough. I don't want to see your light on again.'

Her mother left, turning the light off on her way out. Jerrica bunched down in the bed, tense and resentful, staring out into the dark.

Jerrica and the other Oak Town children used reading, as an activity, in order both to participate in a consumer economy and to achieve their own social purposes. Jerrica collected books in the same way that she collected stuffed animals; she consumed the books marketed for her in the same spirit in which she consumed Pepsi; and she used reading, as an activity, in order to fill her empty hours, to try on gendered social roles and situations, and to compete for status at school[2].

Jerrica read fiction. European and North American women have been reading fiction in their homes for more than 200 years. The practice began, perhaps, as a form of rebellion against the clergy's control of women's reading (Luke, 1992), and the invention of the printing press, on the one hand, and the rise of the middle class on the other were what made such a practice possible. Texts were produced in greater numbers, leisure time, for some women, was created, and reading matter became available for private uses. In the eighteenth century, moreover, novels began to be written which focused on the private world, and thus allowed the use of reading for private ends (Graff, 1987).

Late in the twentieth century, the reading of fiction formed part of Jerrica's own rich and complicated lifestyle. Indeed, the reading of fiction at home served the purposes of many women in her community. Jerrica's reading of fiction at home was in many ways a manifestation of the cultural ideology of individualism (Apple, 1982) that supported the consumer economy in which she lived: books were among the many material possession which she enjoyed in the comfortable isolation of her own bedroom; books supported her in her time alone, a condition made inevitable by a cold climate, by single-family homes, and by individual schedules of activity; and the reading of fiction was an activity which Jerrica's parents approved of, both because it served as a gender-appropriate time-filler, and because they saw it as a worthwhile personal achievement.

Reading at School

Ethnographic studies of literacy in children's lives are very useful to teachers, who can see and understand more of what is happening in their classrooms when they can use a 'cultural lens' to examine what goes on there. For example, an analysis of culture can provide an explanation for why girls and boys tend to have different reading interests, as well as different test scores. Girls may learn to 'read', and to do school tests, more easily than boys do when what counts as reading requires compliance. That is because the gender-specific norms that govern *their* behavior in and out of school are more conducive to cooperation and compliance with adult authority than are those norms that govern the *boys*' behaviour in these places.

Even when something *other* that compliance is involved in the practice of reading, teachers still gain in understanding when they examine their classrooms both with cultural messages and with cultural constraints in mind. Walkerdine (1985) and Solsken (1993) suggest that, in 'child-centred' classrooms, girls may be at a disadvantage when taking part in activities that require risk-taking and creative behavior. This is because the patriarchal culture is signaling, and the usually female teacher, in turn, is acting as a model for gender-appropriate behavior that is intuitive and supportive in character, and *not* concerned with taking risks or with leaving others behind in the pursuit of individual glory or achievement. I agree that girls can indeed be at a disadvantage when the curriculum calls for divergent thinking and creative problem-solving, because in these cases the gender-appropriate norms for girls' behavior cartainly are in conflict with what is being called for in the classroom. My point here is that teachers can see and understand more of what happens in their classrooms when they take the trouble to consider the influences of cultural discourses in the children's lives.

Certainly, the kind of reading that the Oak Town girls were encouraged, by their culture, to do at home did contribute to their success in the sixth-grade classrooms at Oak Town School. To begin with, the school *approved* such reading activity. Reading for leisure became a central curricular goal early in the twentieth century (Luke, 1988), emerging as part of the progressive approach to literacy. The reading of popular literature is encouraged, in Oak Town and in many other places, as supportive of the school's literacy training. And it was the Oak Town *girls* who were doing this leisure reading, thus receiving extra practice in getting meaning from print, and acquiring a greater degree of familiarity with the conventions of fiction. In this sense, the girls had the advantage in any classroom where fictional reading was valued.

What is Being Read

Cultural norms and values also have an important role in determining *what* it is that children read. As seen in Chapter 2, the Oak Town boys, on the one hand, were encouraged and guided by gendered cultural values to read *non-*fiction, while the Oak Town *girls*, on the other hand, were encouraged by their own set of such values, to read *fiction* instead. The girls *were* able to understand the *concept* of 'fiction', although they did not often use the word. They spoke instead of the 'stories' they read, and of the fact that they preferred to read books about people and their lives and relationships. What they did *not* understand was the distinction that their teachers and I made between 'literature' and 'fiction'. For the girls, stories were stories.

Any writing can be considered to be 'literature', because literature is 'a *construct*, fashioned by particular people for particular reasons at a particular time' (Eagleton, 1983, p. 11). So what gets 'constructed' as literature? Once, as a classroom teacher, I would have said that what counts as literature, on the one hand, is any well-crafted writing on subjects that are of significance to people, but that fiction is a broader category that includes *all* imaginative writing — whether worthy or not, whether significant or not. Now, however, I would no longer make such a simple binary distinction. Since the Oak Town study, I have had to turn away from attempts to establish a theoretical category of 'literature', one based on certain intrinsic character-istics of the text, and I have had to reject the definition of literature as 'that body of writing that exists because of inherent imaginative and artistic qualities' (Lukens, 1986, p. 3). I no longer believe that literature is somehow better than other writing because it is beautifully written, appeals to universal aesthetic standards, expresses ideas of lasting and universal inter-est, and is shaped by universal psychological processes (Bettelheim, 1989; Frye, 1974; Sloan, 1984; Vandergrift, 1986).

Since my year in Oak Town, I have been able to 'deconstruct' these definitions and see how impossible it is to establish and compare the 'worth' of different fictional works. Literature is any kind of writing which, for some reason or another, *somebody* values highly (Eagleton, 1983). Value judgments have a lot to do with what is judged to be literature and what isn't, and value judgments have their basis in ideology. Ideology consists of 'those modes of feeling, valuing, perceiving and believing which have some kind of relation to the maintenance and reproduction of social power' (Eagleton, 1983, p. 15).

Prevailing social power structures are reproduced in part as a result of the fact that what gets counted as literature becomes the *literary canon* — i.e. the approved works of fiction that will be taught and studied in schools. The values inherent in what gets chosen as literature are those endorsed by the dominant culture and its institutions — such as schools, libraries, and publishing houses. And what counts, in the first place, both as adult literature and as children's literature are written works that are consistent with selective gender, race and class interests, with the unfortunate result that children's books in general have upheld White male views of reality at the expense of those of both women and people of color (Christian-Smith, 1989b). The school's literature curriculum is a powerful cultural discourse which all children are required to encounter and consider.

In imposing upon the children one definition of literature through Tom Penner's 'Structured Tales Curriculum', Oak Town School effectively privileged Penner's particular choices of text, and perpetuated a 'selective tradition' (Williams, 1977) that offered a narrow view of human experience. In Oak Town, knowledge in the text was first identified and then 'handed down' to the people in school. The people themselves had no role in constructing knowledge. And because this 'selective tradition' valued *male* experience only, girls involved could not benefit from its study in the way that the boys, on the other hand, could. If the girls accepted the canon, they were forced to identify with someone else's experience of the world, and to see their own experience as peripheral or deviant (Fetterley, 1978). If, on the the other hand, the girls *refused* to take the canon seriously, they then risked being seen as uncooperative (and thus as 'unfeminine') in school. They were also more likely to turn away from literature in school and toward mass-marketed fiction instead, because this latter kind of fiction took girls' experiences seriously, and offered them a world that they knew. The girls thus chose fiction that valued and validated their own female experience, but at the same time they remained aware that such experience was *devalued* by the prevailing culture in which they were growing up.

Focus on Gender

I believe that the gender messages that I have identified as emerging from the dominant discourses of North American culture in fact reach almost *all* Canadian children. Almost all Canadian children are exposed to the idea that the genders are opposite and antagonistic, and that boys are more active than girls. Almost all would see that the culture privileges emotional experience and friendship for girls, and the violent assertion of the will for boys. But it is also true that those cultural messages are received and acted upon in different ways in different communities. The ways in which the Oak Town sixth-graders experienced gender are not necessarily the ways in which other 11-year-old children experienced gender.

Gender is 'nested within class and race realities' (Weis, 1990, p. 55). By this, I mean that the business of constructing a gendered subjectivity takes on a different character for people of different races, and for people of different social classes, because the discourses of race and class and the life experiences which position people as certain kinds of subjects, are not the same for separate groups. Consider, for example, the ways in which two men might 'construct' themselves as capable of acting. A White male teacher at Oak Town school and a male aboriginal teacher in a nearby Canadian Indian community would be unlikely to construct the same expectations concerning the exercise of their agency at the workplace. The Oak Town teacher could reasonably 'contruct' himself as someone free to choose — or invent, perhaps — a new Language Arts curriculum. Growing up with racial privilege, and interacting with cultural discourses of gender, he could come to see himself as quite capable of acting on behalf of the children that he teaches, and, moreover, as likely to judge well. (I don't think it likely that a *female* teacher of his race would have been positioned in the same way as similarly capable of such wise judgments.) The male Indian teacher, on the other hand, who would not have been surrounded by any such cultural discourses positioning him as a capable and independent actor in the world, would be more likely, as a result, to construct himself as someone who is aligned to the authority of the school. He might not be as likely to risk curricular innovation because those racial discourses which position him as inferior in intellect and judgment have also made him less likely to expect success. I am speculating here about the ways in which subjects of the same gender might respond to a similar task in different ways, because I want to show that gender is constructed according to class and race positions.

In a similar way, the gendered subjectivities constructed in relation to the prevalent cultural ideals of beauty would be different for an Oak Town woman, on the one hand, and for a single mother living in poverty in a nearby city on the other hand. It seems to me to be likely that both women would have been positioned, by certain cultural images delivered through mass media, as people whose worth is founded on their physical appearance; and that both would be likely to desire the kind of beauty that is presented in those images. But what such cultural discourses do not make explicit is the role that *money* has to play in the achievement of beauty. A woman without money for cosmetics, and without the leisure time in which to carry out the various rituals of grooming, will not find it easy to achieve the culture's ideal image of beauty, no matter what she looks like. The Oak Town woman, who *does* have money and time for the requirements of beauty, would find it easier to 'construct' herself as worthy and successful. On the other hand, the woman living in poverty, deprived of the means to 'acquire' beauty, would be more likely to construct herself as *unworthy*.

My point here is that gender is not merely a relational category — i.e., not merely a simple category whose definition becomes clear only in relation to its opposite. People will also respond to gender beliefs according to their specific racial and class positions within society. And gender is also intimately affected both by other aspects of culture and by other forms of experience (Purcell-Gates, 1993). There are rich and complex connections between gender identity and all various cultural representations of gender. This may become clearer if we examine in greater detail the greeting-card phenomenon mentioned in Chapter 3. During the course of the Oak Town study, I collected more than 30 notecards, postcards, and birthday cards, all of which bore pictures of girls and women reading. I found only *two* representations of boys and men reading; one was a bookmark published by the Canadian Children's Book Centre, and the other was an advertisement for the Literary

Guild. The notecards that I collected often bore reproductions of nineteenth-century paintings. What is remarkable here is not the fact that many painters of the past chose women who are reading as their subjects, but the fact that twentieth-century entrepreneurs should now have chosen to reproduce and market these same images. (Appendix C contains descriptions of these cards.) Certain images were chosen for these greeting cards for the reason that these images represent certain cultural ideals. And the cards sell because the pictures on them represent something lovely and desirable, something that, for the women who buy them, reverberates with meaning[3]. A semiotic analysis of these images reveals messages about race and class and gender that appear very appealing to the women in question.

None of the people on these notecards are people of color. All appear to be people of means, well-fed and well-dressed, and to be living somewhere in times past. The past is represented nostalgically: sunlight and light from the fire bathe interiors and gardens in a warm glow; animals recline at a mistress's feet; and a basket of knitting lies nearby. Old-fashioned ruffled white dresses with blue sashes are the costume of choice, and the women have long hair, carefully dressed in curls or swept up on the head.

Elaborate white dresses and hairstyles like these cannot be worn by any women who work. The women on the notecards are women who are instead at leisure to read. Nothing about their posture or their attitude suggests that they are doing thoughtful or academic reading. This is relaxing private reading, and strictly a woman's sphere. The cultural message of the notecards is that reading is appropriate for those White women who have youth, beauty, money, leisure time, and who are required, by the gendered imperatives of their culture, to live only in the private sphere. A further subtext is that women are, ideally, *peripheral* to the real and public world.

The world of the notecards is redolent of a past that, if it existed at all, existed only for very few women indeed. I believe that for the women of Oak Town, and for other women of similar race and class, this is an ideal that brings pleasant associations, and that presents a state to which they feel they might themselves aspire. The notecards sell because they provide a means to the women's vicarious participation in that ideal — a means for them to insert themselves into the text and then fantasize about their participation in the world conveyed to them through that text (Walkerdine, 1985). The notecards are thus part of one cultural discourse that positions women as out of place in the public world.

What can it mean for other women of a different race and class to have reading presented in this way? Perhaps, for women of a different race but in similar economic position, the notecards encourage similar sorts of fantasy experience. Perhaps still other women, because they only shop for groceries and other such necessities, do not see the notecards at all. For *all* those people who do see them, however, the notecards present a *false* picture of women's place in society. They provide yet another textual framework in which women are positioned as peripheral to the work of the world, and in which women of color and poor women are made invisible.

In a similar way, the discourses presented through the series books written for girls again make people of color, working women and single mothers invisible. Most of the series books deal only with the lives of affluent White girls. The *Babysitters Club* does include, in its membership, one Japanese American girl and one Black American, but both are clearly portrayed as middle class. And in all the *Sweet Valley* books, consumerism is taken for granted, the connections between race and poverty are obscured, and the wide variations in different families' incomes and degrees of education do not appear at all. The series books also take gender for granted, and treat the negative consequences of cultural gender constructions (such as the threat of violence) as something natural and inevitable.

A cultural analysis of gender in the classroom could begin to counter these unfavorable discourses, first perhaps by making them visible, and secondly by helping teachers and children to appreciate the negative consequences associated with the way in which gender is constructed by the prevailing culture. What does it mean for girls and women to live with the threat of violence, and with harassment in their daily lives? What does homophobia cost when it is enacted in daily life? How is the experience of the peer group different for girls and for boys? What happens when an individual is positioned by the culture as a person of feeling or a person of action, on the basis of gender? What are the consequences when cultural constraints work to maintain the boundaries between women and men, and to reproduce the social inequalities with which we live?[4] Teachers need to consider these questions with children, in order both to help them see how gender shapes their lives, and to help them understand the power differentials that operate in society. Classroom talks with children about these texts and issues would be a beginning. There are, however, other practices, too, that would both help teachers in their attempts to do justice to the complexity of gender, and, at the same time, shed light on the role of gender in literacy learning and in literate behavior. I would like now to go on to describe some of these other practices.

Focus on Schooling: Literacy, Curriculum and Pedagogy

Education is a political enterprise. It is possible to think of 'politics' simply as involving arrangements of tacit rules for the conduct of human life, but such a definition does not account for the fact that those rules refer, in turn, to power-structured relationships of a kind which allow one group of people to control another. Politics thus concerns power, and education is *not* politically neutral. The schooling process plays an important role in the reproduction of culture and society, with all its power differentials and inequalities. As we have seen in Chapter 4, the schooling process can place limits on children's lives, and can work, moreover, *against* the children's best interests.

What this means is that teachers need to be more aware of the political nature of their work, if they hope to counter the injustices of schooling and not instead blindly participate in them. The awareness that schooling works to reproduce social inequality and injustice has implications for educational premises and educational *practices*. Each of the following, for example, can be considered as a political arena: *literacy, curriculum,* and *pedagogy*. Teachers need to see that when children emerge from the school system with competence in certain kinds of literacy but not others, that very fact has political implications. They also need to realize that what the curriculum identifies as appropriate content has been chosen in order to serve certain political interests. Finally, teachers need to be aware that certain pedagogical practices do support cultural reproduction, while others, on the other hand, do not.

Literacy

Literacy learning also always has political implications. Literature on the history and sociology of literacy provides many examples of the reproduction of unequal levels of competence in reading and writing for different social classes and for people from different cultural backgrounds (Luke, 1994). Recent studies have added to this body of literature by contributing evidence supporting the role of gender in the production of differences in literacy (Solsken, 1993; Blenkinsop, 1993; Kamler, 1993). Certainly, the Oak Town girls' reading of fiction was a factor in creating and maintaining gender divisions, whether we choose to see it either as a gender practice, or as a gender 'display' (Goffman, 1976), or again as an enactment of certain gendered values.

Gendered literacy helps to construct not only gender division, but also inequalities between the genders, as well as the use of violence on the part of one gender against the other. Mine is not the only study that reaches these conclusions. Moss, who examined (1989) high-school students' writing in

English classes in Britain, showed how the content of the popular works of fiction that the girls were reading had an influence on their writing. The girls that she studied used writing to recreate the kinds of romantic fictional worlds in which they thought they ought to live. Lankshear and Lawler, described (1987) the ways in which the Australian high-school girls that they studied took notes, memorized, and wrote recall answers on tests. These working-class girls believed that these forms of literacy were appropriate expressions of what the culture demanded of them: unquestioning compliance. Other researchers have suggested that boys may use writing to 'do boy' in thoroughly alarming ways. Gilbert summarized (1989) a story, written in school by four 9-year-old boys, in which the boys ward off an attack on their classroom by Easter bunnies armed with grenades and other artillery. With incredible feats of skill and heroism, the Easter bunnies (named after the boy authors) defend themselves and triumph, while the girls in the class, and some of the 'weaker' boys, are either blown up, killed by firing squads, or crucified. These boys used writing to construct themselves as the people that their culture was instructing them to be: people who win the day, and maintain their own superior status, through acts of violence. Finally, Hu studied (1992) the recreational writing of her 14-year-old son, and came to similar conclusions. This boy and his friends, all of whom read Stephen King novels and other horror novels, wrote stories about overwhelmingly powerful male characters who engaged in violent and sadistic acts. Hu, after analyzing the stories and interviewing the authors, concluded that the boys were reading and writing both to 'try on' extreme and culturally ideal forms of masculinity, and to distance themselves from the opposite sex.

I cite these other studies to show that I am not alone in believing that gendered differences in literacy practices are harmful. Children do not *freely* choose to do literacy differently: they are *positioned*, on the basis of their gender, to choose certain ways of doing literacy. And those choices are made within a political context in which men have more power than women. They become part of patterns of difference that cannot be valued equally in a world where the two genders are not valued equally.

Curriculum

It was Language Arts time in Matt Peterson's room and the children were working on their activity cards. I picked another one up off the counter. It said, 'The *protagonist* is the leading character or hero of the story.

Name the protagonist of your novel. Give reasons for your choice. What does the protagonist of your book look like? Use information from your story to write a physical description of the main character. Paint his or her portrait.'

I returned the card to the counter and went over to examine the paintings on the bulletin board. Three different versions of Taran, it seemed. They must have been done to complete the activity card I'd just read.

I sat in my chair and made notes. Matt brought me a booklet and asked, 'Have you seen this?' I hadn't. It was *Reading: A Novel Approach*, written by Janice Szabos, and illustrated by Vanessa Filkins. It called itself a 'Good Apple Activity Book, Carthage, Illinois, for Grades 4–8'. It didn't seem to be the source for the activities shown on the activity cards.

I read the introduction: 'This booklet can help to enrich the reading experiences of children in Grades Four through Eight.' It spoke of the novel as 'a vehicle for explorations which involve critical and creative thinking'.

I saw that it had reproducible activity sheets.

It also said that the center of the program was 'discussion group training'. Students would be taught to run their own discussion groups and then evaluate them. The reproducible sheets were lists of questions for the group discussions. The program also included a system of record-keeping.

I closed the booklet. It occurred to me that I have never seen Matt use discussion groups for any subject. I returned the book to Matt's tidy desk. His day book was neatly and completely filled out.

Curriculum, like literacy, is located in a political arena. Ideology is both explicit and implicit in what is taught. Eisner says it this way (1982): 'What pupils learn is not only a function of the formal and explicit content that is selected; it is also a function of the manner in which it is taught. The characteristics of the tasks and the tacit expectations that are a part of the structured program become themselves a part of the content' (p. 414). I believe that the children of Oak Town School were influenced both by the formal content of the literature curriculum and by its 'tacit expectations'. Its formal content excluded the world-views and values of women, racial and ethnic minorities, and working people; and by representing and naturaliz-ing the ways and the beliefs of mainstream culture, this content contributed to the reproduction of cultural values from one generation to the next. From the characteristics of the tasks that they were given, the children learned that the study of literature should focus upon those characters who were important both for the roles that they played in relation to plot, and for what they looked like. The children learned not to look too deeply, but instead to value the individual acquisition of those 'facts' that had been identified both by an external authority and by a cultural tradition. The Oak Town children were being positioned as intellectually limited — as people who wrote merely in order to meet certain requirements, and to display what they knew. They were being 'constructed' as people who read only to locate certain information, or to entertain themselves. They were *not* being constructed as people who read and wrote in order to be able to think critically about the world around them, and about what might be done to improve it.

Oak Town's curriculum for the teaching of writing also had political implications. This curriculum centred on those particular genres (such as expositions, reports, certain forms of poetry) that privileged specific forms of knowledge, and that served the purposes of the education system that had been designed to transmit that knowledge. Students were expected to use their writing activities in order to demonstrate a limited form of competence with written language, to comply with teachers' demands, and to learn a *hidden curriculum* promoting compliance with authority. In a city near Oak Town a 'process writing' curriculum offered students a choice of genres and topics, and valorized student 'voice'. But the process-writing curriculum has been criticized both for limiting student writers to personal and narrative genres, and for not explicitly teaching them about those genres of power which could provide them with access to broader educational and employment opportunities (Comber and O'Brien, 1993).

What form, then, *should* the literacy curriculum have taken? Because I believe that all forms of curriculum are political, and that all such forms further involve a hidden curriculum, I would like to see a *curriculum of critique*: one which includes the literature of women and of minorities, as well as some of the traditional canon, but which treated all literature as the subject of critical analysis by asking questions about *whose perspectives* a text represents and *whose interests* it serves. I would like to see a curriculum for writing which challenges the status quo by valuing both originality and the ability to shape language to a specific (political) purpose. With the help of others who also value such a critical perspective in education, I am beginning to develp a vision of what this curriculum might look like in action.

It could take the form of Fairclough's (1989; 1992) Critical Language Studies (CLS) scheme, in which a curriculum involves a form of language-study that is designed to highlight the connections between the use of language, on the one hand, and unequal relations of power on the other. Classroom texts (whether those that are part of the literary canon or those that are produced by the students themselves) could be described and then interpreted in terms of the *social contexts* which frame them. Such an interpretation of a text would involve showing just how the particular genre and discourse modes which it involves have been used to 'construct' meaning. Students could be asked to identify the presuppositions and world-views implicit in their texts, texts which they would then explain by reference to the social power structures and cultural contexts surrounding them. The curriculum could then help the students to develop a cricital awareness of the ways in which history, on the one hand, and the vested interests of certain groups of people, on the other hand, serve to determine the way in which language is used. The curriculum could furthermore require that students become researchers of language by *problematizing* both classroom and literary texts. This could be achieved through the use of critically framed conversations, questions and tasks. Comber and O'Brien suggest (1993) that the critical analysis could begin in primary grades with discussions of such questions as 'Who had the power in this story?' or 'How has the author made some characters very wicked and some very good?' This kind of curriculum could help to increase the students' awareness of those devices that work both to construct powerful textual meanings and to represent one particular world-view.

I would like to see a literacy curriculum which highlights the relationship between language and power by placing 'the role of language in perpetuating or constituting systems of domination' at the center of our inquiry (Edelsky, 1993). This kind of curriculum would make it more difficult both for schools to promote, and for teachers to participate in, the reproduction of social inequality. It might also work to alleviate some of the feelings of alienation and boredom which have plagued traditional curriculums, and countered teachers' best efforts with resistance.

Pedagogy

Pedagogy has the power to oppress. Where education takes the form of imposition and inculcation, where the teacher's power is the precondition for the establishment of pedagogic communication, pedagogy itself becomes a form of symbolic violence (Bourdieu and Passeron, 1990). Many brilliant teachers have objected to this form of symbolic violence, and have worked to develop alternative pedagogies that 'guide' rather than control the child in his or her learning. Bernstein (1990) recognizes their work by distinguishing between 'visible' and 'invisible' pedagogies. 'Visible' pedagogies are those in which the teacher's teaching is explicit and aimed at knowledge transmission (as in the lesson described at the start of Chapter 4). 'Invisible' pedagogies are those that require the teacher to facilitate and guide the children in such a way that they appear to be learning without direct instruction. Child-centred classrooms and whole-language programs would fall into this latter category, as would process-writing classrooms and readers' workshops, which also involve invisible pedagogies where the child appears to lead the way, while in fact being supported and guided by an attentive teacher. Although these pedagogies have many benefits for the individual child — including both opportunities for the child to collaborate with others in constructing knowledge, and opportunities for the child to exercise agency — they also present serious problems. Their personal and private focus tends to support cultural values of individualism and personalism, and ignores the influence of the larger cultural context in people's lives (Gilbert, 1989; 1991). These pedagogies also place *women* teachers, in particular, in conflict, because they require that women suppress in themselves the capacity for initiative and the independence that they seek to nurture in *children* (Walkerdine, 1985). Female children, moreover, must deal with the adult teacher's demonstration of gender appropriate behavior, behavior which differs from the behavior being asked of them in the classroom (Solsken, 1993). Finally, invisible pedagogies offer to the children only the *illusion* of choice and control: in the end, the teacher's power remains implicit, and children are not deceived.

Both the visible and invisible forms of pedagogy, as already pointed out, amount to manifestions of symbolic power. Mr Peterson's visible pedagogy, transmitted to students certain norms, values, and beliefs that served to express a particular ideology of hierarchical social relations (Simon, 1983). These norms, beliefs and practices concerning literacy are non-negotiable, and part of the 'hidden curriculum' through which ideologies of authority are taught — ideologies that restrict the individual. Alisa, for example, whose parents were anxious to have her attend law school some day, was in fact learning a form of literacy that would actually hinder her there[5]. She read for facts, she memorized diligently, and she wrote neatly, but these things were likely to be more helpful to her in a job as a bookeeper. She was learning what Anyon would classify (1980) as a lower-middle-class form of literacy, where all that was required was to find and to present the right answer. Alisa did not get any practice or guidance in school in thinking critically, in analyzing texts, or in developing either an argument or an informed opinion.

Current pedagogies of knowledge-transmission thus serve to discourage children from independent critical thought. When teachers approach the study of literature as if its first purpose were the acquisition of 'facts' about the text, and as if knowledge of the text were something that comes from experts *outside* the classroom, children end up believing that they should read only in a passive way, and that they should look to others for the *meaning* of what they are reading. When teachers do not value the children's own ideas, when they do not provide time for discussion, when they keep the children dependent upon themselves (the teachers) for the right answers, they end up teaching them that 'learning' process amounts to the obedient absorption of information, and that critical enquiry is something irrelevant.

It seems to me that there must be other kinds of pedagogy that implicitly teach values that teachers would *like* to impart. Bleich suggests (1989) that it has been possible for some teachers to move from a study of 'language as an individual skill and literacy as a remedial subject to language as an intersubjective experience and literacy as an investigatory subject which one learns actively and in community with others' (p. 6). Consider, for example, a pedagogy that supports both literature-response groups and literature-study groups. Literature-*response* groups allow children the responsibility for expressing their own individual views concerning a book that all the children in the group have read. Literature-*study* groups require that the children work *collaboratively* toward 'constructing' meaning from the text that (again) they have all read, exploring possible interpretations and analyzing the author's craft (Edelsky, 1988; Peterson and Ees, 1990. The form of pedagogy expressed in these groups assumes that knowledge is something that must be created with other people; that people should be active participants in their own education; that they learn only by thinking deeply; and that everyone can contribute something of value. The problem with this pedagogy, of course, is both that the individual responses that the children bring to the groups have already been constructed through various cultural discourses, and that the ways of analyzing text that have already been taught to the children have promoted the veneration of literature and discouraged any critical questions or challenges.

My own belief is that although collaborative pedagogies are less damaging to children than pedagogies of knowledge transmission, such pedagogies do not help children to understand the wide variety of reading positions that are available to them, or foster any understanding of the various cultural discourses that produce both a body of literature and aesthetic responses to the work created. Pedagogy can do more to foster both an aptitude for critical thought and the development of egalitarian values. Requiring that children think critically in school would be a beginning. By 'critically', I mean thinking from a position that makes connections between the use of language and unequal relations of power. Certainly, the Oak Town study suggests some important questions for teachers to discuss with their children within a 'critical' framework. The critical analysis of horror, and of its appeal, ought, for a start, to be undertaken in school; and the necessity for *de-eroticizing* violence also ought to be made the subject of critical discussions. What needs to be modelled for children is a critical stance that grows out of the teacher's awareness of the influence of both language and culture upon our lives.

This critical stance ought then to inform the study of literature. The foundation of this critical stance is the teacher's realization both that texts are constructed in ways which represent certain vested interests, and that readers are positioned, by cultural discourses of race and class and gender, to read and respond in certain ways. Purely personal responses do not exist. Initial readings are likely to be *cultural* readings rather than personal, individual readings. This is because the meanings that readers assign to the texts they are reading have already been shaped for them by certain discourses before they have even begun to read (O'Neill, 1993). Children need to understand this fact in order to gain some measure of influence over their own lives. Readers are positioned to read a text in a certain way, and this process is neither a natural nor a neutral one. But we can at least teach our children to think *critically* about these cultural readings — to recognize them and analyze them, and not pretend that they don't exist. Teachers can also show their children how the same work of literature can be interpreted in several different ways, ways that are positioned or created by particular sets of values and beliefs. In Oak Town, literacy was a means to compliance. It ought, instead, to be at the center of a critical approach to the study of texts.

Many teachers are involved in the struggle to find pedagogies that will teach social and ideological analysis. This includes work toward identifying those reading and writing strategies that will produce 'proper literacy' — strategies that will allow the students both to know the world and to have an impact on it. Shor's (1990) suggestions for 'liberation education', Shor and Friere's (1987) 'dialogical method', and Ellsworth's (1992b) continuing negotiations of feminist pedagogies all point the way. Others are describing classroom practices which consider the acquisition of knowledge by asking critical questions about *whose* knowledge it is and *whose* interests it serves (Comber and O'Brien, 1993; Greifenhagen, 1994; Shannon, 1989; Taylor, 1993).

These people have provided teachers with a place at which to begin. Because the construction of social inequality is such a complicated matter, and because individual contexts differ so much, more teachers will need to take responsibility for creating new, alternative pedagogies that are work-able and effective in specific local contexts.

Final Thoughts

The Oak Town study has a contribution to make to the struggle. Ethnographic research can be criticized — and it *has* been — for failing to empower, or otherwise benefit, the people being researched (Lather, 1986). This study did not benefit the people of Oak Town. But if psychological reality is shaped by relations of status and power, then educators need to see how this shaping process occurs in the daily lives of the children they work with. Private reading practices are *publicly* constructed. They are private only in that they are not easily available to public view.

The private lessons of the Oak Town study are private only in that they must be accepted by individual teachers if they are to have an effect. Perhaps the most important lesson of the Oak Town study is one that I want to believe: if reality is socially constructed, then it can be changed. Yes, the culture imposes limitations on our lives. Gender, race and class all have a profound influence upon how we see the world, and what we can accomplish in it. But, 'social arrangements are not immutable because hegemonic practices are produced in and sustained by a system that is socially constructed' (Brodkey, 1987, p. 68). *Understanding what is happening* is the first step toward cultural change.

I hope that teachers and parents and others concerned with both educational problems and 'private' practices will take three important realizations away from this book: firstly, that the world is a different place for girls and for boys — we need to *see* gender at work in children's lives if we are to understand what happens in classrooms and at home, and if we are to understand how inequality is both 'constructed' and reproduced; secondly, that children are not passive consumers of cultural meanings: they can, and do, resist, and their resistance can give teachers a starting point for working toward change; and finally, that because literacy plays a part in the creation of gender, race and class, because literacy provides us with ways of being in and influencing the world, we need deeper knowledge of literacy as a situated social practice in order to support social transformation.

Notes

1 Only Samantha's father was unemployed, and because he *had*, previously, been employed for a period of years, he was able to collect unemployment insurance during the year of the study.
2 The data for the Oak Town study show that Jerrica, perhaps more than any other girl, used the reading of fiction to help maintain her high social status at school. In

a number of subtle ways, Jerrica let people know that she read between 15 and 20 novels a month — more than anyone else in the class managed to read. Jerrica saw her status as 'the girl who read the most' as an *individual* achievement, and she continued to compete successfully with Cara and Samantha to keep her title.

3 We have seen in Chapter 4 that there exists what Luke refers to (1994) as a 'sexual division of literacy'. In Oak Town, and in other middle-class Canadian communities, it is a woman's job to buy and write and send both notecards and greeting cards.

4 Teaching boys — like Gilligan's (1982) boy Jake — to embrace abstract conceptions of justice, while encouraging girls, on the other hand, to live by a contrasting ethic of caring (like Gilligan's girl Amy did) makes it possible for grown-up boys to create and to participate in war. Marilyn French (1985) and other feminists have suggested that war and blatant abuse are two consequences of investing power in one gender while denying it to the other.

5 The fact that Alisa's parents want her to become a lawyer may reflect their desire for her to improve her social-class standing. Moving up in one's social class is not as easy as cultural ideologies (like those inherent in the Horatio Alger stories of the nineteenth century) would suggest. Hard work alone is not likely to enable someone to acquire the right kind of education for 'moving up'. I am suggesting that 'improper literacy' helps to prevent the necessary educational achievement.

References

ALTHUSSER, L., 1971, *Lenin and Philosophy and Other Essays*, New York: Monthly Review Press.

ANDERSON, G. L., 1989, Critical ethnography in education: Origins, current status and new directions, *Review of Educational Research*, **59**, pp. 249–270.

ANSARA, A., GESCHWIND, N., GALABURDA, A., ALBERT, M., and GARTELL, N. (Eds), 1981, *Sex Differences in Dyslexia*, Towson, MD: Orton Dyslexia Society.

ANYON, J., 1984. Intersections of gender and class: Accommodation and resistance by working-class and affluent females to contradictory sex role ideologies, *Journal of Education*, **166**, pp. 25–47.

ANYON, J., 1980, Social class and the hidden curriculum of work, *Journal of Education*, **162**, pp. 67–92.

ANYON, J., 1981, Social class and school knowledge, *Curriculum Inquiry*, **1**, pp. 3–42.

APPLE, M. W., 1982, *Education and Power*, Boston: Routledge & Kegan Paul.

APPLE, M. W., 1979, *Ideology and Curriculum*, Boston: Routledge.

APPLE, M. W., 1993, *Official Knowledge*, New York: Routledge.

ASHTON-WARNER, S., 1963, *Teacher*, New York: Bantam Books.

ATWELL, N., 1987, *In the Middle: Writing, Reading and Learning with Adolescents*, Upper Montclair, NJ: Boynton-Cook.

AU, K. H., 1980, Participation structures in a reading lesson with Hawaiian children: Analysis of a culturally appropriate instructional event, *Anthropology & Education Quarterly*, **11**, 2, pp. 91–115.

BARONE, T. E., 1990, 'On the demise of subjectivity in educational inquiry', paper presented at the annual meeting of the American Educational Research Association, Boston.

BARTON, D. and IVANIC, R. (Eds), 1991, *Writing in the Community*, Newbury Park, CA: Sage.

BERNSTEIN, B., 1990, *Structuring of Pedagogic Discourse: Class, Codes and Control, Vol. 4*, London: Routledge.

BETTELHEIM, B., 1989, *The Uses of Enchantment: The Meaning and Importance of Fairy Tales*, New York: Random House.

BLEICH, D., 1978, *Subjective Criticism*, Baltimore: Johns Hopkins University Press.

BLEICH, D., 1989, 'Feminism and the teaching of literacy', paper presented at the annual meeting of the International Reading Association, New Orleans, LA.

BLENKINSOP, S. J., 1993, 'Children's acquisition of classroom literacy experience', unpublished doctoral dissertation, University of Oregon, Eugene, Oregon.

BLOOME, D. and BAILEY, F., 1989, 'From linguistics and education: A direction for the study of language and literacy', draft prepared for the National Council on Research on English and NCTE Assembly for Research, Conference on Multidisciplinary Perspectives on Literacy Research, Chicago.

BLOOME, D. and SOLSKEN, J., 1988, 'Cultural and political agendas of literacy learning in two communities: Literacy as a verb', paper presented at the meeting of the American Anthropological Association, Phoenix, Arizona.

BLUMER, H., 1969, *Symbolic Interactionism: Perspective and Method*, Englewood Cliffs, NJ: Prentice-Hall.

BOURDIEU, P. and PASSERON, J., 1990, *Reproduction in Education, Society and Culture*, London: Sage.

BOURDIEU, P., 1991, *Language and Symbolic Power*, Cambridge, MA: Harvard University Press.

BOWLES, S. and GINTIS, H., 1976, *Schooling in Capitalist America*, New York: Basic Books.

BRODKEY, L., 1987, Writing critical ethnographic narratives, *Anthropology & Education Quarterly*, **18**, pp. 67–76.

BROWNMILLER, S., 1975, *Against Our Will: Men, Women and Rape*, New York: Simon and Schuster.

CAMITTA, M., 1993, Vernacular writing: Varieties of literacy among Philadelphia high school students, in STREET, B. V. (Ed.) *Cross-cultural Approaches to Literacy*, pp. 228–246, Cambridge: Cambridge University Press.

CHRISTIAN-SMITH, L. K., 1987, Gender, popular culture, and curriculum: Adolescent romance novels as gender text, *Curriculum Inquiry*, **17**, 4, pp. 365–406.

CHRISTIAN-SMITH, L. K., 1989a, 'Going against the grain: Gender ideology in selected children's fiction', paper presented at the annual meeting of the American Educational Research Association at San Francisco.

CHRISTIAN-SMITH, L. K., 1989b, 'Reading and gender', paper presented at the International Reading Association's Annual Convention in New Orleans, LA.

CHRISTIAN-SMITH, L. K. (Ed.), 1993, *Texts of Desire: Essays on Fiction, Femininity and Schooling*, London: Falmer Press.

CLIFFORD, J., 1986a, Introduction: Partial truths, in CLIFFORD, J. and MARCUS, G. (Eds) *Writing Culture*, pp.1–26, Berkeley, California: University of California Press.

CLIFFORD, J., 1986b, On ethnographic allegory, in CLIFFORD, J. and MARCUS, G. (Eds) *Writing Culture*, pp. 98–121, Berkeley, California: University of California Press.

COLTHEART, M., HULL, E., and SLATER, D., 1975, Sex differences in imagery and reading, *Nature*, **253**, pp. 438–440.

COMBER, B. and O'BRIEN, J., 1993, Critical literacy: Classroom exploration, *Critical Pedagogy Newsletter*, **6**, pp. 1–11.

CONROY, P., 1972, *The Water is Wide*, New York: Bantam Books.

COOK-GUMPERZ, J., 1986, Introduction, in COOK-GUMPERZ, J. (Ed.) *The Social Construction of Literacy*, pp.1–15, Cambridge: Cambridge University Press.

CULLER, J., 1982, *On Deconstruction: Theory and Criticism After Structuralism*, New York: Cornell University Press.

DALY, B. O., 1989, Laughing *with*, or laughing *at* the young adult romance, *English Journal*, **78**, 6, pp. 50–60.

DUROCHER, C., 1990, Heterosexuality: Sexuality or social system?, *Canadian Woman Studies*, **19**, 3/4.

EAGLETON, T., 1983, *Literary Theory: An Introduction*, Minneapolis: University of Minnesota Press.

EDELSKY, C., 1981, Who's got the floor?, *Language in Society*, **10**, pp. 383–421.

EDELSKY, C., 1988, 'Living in the author's world: Analyzing the author's craft, *The California Reader*, **21**, pp. 14–17.

EDELSKY, C., 1993, 'Education for democracy', paper presented at the National Council of Teachers of English Annual Meeting in Pittsburgh.

EDER, D. and HALLINAN, M. T., 1978, Sex differences in children's friendships, *American Sociological Review*, **43**, pp. 237–250.

EDWARDS, A., 1987, Male violence in feminist theory: An analysis of the changing conceptions of sex/gender violence and male dominance, in HANMER, J. and MAYNARD, M. (Eds) *Women, Violence, and Social Control*, pp. 13–29, London: The MacMillan Press.

EEDS, M. and WELLS, D., 1989, Grand conversations: An exploration of meaning construction in literature study groups, *Research in the Teaching of English*, **23**, 1, pp. 4–29.

EIDMAN-AADAHL, E., 1988, The solitary reader: Exploring how lonely reading has to be, *The New Advocate*, **1**, 3, pp. 165–176.

EISENHART, M.A. and HOLLAND, D.C., 1983, Learning gender from peers: The role of peer groups in the cultural transmission of gender, *Human Organization*, **42**, 4, pp. 321–332.

EISNER, E., 1982, *Cognition and Curriculum: A Basis for Deciding What to Teach*, New York: Longman.

EISNER, E., 1981, On the differences between scientific and artistic approaches to qualitative research, *Education Researcher*, **10**, 4, pp. 5–9.

ELLSWORTH, E., 1984, 'The power of interpretive communities: Feminist appropriations of "Personal Best"', doctoral dissertation, University of Wisconsin, *Dissertation Abstracts International*, *45, 1225A*.

ELLSWORTH, E., 1992, Teaching to support unassimilated difference, *Radical Teacher*, **42**, pp. 4–9.

ELLSWORTH, E., 1992, Why doesn't this feel empowering? Working through the repressive myths of critical pedagogy, in LUKE, C. and GORE, J. (Eds) *Feminisms and Critical Pedagogy*, pp. 90–119, New York: Routledge.

ERICKSON, F., 1986, Qualitative methods in research on teaching, in WITTROCK, M. (Ed.) *Handbook of Research on Teaching*, 3rd edition, pp. 119–161, New York: Macmillan.

EVERHART, R. B., 1980, *Reading, Writing and Resistance*, New York: Routledge.

EVERHART, R. B., 1983, Classroom management, student opposition, and the labor process, in APPLE, M. W. and WEIS, L. (Eds) *Ideology and Practice in Schooling*, pp. 169–192, Philadelphia: Temple University Press.

FAIRCLOUGH, N., 1989, *Language and Power*, London and New York: Longman.

FAIRCLOUGH, N. (Ed.) 1992, *Critical Language Awareness*, London: Longman.

FETTERLEY, J., 1978, *The Resisting Reader: A Feminist Approach to American Fiction*, Bloomington: Indiana University Press.

FINE, M., 1988, Sexuality, schooling, and adolescent females: The missing discourse of desire, *Harvard Educational Review*, **58**, 1, pp. 29–52.

FISHMAN, A. R., 1991, Because this is who we are: Writing in the Amish community, in BARTON, D. and IVANIC, R. (Eds) *Writing in the Community*, pp. 14–37, Newbury Park, California: Sage.

FISHMAN, P., 1978, Interaction: The work women do, *Social Problems*, **25**, pp. 397–406.

FISKE, D. and SHWEDER, R. (Eds), 1986, *Metatheory in Social Science: Pluralisms and Subjectivities*, Chicago: University of Chicago Press.

FOUCAULT, M., 1979, *Discipline and Punish*, Harmondsworth: Penguin.

FOX, T., 1990, *The Social Uses of Writing: Politics and Pedagogy*, Norwood, NJ: Ablex Publishing.

FREIRE, P., 1973, *Pedagogy of the Oppressed*, New York: Seabury Press.

FREIRE, P. and MACEDO, D., 1987, *Literacy: Reading the Word and the World*, South Hadley, MA: Bergin & Garvey.

FRENCH, M., 1985, *Beyond Power: On Women, Men, and Morals*, New York: Summit Books.

FRYE, N., 1974, *The Educated Imagination*, Bloomington: Indiana University Press.

GARFINKEL, H., 1967, *Studies in Ethnomethodology*, New York: Prentice-Hall.

GILBERT, P., 1989, Personally (and passively) yours: Girls, literacy, and education, *Oxford Review of Education*, **15**, 3, pp. 257–265.

GILBERT, P., 1991, 'The story so far: Gender, literacy, and social regulation', paper prepared for the Center for the Expansion of Language and Thinking Conference, Mount Holyoke College, South Hadley, MA.

GILLIGAN, C., 1982, *In a Different Voice: Psychological Theory and Women's Development*, Cambridge, MA: Harvard University Press.

GILLIGAN, C., 1989, Preface, in GILLIGAN, C., LYONS, N. P. and HANMER, T. J. (Eds) *Making Connections: The Relational Worlds of Adolescent Girls at Emma Willard School*, Troy, New York: Emma Willard School.

GILLIGAN, C., LYONS, N.P. and HANMER, T.J. (Eds), 1989, *Making Connections: The Relational Worlds of Adolescent Girls at Emma Willard School*, Troy, New York: Emma Willard School.

GIROUX, H., 1992, *Border Crossings: Cultural Workers and the Politics of Education*, New York: Routledge.

GIROUX, H., 1986, Foreword, in MCLAREN, P. (Ed.), *Schooling as a Ritual Performance*, London: Routledge & Kegan Paul.

GIROUX, H. (Ed.), 1988, *Teachers as Intellectuals: Toward a Critical Pedagogy of Learning*, Granby, MA: Bergin & Garvey.

GIROUX, H., 1983, *Theory and Resistance in Education: A Pedagogy for the Opposition*, South Hadley, MA: Bergin & Garvey.

GIROUX, H. and MCLAREN, P. (Eds), 1989, *Critical Pedagogy, the State, and Cultural Struggle*, Albany: State University of New York Press.

GIROUX, H. and PURPEL, D. (Eds), 1982, *The Hidden Curriculum and Moral Education: Illusion or Insight*, Berkeley, CA: McCutchan Publishing.

GLASER, B., 1978, *Theoretical Sensitivity: Advances in the Methodology of Grounded Theory*, Mill Valley, California: Sociology Press.

GOFFMAN, I., 1976, Gender display, *Studies in the Anthropology of Visual Communication*, **3**, pp. 69–77.

GOFFMAN, I., 1977, The arrangement between the sexes, *Theory and Society*, **4**, pp. 301–331.

GOODWIN, M., 1980, Directive response speech sequences in girls' and boys' task activities, in MCCONNELL-GINET, S., BORKER, R. and FURMAN, N. (Eds), *Women and Language in Literature and Society*, pp. 157–173, New York: Praeger.

GOODWIN, M., 1985, The serious side of jump rope: Conversational practices and social organization in the frame of play, *Journal of American Folklore*, **98**, pp. 315–330.

GRAFF, H. J., 1987, *The Legacies of Literacy: Continuities and Contradictions in Western Culture and Society*, Bloomington: Indiana University Press.

GREIFENHAGEN, F. V., 1994, *Transference in the Hebrew Bible Classroom: The Dynamics of Authority*, Unpublished manuscript.

HANMER, J. and MAYNARD, M., 1987, *Women, Violence and Social Control*, London: Macmillan Press Ltd.

HARDING, S. (Ed.), 1987, *Feminism and Methodology*, Bloomington: Indiana University Press.

HEATH, S. B., 1983, *Ways with Words: Language, Life and Work in Communities and Classrooms*, Cambridge: Cambridge University Press.

HENLEY, N., 1977, *Body Politics: Power, Sex and Nonverbal Communication*, Englewood Cliffs, NJ: Prentice-Hall.

HERNDON, J., 1968, *The Way It Spozed to Be*, New York: Simon & Schuster.

HOLLAND, N., 1975, Unity, identity, text, self, *PMLA*, **90**, pp. 813–822.

HOSKINS, J., 1987, Complementarity in this world and the next: Gender and agency in Kodi mortuary ceremonies, in STRATHERN, M. (Ed.), *Dealing With Inequality*, pp. 174–206, Cambridge: Cambridge University Press.

HU, Y. T., 1992, 'What writing means to a fourteen-year-old boy', unpublished manuscript.

ISER, W., 1974, *The Implied Reader: Patterns in Communication in Prose Fiction from Bunyan to Beckett*, Baltimore: Johns Hopkins University Press.

JACKSON, P., 1968, *Life in Classrooms*, New York: Holt, Rinehart & Winston.

JENISH, D., 1993, The king of porn, *Maclean's*, **106**, 41, pp. 52–56.

KAMLER, B., 1993, Constructing gender in the process writing classroom, *Language Arts*, **70**, 2, pp. 95–103.

KAPLAN, E. A., 1987, *Rocking Around the Clock: Music Television, Postmodernism, and Consumer Culture*, New York: Routledge.

KLASSEN, C., 1991, Bilingual written language use by low-education Latin American newcomers, in BARTON, D. and IVANIC, R. (Eds), *Writing in the Community*, pp. 38–57, Newbury Park, California: Sage.

KOZOL, J., 1967, *Death at an Early Age: The Destruction of the Hearts and Minds of Negro Children in the Boston Public Schools*, Boston: Houghton Mifflin.

LAKOFF, R., 1990, *Talking Power: The Politics of Language in our Lives*, New York: Basic Books.

LANKSHEAR, C. and LAWLER, M., 1987, *Literacy, Schooling, and Revolution*, New York: Falmer Press.

LATHER, P., 1986, Research as praxis, *Harvard Educational Review*, **56**, 3, pp. 257–277.

LATHER, P., 1992, Critical frames in educational research: Feminist and post-structural perspectives, *Theory into Practice*, **XXXI**, 2, pp. 87–99.

LESKO, N., 1988, *Symbolizing Society: Stories, Rites and Structure in a Catholic High School*, London: Falmer.

LEVER, J., 1976, Sex differences in the games children play, *Social Problems*, **23**, pp. 478–487.

LEWIS, I. M., 1993, Literacy and cultural identity in the Horn of Africa: The Somali case, in STREET, B. V. (Ed.) *Cross-cultural Approaches to Literacy*, pp.143–155, Cambridge: Cambridge University Press.

LIBERMAN, I. Y. and MANN, B., 1981, Should reading instruction and remediation vary with the sex of the child?, in ANSARA, A., GESCHWIND, N., GALABURDA, A. ALBERT, M. and GARTELL, N. (Eds.) *Sex Differences in Dyslexia*, pp. 161–186, Towson, MD: Orton Dyslexia Society.

LUKE, A., 1993, Series editor's introduction, in CHRISTIAN-SMITH, L. K. (Ed.) *Texts of desire: Essays on Fiction, Femininity and Schooling*, London: The Falmer Press.

LUKE, A., 1988, *Literacy, Textbooks and Ideology*, London: Falmer Press.

LUKE, A., 1994, On reading and the sexual division of literacy, *Journal of Curriculum Studies*, **25**, 4, pp. 491–511.

LUKE, A. and BAKER, C., 1991, Introduction, in BAKER, C. and LUKE, A. (Eds) *Towards a Critical Sociology of Reading Pedagogy: Papers of the XII World Congress on Reading*, Amsterdam: John Benjamins.

LUKE, C. and GORE, J. (Eds), 1992, *Feminisms and Critical Pedagogy*, New York: Routledge.

LUKENS, R. J., 1986, *A Critical Handbook of Children's Literature*, 3rd edition, Glenview, IL: Scott, Foresman and Co.

MACCOBY, E. and JACKLIN, C., 1974, *The Psychology of Sex Differences*, CA: Stanford University Press.

MACKINNON, C., 1982, Feminism, Marxism, method and the state: An agenda for theory, *Signs*, **7**, 3, pp. 515–544.

MACKINNON, C., 1983, Feminism, Marxism, method and the state: Toward feminist jurisprudence, *Signs*, **8**, 4, pp. 635–658.

MALTZ, D. N. and BORKER, R. A., 1983, A socio-cultural approach to male–female miscommunication, in GUMPERZ, J. (Ed.) *Language and Social Identity*, pp. 195–216, Cambridge: Cambridge University Press.

MCCONNELL-GINET, S., 1984, The origins of sexist language in discourse, *Annals of the New York Academy of Sciences*, **433**, pp. 123–135.

MCLAREN, P., 1989, *Life in Schools*, New York: Longman.

MCLAREN, P., 1986, *Schooling as a Ritual Performance*, London and Boston: Routledge & Kegan Paul.

MCROBBIE, A. (Ed.), 1989, *Zootsuits and Second-hand Dresses: An Anthology of Fashion and Music*, New York: Unwin Hyman.

MCROBBIE, A., 1978, Working class girls and the culture of femininity, in Women's Study Group (Eds), *Women Take Issue: Aspects of Women's Subordination*, pp. 96–108, London: Hutchinson.

MEAD, G. H., 1934, *Mind, Self, and Society: From the Standpoint of a Social Behaviorist*, Chicago: University of Chicago Press.

MEHAN, H. and WOOD, H., 1975, *The Reality of Ethnomethodology*, New York: Wiley.

MICHAELS, S., 1986, Narrative presentations: An oral preparation for literacy with first graders, in COOK-GUMPERZ, J. (Ed.) *The Social Construction of Literacy*, pp. 94–116, Cambridge: Cambridge University Press.

MILLET, K., 1970, *Sexual Politics*, New York: Doubleday & Co.

MORGAN, D., 1987, Masculinity and violence, in HANMER, J. and MAYNARD, M. (Eds) *Women, Violence and Social Control*, pp. 180–192, London: The Macmillan Press.

MORGAN, R., 1990, *Demon Lover: On the Sexuality of Terrorism*, New York: W. W. Norton.

MOSS, G., 1989, *Un/Popular Fictions*, London: Virago Press.

OGBU, J., 1985, Research currents: Cultural-ecological school learning, *Language Arts*, **62**, 8, pp. 860–869.

OGBU, J., 1990, Cultural mode, identity and literacy, in STIGLER, J. W. (Ed.) *Cultural Psychology*, Cambridge: Cambridge University Press.

OMNI, M. and WINANT, H., 1986, *Racial Formation in the United States*, New York: Routledge.

O'NEILL, M., 1993, Teaching literature as cultural criticism, *English Quarterly*, **25**, 1, pp. 19–25.

ORNER, M., 1992, Interrupting the calls for student voice in 'liberatory' education: A feminist poststructuralist perspective, in LUKE, C. and GORE, J. (Eds) *Feminisms and Critical Pedagogy*, pp. 74–89, New York: Routledge.

ORTNER, S.B. and WHITEHEAD, H. (Eds), 1981, *Sexual Meanings: The Cultural Construction of Gender and Sexuality*, Cambridge: Cambridge University Press.

PETERSON, R. and EEDS, M., 1990, *Grand Conversations: Literature Groups in Action*, New York: Scholastic.

POGREBIN, L. C., 1980, *Growing Up Free*, New York: McGraw-Hill.

POSTMAN, N., 1981, The day our children disappear: Predictions of a media ecologist, *Phi Delta Kappan*, **62**, 1, pp. 382–386.

PROTHROW-SMITH, D. and WEISSMAN, M., 1991, *Deadly Consequences*, New York: Harper Collins Publishers.

PURCELL-GATES, V., 1993, Focus on research: Complexity and gender, *Language Arts*, **70**, 2, pp. 124–127.

RADWAY, J., 1984, *Reading the Romance: Women, Patriarchy, and Popular Literature*, Chapel Hill: University of North Carolina Press.

REED, T., 1989, *Demon Lovers and Their Victims in British Fiction*, University of Kentucky Press.

RICH, A., 1979, Vesuvius at home: The power of Emily Dickenson, in *On Lies, Secrets, and Silence: Selected Prose, 1966–1978*, pp. 157–183, New York: W.W. Norton.

RICH, A., 1978, Natural resources, in *The Dream of a Common Language: Poems 1974–1977*, New York: W.W. Norton.

ROGERS, A. G., 1993, Voice, play and a practice of ordinary courage in girls' and women's lives, *Harvard Educational Review*, **63**, 3, pp. 265–295.

ROCKHILL, K., 1993, Gender, language and the politics of literacy, in STREET, B. V. (Ed.) *Cross-cultural Approaches to Literacy*, Cambridge: Cambridge University Press.

ROSENBLATT, L. M., 1938, *Literature as Exploration*, New York: D. Appleton-Century.

ROSENBLATT, L. M., 1978, *The Reader, the Text and the Poem: The Transactional Theory of the Literary Work*, Carbondale, Illinois: Southern Illinois University Press.

SAVIN-WILLIAMS, R. C., 1976, An ethological study of dominance formation and maintenance in a group of human adolescents, *Child Development*, **47**, pp. 972–979.

SCHLEGLOFF, E., 1974, Opening up closings, in TURNER, R. (Ed.) *Ethnomethodology*, pp.197–215, Middlesex, England: Penguin Education.

SCRIBNER, S. and COLE, M., 1981, *The Psychology of Literacy*, Cambridge, MA: Harvard University Press.

SEARS, J. T., 1992, Researching the other/searching for self: Qualitative research on (homo)sexuality in education, *Theory into Practice*, **XXXI**, 2, pp. 147–156.

SEGEL, E., 1986, 'As the twig is bent . . .': Gender and childhood reading, in FLYNN, E and SCHWEICKART, P. (Eds) *Gender and Reading: Essays on Readers, Texts and Contexts*, pp. 165–186, Baltimore: Johns Hopkins.

SHANNON, P., 1989, The struggle for control of literacy lessons, *Language Arts*, **66**, 6, pp. 625–634.

SHOR, I., 1990, Liberation education: An interview with Ira Shor, *Language Arts*, **67**, 4, pp. 342–352.

SHOR, I. and FREIRE, P., 1987, *A Pedagogy for Liberation: Dialogues on Transforming Education*, South Hadley, MA: Bergin & Garvey.

SIMON, R. I., 1983, But who will let you do it? Counter-hegemonic possibilities for work education, *Journal of Education*, **165**, 3, pp. 235–256.

SLOAN, G. D., 1984, *The Child as Critic*, 2nd edition, New York: Teachers College Press.

SMITH, F., 1986, *Understanding Reading*, 3rd edition, Hillsdale, NJ: Erlbaum.

SMITH, M. O., 1981, Sex differences in the perceptual and cognitive skills essential to reading acquisition, in ANSARA, A., GESCHWIND, N., GALABURDA, A., ALBERT, M. and GARTELL, N. (Eds) *Sex Differences in Dyslexia*, pp. 119–127, Towson, MD: Orton Dyslexia Society.

SOLSKEN, J., 1993, *Literacy, Gender & Work in Families and in School*, Norwood, NJ: Ablex.

SPENDER, D. and SARAH, E. (Eds), 1980, *Learning to Lose*, London: The Women's Press.

STANLEY, L. and WISE, S., 1993, *Breaking Out Again: Feminist Ontology and Epistemology*, London and New York: Routledge.

STOKES, R. and HEWITT, J., 1976, Aligning actions, *American Sociological Review*, **41**, pp. 838–849.

STREET, B. V. (Ed.), 1993, *Cross-cultural Approaches to Literacy*, Cambridge: Cambridge University Press.

TANNEN, D., 1990, *You Just Don't Understand: Women and Men in Conversation*, New York: Ballantine Books.

TAYLOR, D. and DORSEY-GAINES, C., 1988, *Growing Up Literate: Learning from Inner-City Families*, Portsmouth, NH: Heinemann Educational Books.

TAYLOR, S., 1993, Transforming the texts: Towards a feminist classroom practice, in CHRISTIAN-SMITH, L. K. (Ed.) *Texts of Desire: Essays on Fiction, Femininity and Schooling*, pp. 126–144, London: Falmer Press.

THORNE, B., 1993, *Gender Play: Girls and Boys in School*, New Brunswick, NJ: Rutgers University Press.

THORNE, B., 1986, Girls and boys together . . . but mostly apart: Gender arrangements in elementary schools, in HARTUP, W. W. and RUBIN, Z. (Eds) *Relationships and Development*, pp. 167–183, Hillsdale, NJ: Erlbaum.

THORNE, B. and LURIA, Z., 1986, Sexuality and gender in children's daily worlds, *Social Problems*, **33**, 3, pp. 176–190.

TROEMEL-PLOETZ, S., 1991, Review essay: Selling the apolitical, *Discourse and Society*, **2**, 4, pp. 48–52.

TWITCHELL, J. B., 1985, *Dreadful Pleasures: An Anatomy of Modern Horror*, New York: Oxford University Press.

VANDERGRIFT, K. E., 1986, *Child and Story: The Literary Connection*, New York: Neal-Schuman.

WALDROP, M. F. and HALVORSEN, C. F., 1975, Intensive and extensive peer behavior: Longitudinal and cross-sectional analysis, *Child Development*, **46**, pp. 19–26,

WALKERDINE, V., 1985, On the regulation of speaking and silence: Subjectivity, class and gender in contemporary schooling, in STEEDMAN, C. UNWIN, C. and WALKERDINE, V. (Eds) *Language, Gender and Childhood*, pp. 203–241, London: Routledge & Kegan Paul.

WALKERDINE, V., 1990, *Schoolgirl Fictions*, London: Verso.

WALKERDINE, V., 1984, Someday my prince will come: Young girls and the preparation for adult sexuality, in MCROBBIE, A. and NIVA, M. (Eds) *Gender and Generation*, pp. 162–184, Houndmills, England: Macmillan.

WEEDON, C., 1987, *Feminist Practice and Poststructuralist Theory*, Oxford: Basil Blackwell.

WEILER, K., 1988, *Women Teaching for Change: Gender, Class and Power*, South Hadley, MA: Bergin & Garvey.

WEINSTEIN-SHR, G., 1993, Literacy and social process: A community in transition, in STREET, B. V. (Ed.) *Cross-cultural Approaches to Literacy*, pp. 272–293, Cambridge: Cambridge University Press.

WEIS, L., 1990, Issues of disproportionality and social justice in tomorrow's schools, in WEIS, L., CORNBLETH, C., ZEICHNER, K. and APPLE, M. (Eds) *Curriculum for Tomorrow's Schools*, pp. 32–67, Buffalo, NY: Buffalo Research Institute for Teaching, Graduate School of Education, State University of NY at Buffalo.

WEST, C. and ZIMMERMAN, D. H., 1987, Doing gender, *Gender and Society*, **1**, 2, pp. 125–151.

WILLIAMS, R., 1977, *Marxism and Literature*, Oxford: Oxford University Press.

WILLIS, P., 1977, *Learning to Labour*, Westmead, England: Saxon House.

WOLF, M. and GOW, D., 1986, A longitudinal investigation of gender differences in language and reading development, *First Language*, **6**, pp. 81–110.

Appendix A

Methodology for the Study

Research Questions

These are the questions that guided the study:

- What did the reading of fiction mean to 7 sixth-grade girls in Oak Town who read 10 or more novels a month?
- How did these girls read, why did they read, and what did reading feel like to them?
- What patterns of social organization framed and defined the activity of reading fiction in their classrooms, in their homes, and in their personal relationships?
- What are the cultural assumptions that shaped and influenced what the reading of fiction meant to these girls?

Access and Ethics

I wanted to do research in Oak Town because it was only a short drive from the university where I was doing graduate work in the late 1980s. I approached the principal of Oak Town School because he was the friend of a friend, and because I knew he was interested in the teaching of literature. Because he was interested in what I had to say, he arranged for me to speak with the two sixth-grade teachers. The teachers, too, were interested and gracious, although I do not think they either understood the nature of interpretive research or had a clear idea of the kind of report that I would be writing.

I began participant observation on the first day of school, spending 10 hours a week there until the last day of that school year. I got to know the teachers and the children well. When, after Christmas, I sent letters home to the parents of seven friendly girls who read between 10 and 15 novels a month, asking for the parents' permission to work with their daughters, all accepted. They welcomed me into their homes for interviews.

All the people involved in the study were kind to me, and my relationships with the seven focal girls were especially satisfying. Because I had no responsibilities as a teacher, I did not have to enforce school rules or timetables. I was free to listen to their stories of their lives, and I was keenly interested. They responded with affection, and I believe that they were open and honest with me.

But it needs to be noted that, in the interests of telling a story clearly, I have obscured certain inequalities and certain power relationships. One of these is the fact that various power differentials between adult and child on the one hand, and between researcher and subject, on the other, exerted an influence over the data-gathering process. Another is the fact that my university status and my educational background meant something to the parents and teachers that I interviewed.

I chose to work with 7 of the 12 or so sixth-grade girls who were avid readers of fiction. I chose the seven girls who were most willing and most able to talk to me about their reading.

I did not choose to work as closely with the boys. This was, most importantly, because I had chosen to do feminist research, which privileges the experiences of women and girls. Girls were reading more and reading differently from boys, and that is the phenomenon that I wished to study — and from the *girls'* point of view. However, there were also culturally shaped reasons why the boys were not as willing as the girls to talk to me, an older female, about their reading activities.

Data Collection

Data collection took four forms. The first two forms (participant observation and ethnographic interviews) are traditional ones in the field of ethnographic research. The last two forms (literature-response groups and dialogue journals) have been the bases for recent and distinguished classroom research into the teaching of children's literature (Eeds and Wells, 1989; Atwell, 1987).

Four methods in all were used in order that the weaknesses inherent in any one method would be eliminated by the relative strengths of another. Erickson's (1986) six criteria for validity in qualitative research studies were frequently examined and addressed during both the data-collection and the analysis stages (see below).

Participant observation and field notes

800 single-spaced pages of field notes were written which gave a detailed record of more than 400 hours spent in participant observation at Oak Town School. These notes retold events, recounted conversations (with the help of a tape recorder), tried to capture the feeling tone of certain scenes, and described certain people and places.

Ethnographic interviews and transcripts

Open interviews were conducted with individual children, parents in their homes, teachers at the school, and groups of three to six children. The interviews in question were 'open' in that they did not make use of a prepared and uniform set of questions. Instead, I prepared an *interview guide* (i.e. a list of topics that I hoped would be covered) and used that toward the end of each interview in order to address any areas of interest that the person being interviewed had not mentioned. Interviews were audiorecorded and transcribed.

Literature-response group transcripts

I organized 14 literature-response groups for this study. There were three to five children in each group. Seven girls and four boys, all avid readers and all members of the two sixth-grade classes, read novels that I suggested. Then, during class time, I brought together children who had read the same book and asked them to talk about the book in any way that they chose. Their conversation was audiotaped and later transcribed.

Of the 14 groups, seven were all-girl groups, two were all-boy groups, and five were mixed-gender groups. I assigned the group memberships myself, making sure that each of the 11 children participated in at least two of the mixed-gender groups and in at least two of the same-gender groups. The groups in question met in a private conference room at school for sessions lasting from 20 to 45 minutes. I was the only other person present when each group met. I participated in the conversation as little as possible.

Dialogue journals

From January through to June, each of the seven focal girls for the study wrote dated letters to me, in a spiral notebook, about the books that she was reading. I wrote replies to her letters in the same notebook. All entries were transcribed.

Data Analysis

There were over 2000 pages of data for this study. Data analysis followed Erickson's (1986) guidelines, beginning at an early stage and proceeding inductively. The field notes made were read repeatedly, and the first analytic memo, in which the first codes and categories emerged, was written three months after the study began.

Other analytic memos were also written, each of which was based on a re-reading of the entire body of data collected thus far, and each of which described my understanding, at that time, of the codes and categories that had emerged from the data. Later analytic memos attempted to make connections between and among these various codes and categories.

Theoretical memos were also written as the data-collection process continued. These involved explorations of ideas that came from the reading that I was doing, reading that connected with themes that I had constructed from the data. I 'tried on' different theories, discarding those that were not useful in explaining the data. Before the school year had ended, I had established the core categories of *time, gender* and *individualism,* and had settled on *critical theory* as the basis for my analysis.

After the data-collection process had ended, I spent one year writing a report, explaining the practice of reading in Oak Town in terms of both cultural reproduction and resistance.

Validity

Erickson outlines (1986) six criteria upon which the validity of a qualitative research study rests. The first criterion is that there must be an adequate relationship between the researcher, on the one hand, and the participants on the other. The second is that an adequate amount of good-quality data must be collected. The third is that a variety of methods must be used to gather data. I believe I have already shown that these particular criteria have been met.

The fourth criterion, that the analysis must be adequate as regards the identification of recurrent patterns of action and meaning, can only be judged through the actual reading of this text. Erickson's fifth criterion is that a rigorous search for any evidence which *disconfirms* these patterns of meaning must also be conducted. This kind of search was conducted repeatedly, during, and as part of, the data-analysis and memo-writing phases described above. The sixth and final criterion by which the validity of a qualitative study may be judged, is the degree of *credibility* of the final account. That judgment, too, I must leave in the hands of the reader.

Generalizability

Does the theory generated in this book apply only to *these particular* sixth-grade girls in Oak Town, or is it applicable to sixth-grade girls in general? I believe that these findings *are* generalizable beyond the specific setting of this study. What I saw happening was specific to a certain local context, but it was also representative of an *historical* and *cultural type* of situation. Glaser distinguishes (1978) between *analytic* generalizations and *statistical* generalizations. Theory generated from qualitative data is not intended to be generalized to other populations. Rather, it is to be generalized to other basic social processes of the kind that underlie the issues and problems of other settings.

Appendix B

Fiction and Videos Mentioned in the Text

Alexander, L., 1964, *The Black Cauldron*, New York: Dell.

Alexander, L., 1964, *Book of Three*, New York: Dell.

Alexander L., 1967, *Taran Wanderer*, New York: Dell.

Andrews, V. C., 1982, *Flowers in the Attic*, New York: G. K. Hall Paperback.

Andrews, V. C., 1987, *Garden of Shadows*, New York: Pocket Books, Inc.

Andrews, V. C., 1987, *Petals on the Wind*, New York: Pocket Books, Inc.

Babbitt, N., 1975, *Tuck Everlasting*, New York: Bantam.

Bernard, E., 1987, *Satin Slippers #1: To Be a Dancer*, New York: Ballantine Books.

Boissard, J., 1985, *A Question of Happiness*, New York: Fawcett.

Bradford, K., 1985, *The Haunting at Cliff House*, Richmond Hill, Ontario: Scholastic-TAB.

Burnett, F. H., 1938, *The Secret Garden*, New York: Harper and Row.

Burnford, S., 1961, *The Incredible Journey*, Boston: Little, Brown & Co.

Byars, B., 1988, *Summer of the Swans*, New York: Viking Penguin Inc.

Canning, V., 1978, *The Crimson Chalice*, New York: Charter Books.

Carter, A. R., 1985, *Wart, Son of Toad*, New York: Berkley.

Clark, M. H., 1983, *The Cradle Will Fall*, New York: Dell.

Conrad, P., 1987, *Holding Me Here*, New York: Bantam.

DeJong, M., 1987, *The House of Sixty Fathers*, New York: Harper and Row Junior Books.

Duncan, L., 1986, *Locked in Time*, New York: Dell.

Farley, W., 1947, *Black Stallion*, New York: Random House.

Frank, A., 1961, *The Diary of a Young Girl*, Garden City, New Jersey: Doubleday.

Gates, D., 1940, *Blue Willow*, New York: Scholastic.

George, J. C., 1972, *Julie of the Wolves*, New York: Harper and Row.

Gipson, F., 1956, *Old Yeller*, New York: Harper.

Gonzalez, G., 1986, *Deadly Rhyme*, New York: Dell.

Halvorson, M., 1984, *Cowboys Don't Cry*, Toronto: Clarke Irwin.

Hermes, P., 1982, *You Shouldn't Have to Say Good-by*, San Diego: Harcourt, Brace, Jovanovitch.

Houston, J., 1986, *Frozen Fire*, Toronto: McClelland & Stewart, Ltd.

Hughes, M., 1983, *Space Trap*, Toronto: Groundwood Books.

Kjèlaard, J., 1973, *Big Red*, Toronto: Bantom Skylark.

Klein, N., 1974, *Sunshine*, New York: Avon Books.

Knaak, R., 1988, *The Legend of Huma*, New York: Random House.

Konigsburg, E. L., 1967, *The Mixed-Up Files of Mrs Basil E. Frankweiler*, New York: Dell.

Krumgold, J., 1959, *Onion John*, New York: Harper & Row.

Landis, J. D., 1981, *The Sisters Impossible*, New York: Bantam.

L'Engle, M., 1962, *A Wrinkle in Time*, New York: Dell.

Little, J., 1988, *Mama's Going to Buy You a Mockingbird*, New York: Viking Penguin Inc.

Martin, A. M., 1987, *Boy-Crazy Stacey*, New York: Scholastic.

Martin, A. M., 1988, *Kristy and the Snobs*, New York: Scholastic.

Martin, A. M., 1987, *Mary Anne Saves the Day*, New York: Scholastic.

Mazer, N. F., 1986, *I, Trissy*, New York: Dell.

Miles, B., 1979, *The Trouble with Thirteen*, New York: Knopf.

Montgomery, L. M., 1987, *Anne of Green Gables*, New York: Bantam.

Nathanson, L., 1987, *The Trouble with Wednesdays*, New York: Bantam.

Naylor, P. R., 1991, *Shiloh*, New York: Dell.

O'Brien, R. C., 1971, *Mrs Frisbee and the Rats of NIMH*, New York: Macmillan.

Pascal, F., 1989, *All Night Long*, Lakeville, CT: Grey Castle.

Pascal, F., 1984, *Dear Sister*, New York: Bantam.

Pascal, F., 1986, *Hostage!*, New York: Bantam.

Pascal, F., 1989, *Out of Reach*, Lakeville, CT: Grey Castle.

Pascal, F., 1988, *Slam Book Fever*, New York: Bantam.

Pascal, F., 1989, *White Lies*, Lakeville, CT: Grey Castle.

Paterson, K., 1977, *Bridge to Terabithia*, New York: Dell.

Pfeffer, S. B., 1977, *Kid Power*, New York: F. Watts.

Pike, C., 1985, *Slumber Party*, New York: Scholastic.

Pike, C., 1986, *Weekend*, New York: Scholastic.

Porter, G. S., 1986, *Girl of the Limberlost*, New York: Dell Publishing.

Saul, J., 1988, *The Unloved*, New York: Bantam.

Schaefer, J., 1975, *Shane*, New York: Bantam Books.

Snyder, Z. K., 1967, *The Egypt Game*, New York: Dell.

Sperry, A., 1971, *Call It Courage*, New York: Macmillan.

Spinelli, J., 1990, *Maniac McGee*, New York: Scholastic.

Stevenson, R. L., 1911, *Treasure Island*, New York: Charles Scribner's Sons.

Stine, R. L., 1986, *Blind Date*, New York: Scholastic.

Taylor, C., 1987, *The Doll*, Saskatoon, Sask: Western Producer Prairie Books.

Tolkien, J. R. R., 1986, *The Fellowship of the Ring*, New York: Ballantine Books.

Tolkien, J. R. R., 1984, *The Hobbit*, Boston: Houghton Mifflin.

Tolkien, J. R. R., 1985, *The Lord of the Rings*, London: George Allen & Unwin, Ltd.

Watkins, Y. K., 1986, *So Far From the Bamboo Grove*, New York: Viking Penguin Inc.

Wieler, D. J., 1986, *Last Chance Summer*, Saskatoon, Sask: Western Producer Prairie Books.

Wojciechowska, M., 1964, *Shadow of a Bull*, New York: Macmillan.

Young, S., 1985, *Scrubs on Skates*, Toronto: McClelland & Stewart.

Videos

Billy Idol
'White Wedding'
Billy Idol
Chrysalis Records, 1983

Michael Jackson
'Thriller'
Thriller
Epic/CBS Records, 1983

Rod Stewart
'Infatuation'
Camouflage
Warner Bros Records, 1984

Descriptions of Notecards

The following pictures were found on notecards, postcards, and advertisements collected in the United States and Canada between March 1988 and June 1993. The pictures on the notecards form part of the cultural discourses surrounding race, class, and gender with which the Oak Town children engaged. In Chapter 6, I provide a brief semiotic analysis of the messages which these visual images provide.

A Rival Attraction, 1887. This painting by Charles Burton Barber (1845–1894) pictures a young girl reclining in a wicker rocker with a book open on her lap. She is wearing black tights and a white ruffled dress, and she is gazing up at a small black kitten on the back of her chair. The predominant colors of the painting are beige, tan, and cream. It appears on a notecard printed for the Marcel Schurman Company of San Francisco, and was purchased at a children's bookstore in Regina, Saskatchewan.

Hearthside Afternoon. This watercolor by Helen Downing Hunter pictures a woman reading on a sofa in a light, well-ordered, pink and blue room. Her back is toward to us. The room is large and airy, and features finely drawn details: a fire in a fireplace, a knitting basket, a cat, flowers in an earthen pot, and two large bookcases full of books. The watercolor appears on a large notecard printed by Canadian Art Prints, Inc., Vancouver, B.C., and was purchased in the gift shop of the aquarium in Vancouver.

Compulsory Education. This oil painting by Briton Rivière pictures a Victorian child in a white dress with a blue sash, white stockings and black patent leather shoes. She is leaning back against a wall, reading a book that she holds in her hands while her arms encircle the neck of a huge dog. It appears on a birthday card printed for Marian Heath, Wareham, Massachusetts and was purchased at a card shop in Scottsdale, Arizona.

The Lesson. This drawing by Mary Lake-Thompson features a wide frame with the letters of the alphabet and numbers inscribed across the top and the bottom of the frame. Within the frame, a little girl, drawn in a stylized, child-like fashion, sits on the floor and reads to her toys: a doll, a stuffed rabbit, and two teddy bears. It appears on a notecard printed by the artist in Oroville, California. It was purchased in a toy store in Bellingham, Washington.

Summer Sonnets. This watercolor by Lynn Gertenbach features a teenage woman reading in a colorful flower garden. She wears a long white ruffled dress with pink trim and a wide-brimmed straw hat trimmed with flowers. She holds the book in her left hand and rests her right hand on the head of a large dog. The watercolor appears as a 5″-by-7″ print, encased in glass with a brass edging. It is published and distributed by Canadian Art Prints of Vancouver, and was purchased in the gift shop of the Hotel Lac Louise in Banff, Alberta.

The Children's Afternoon in Vargemont. This painting by Pierre-Auguste Renoir (1841–1919) pictures three girls in a sunny, comfortable sitting room. To the right, a teenage girl in a red and white dress sits, helping a small child with her doll. To the left, a girl of 10 or so sits on a blue sofa, her ankles crossed, reading a book. The painting is reproduced on a UNICEF notecard.

Far Away Places. This watercolor by Helen Downing Hunter pictures a young girl sitting on a sofa under a window that looks out to sea. She has a book open beside her, but she is gazing out the window. She sits in a pink and blue room that is delicately decorated, with books and a teddy bear on the floor in the foreground. The watercolor appears on a large notecard published and distributed by Canadian Art Prints in Vancouver. It was purchased in the gift shop at the aquarium in Vancouver, British Columbia.

The Third Volume, 1885. This painting by Edward Killingworth Johnson (1825–1923) pictures a young woman sitting in a green and flowering garden. She wears a long cream-colored gauzy dress and a hat to match. She holds a book up against her shoulder with her right hand, while stirring a cup of tea on the table beside her with her left hand. The picture appears on a birthday card printed for the Marcel Schurman Company of San Francisco. It was purchased at a card shop in Scottsdale, Arizona.

A Schoolgirl. This 1887 oil painting by Sir Luke Fields shows a teenage woman from the waist up against a dark brown background. She wears a cream-colored smock and a dark hat. She is looking down at the book that she is holding. She holds a small slate between her left elbow and her body. The painting is reproduced on a 'congratulations' card printed in England by the Evergreen Press of Pleasant Hill, California. It was purchased in a card shop in Scottsdale, Arizona.

Reading by a Window, Hastings. This watercolor by C. J. Lewis (1830–1892) pictures a teenage woman reading on a bench before a long open window that looks out onto several boats on the seashore. She wears a long white dress trimmed with blue. Gauzy curtains blow at either side of the window. The painting is reproduced on a birthday card printed in England for the Marcel Schurman Company of San Francisco. It was purchased in a card shop in Scottsdale, Arizona.

A Woman Reading. This painting by Claude Monet (1840–1926) shows a woman in a voluminous white dress and hat sitting on the grass against a background of green trees. She gazes at the book she holds on her lap. The painting is printed on a notecard published and distributed by Portal Publications of Corte Madera, California. It was purchased in the gift shop of the Boston Museum of Fine Arts.

Girl Reclining on Couch. This oil painting by Lucius Rossi (1846–1913) features a young woman with dark hair reading as she leans back against red cushions on an ornate sofa. Her dress is yellow, with white ruffles at the throat, and her stockings red. The room she sits in is dark and rustic, and features a polar-bear rug in the foreground. The painting is reproduced on a birthday card published in Italy for the Marcel Schurman Company of San Franciso. It was purchased in a card store in Scottsdale, Arizona.

A Young Flaxen Haired Girl. This painting, 'of the Nineteenth Century English School', pictures a young girl in a long white dress reading as she sits on a porch step, framed in red bricks and dark leaves. A cat curls at her feet. In the background is an open door which gives a view of a warm room with pink wallpaper and a white marble fireplace. The painting is reproduced on a notecard printed for Marion Heath of Wareham, Massachusetts. It was purchased in a card shop in Scottsdale, Arizona.

Reading in The Garden. This painting by Agnes M. Richmond shows a young woman with a pink flower in her upswept hair, sitting in a straight-backed chair before a wooden fence. She is surrounded by green grass and there are impressionistic flowers in the background. She wears a long, lavender dress with a white shawl collar. The painting appeared on the cover of

Instructor magazine, May 1989, courtesy of Vixeboxse Art Galleries, Inc., Cleveland Heights, Ohio.

Dream a Little. This watercolor by Thomas L. Cathey, predominantly pink and blue, is framed in pink, and features a caption across the bottom that says 'Dream a Little.' Within the frame a little girl sits before the fire in an overstuffed armchair with an open book in her lap. Her eyes are closed. A small dog and a doll sit and watch her. The painting appears on a notecard printed by Lang Graphics of Delafield, Wisconsin. It was purchased in a toy store in Bellingham, Washington.

A Book Is a Present You Can Open Again and Again. This 'illustration' by Mary Engelbreit is double-framed. The outer border is a small wallpaper print, while the inner border is black and red. Against it, the title appears as a caption in large gold letters. Within the double borders is a painting of a blond girl, kneeling and reading on a red Persian carpet that appears to be flying against a background of moon, stars and night sky. The illustration forms the cover of a notecard published by Sunrise Publications of Bloomington, Indiana. It was purchased at a children's bookstore in Winnipeg, Manitoba.

Fairy Tales. This oil painting by J. J. Shannon (1862–1923) pictures a dark-haired woman, in a straight-backed white chair, reading to two young girls. The girls wear long white dresses, and have steady gazes. The three figures appear against an impressionistic background of blue, with floral figures. The painting appears on a postcard published by the Metropolitan Museum of Art in New York City, and was purchased in the gift shop there.

Gare Saint-Lazare. This painting by Edouard Manet places two figures against a wrought iron fence before a fountain. The figure on the left is a young woman, in dark suit and hat, who looks at the viewer but has a book open in her lap. The other figure is a little girl, in a white dress with a blue sash, who has her back turned to look at the fountain. The painting appears on a notecard published by the National Gallery of Art in Washington, D.C., and was purchased in the gift shop there.

Christmas Love. This painting features two small blond children sitting together and looking at an open picture book. They wear knee-length dresses, white stockings and black patent leather shoes. There are holly leaves in the foreground and a verse in the lower right-hand corner ('This little card has come to say: Merry be your Christmas Day.') The painting appears on a

Christmas card printed in Westgrove, New Jersey, and was sent to the author from Sun City, Arizona.

Best Friends. This watercolor by Thomas L. Cathey is predominantly pink, blue and pale yellow. It pictures two little girls seated facing each other on the floor of a playroom, surrounded by toys. One little girl is reading aloud to the other. The painting appears on a notecard published by Lang Graphics of Delafield, Wisconsin, and was purchased in a toy store in Bellingham, Washington.

Sharing with Friends. This watercolor painting, also by Thomas L. Cathey, is predominantly deep pink, blue and white. It pictures two little girls seated on a low sofa facing each other, with dolls and a plate of cookies and various tea things arranged around them. The girl on the left is reading aloud to the girl on the right, who leans back in comfort, with her hands clasped behind her head.

1990 is International Literacy Year. This illustration by Jessie Willcox Smith (from *An Old-Fashoned ABC Book* by Elizabeth Allen Ashton) shows two pre-school aged children sitting in the same flowered armchair reading an opened picture book. The caption under the picture reads, '1990 is International Literacy Year. Travel to New Worlds through Reading.' The illustration appears on a postcard published by Viking Children's Books in New York. It was purchased at an NCTE conference, and sent to me from Baltimore, Maryland.

Forbidden Books. This painting by Alexander M. Rossi (1870–1903) shows young women reading in what appears to be a library. A group of four sit together at the right, poring over books, and reading aloud to each other. Two more women sit at the left, in the background, by a window, but appear to be listening. The women wear long skirts and high-necked, long-sleeved blouses. There are books open on the floor around them. The painting is reproduced on a birthday card printed in England for the Marcel Schurman Company of San Francisco. It was purchased in a card shop in Scottsdale, Arizona.

A Quiet Moment. This watercolor by Sally Swatland pictures two little girls (perhaps 7 and 4 years old) looking at an open book. They both wear lavender colored dresses and white pinafores. The younger child holds a teddy bear. The older child points to something on the page. The watercolor appears on a birthday card published by Pierre Belvedere of Montreal, and was purchased in a children's bookstore in Regina, Saskatchewan.

Two Girls Reading. This painting by Pierre-Auguste Renoir (1841–1919) pictures a young girl, seated, wearing a white dress and hat with red trim, and reading aloud. A second young girl sits behind and beside the first, resting her chin on her hand, and gazing down at the open book with a smile. The background is dark and green. The painting is reproduced on a notecard published by Pierre Belvedere of Montreal. It was purchased in Canada and given to me.

Ladies Reading. This painting by John Singer Sargent (1856–1925) is painted with bold strokes in shades of blue and yellow and white. It shows two women in voluminous white dresses under blue and purple parasols. One reclines. The other sits. Books are open between them. The painting is reproduced on both sides of a notecard published by the Museum of Fine Arts in Boston. It was purchased in the gift shop there.

Two Great Offers. This advertisement for the Literary Guild features the silhouettes of two young women seated back-to-back and reading. One wears jeans and running shoes, the other a long skirt and glasses. The print on the page reads: 'You revel in real-life dramas, romance and armchair adventures. Your friend relishes revealing autobiographies, cooking, and intricate mysteries. The Literary Guild can please you BOTH with 2 GREAT OFFERS.' This advertisement was sent to my home.

Man Reading. This colored photograph of a man reading appeared on an advertisement for leatherbound volumes of The 100 Greatest Books Ever Written, a series published by the Literary Guild. The man is handsome, gray-haired, and wears gray flannel slacks, a sweater, and a tweed jacket. He sits in a velour armchair, reading a leatherbound book with gold scrolls on the cover. Two more volumes sit on the mahogany table beside him, and there are more on the mahogany bookshelves behind him, along with plants, brass, pottery, and a porcelain sculpture of a stag.

World to Explore. This drawing of two little boys reading appears on a bookmark published by the Canadian Children's Book Centre in Toronto. The boys both sit on a blue-flowered armchair, the younger one seated on the knee of the older. They wear gold-colored sweaters. Both are smiling. Light glows around their faces. The caption in the lower right-hand corner says: 'Canadian Children's Books: World to Explore.'

Index